Scholar Painters of Japan: The Nanga School

Asia House Gallery,
New York City:
January 13-
February 27, 1972

University Art Museum,
University of California,
Berkeley, California:
April 4-30, 1972

Lenders to the Exhibition

Eisei Bunko, Tokyo
Fuse Art Museum, Shiga
Mr. Gihei Hamaguchi, Chiba
Mr. Yoshirō Hasegawa, Yamagata-ken
Mr. Shinji Hiraki, Tokyo
Mr. Ryōtarō Hirayama, Tokyo
Homma Art Museum, Yamagata
Mr. Ryō Hosomi, Osaka
Miss Yoshiko Hosoya, Yamagata
Idemitsu Art Museum, Tokyo
Japanese Imperial Household Collection
Mr. Jōji Kanzaki, Kanagawa
Mr. Tatsuichi Kataoka, Yamaguchi
Mr. Kinjirō Kitamura, Kyoto
Mr. Shōhei Kumita, Tokyo
Mr. Kazuo Kurimoto, Kanagawa
Kyoto National Museum
Mr. Ichiyō Matsushita, Hyogo
Mr. Kōnosuke Matsushita, Hyogo
Mr. Junkichi Mayuyama, Tokyo
Neiraku Art Museum, Nara
Mr. Hikoshirō Nishitani, Chiba
Mr. Sukekurō Satō, Toyama
Seikadō, Tokyo
Mr. Yoshio Sekizumi, Tokyo
Mr. Takaya Shimada, Tokyo
Mr. Jūrō Sōrimachi, Tokyo
Suntory Art Gallery, Tokyo
Tokyo National Museum
Tokyo University of Fine Arts
Mr. Fudō Tomitori, Chiba
Mr. Genichi Tōyama, Tokyo
Umezawa Memorial Hall, Tokyo
Mr. Kinsuke Wanaka, Wakayama
Mr. Kōzō Yabumoto, Hyogo
Mr. Sōshirō Yabumoto, Tokyo
Mrs. Fumiko Yoshikawa, Tokyo
Zakke-in, Kyoto

Mr. and Mrs. Jackson Burke, New York

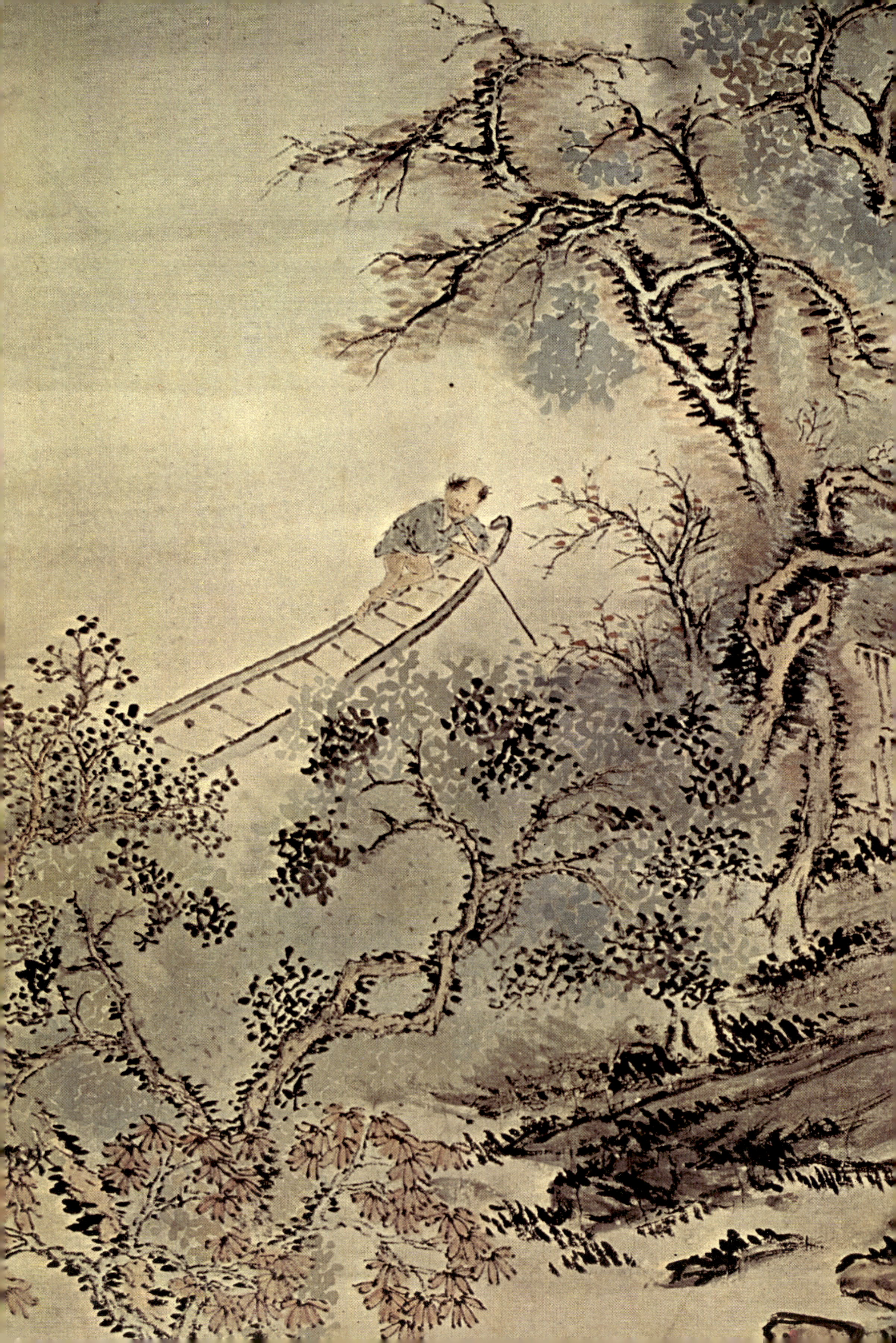

Scholar Painters of Japan: The Nanga School

James Cahill

The Asia Society Inc.

Distributed by New York Graphic Society Ltd.

Scholar Painters of Japan: The Nanga School
is the catalogue of an exhibition selected by Dr.
James Cahill, Professor of the History of Art, the
University of California, and Curator of Oriental
Art at the University Art Museum, Berkeley.
The exhibition was shown at Asia House Gallery
in the winter of 1972 as an activity of The Asia
Society, to further greater understanding
between the United States and the peoples of
Asia.
The exhibition has been made possible by a
grant from the Mary Livingston Griggs and Mary
Griggs Burke Foundation.

An Asia House Gallery Publication

Contents

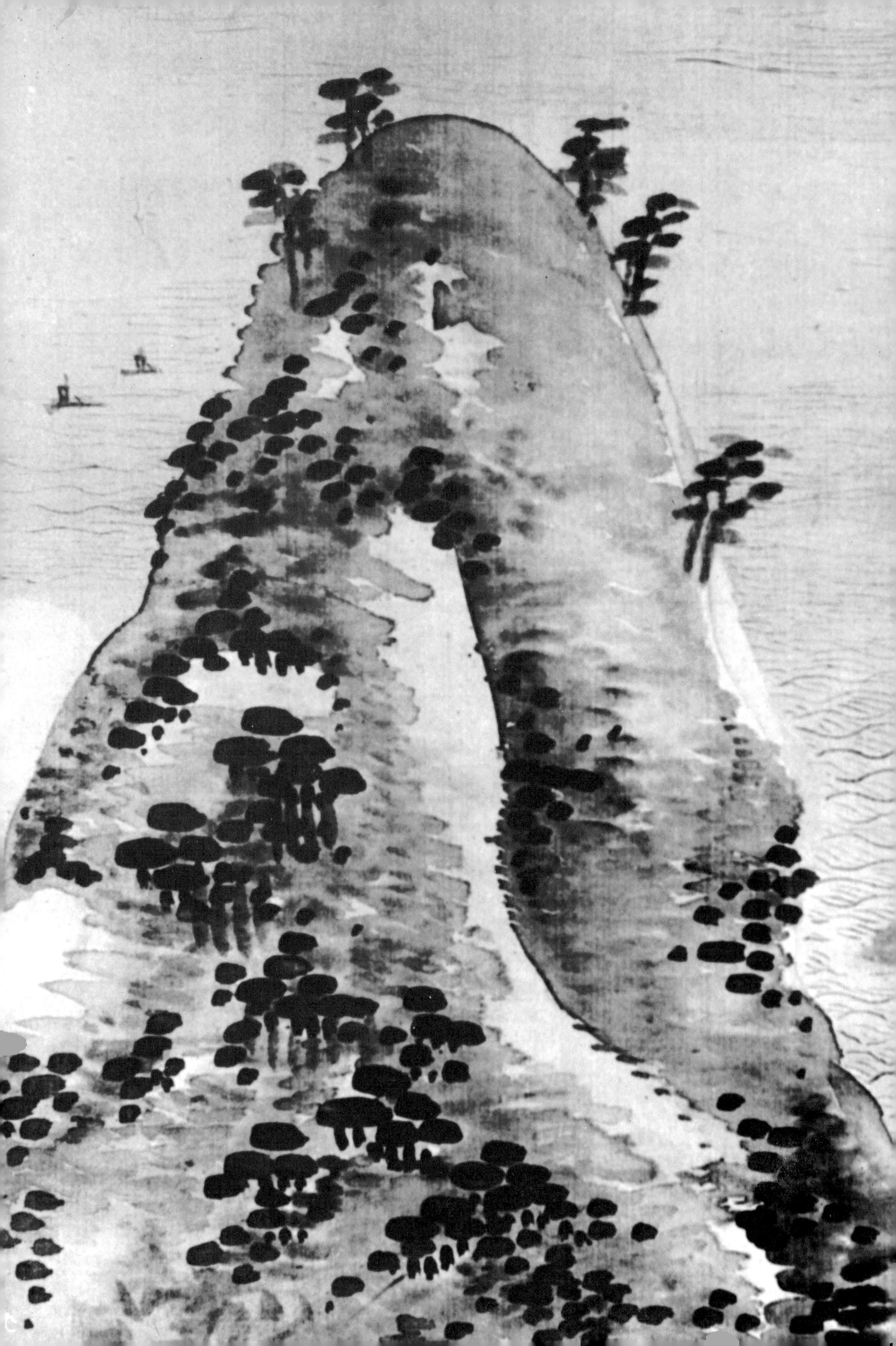

Acknowledgments

14 Ikeno Taiga A Real View of Kojima Bay (detail)

It is little realized that a considerable number of the exhibitions presented at Asia House Gallery have been supported by grants from foundations, corporations, and even by interested groups. As with the exhibition of Japanese folding screens (Byōbu) which was offered last season, this notable showing of Nanga paintings—the work of Scholar Painters of Japan—has been made possible by a grant from the Mary Livingston Griggs and Mary Griggs Burke Foundation. In fact, without the knowledgeable and enthusiastic interest of Mr. and Mrs. Jackson Burke of New York City, it would never have been gathered together or brought to America at all.

"**Scholar Painters of Japan: The Nanga School** represents the first American attempt to present Nanga painting as a whole and to introduce its principal artists at their best," writes Professor James Cahill, the author of this catalogue. As there is no substantial book on Nanga painters in any European language, this study of the subject by Professor Cahill will now fill a serious gap in our current resources. Actually, it was Dr. Cahill, himself, who first urged us to undertake this timely exhibition, and we are profoundly grateful to him for his patient and enthusiastic efforts towards its realization.

The chief support in Japan of the present exhibition has been Dr. Hidemi Kohn, the distinguished Commissioner of the Agency for Cultural Affairs (Bunka-cho) and his learned colleagues. These have included, first and foremost, Mr. Kenji Adachi, Deputy Commissioner, who has earnestly dealt with every difficulty as it appeared. It is through him and his tireless endeavors that Asia House Gallery has been able to borrow these little-known masterpieces by the Scholar Painters of Japan and to bring them to America. We are also grateful for the very considerable contributions of Mr. Jo Okada, and Mr. Tadashi Uchiyama of the Department for the Protection of Cultural Properties, and Mr. Shinji Nishikawa formerly of this same office.

There have been, in fact, a veritable host of helpful Japanese officials, representing in various ways the interests of the Japanese nation and her concern with her artistic treasures. Among these we are happy to thank Mr. Issho Tanaka, the distinguished Japanese scholar for his assistance in the selection of the paintings. In the Ministry of Foreign Affairs (Gaimusho) we are indebted to a number of notable officials including the Director General of the Department of Cultural Affairs, Mr. Takeshi Kanematsu, and Mr. Mitsuo Asaba. Among others who have given us valuable advice during the long period of this undertaking

are Mr. Bunsaku Kurata, Chief Curator of the Tokyo National Museum, to whom
we addressed our first letter when he occupied the leading post in the Bunka-
cho, and Mr. Kikuji Yonezawa, former Director of K.B.S.—the Japan Cultural
Society. So, too, we appreciate the efforts of Mr. Susumu Suzuki of Tokyo, who
had originally collaborated with Professor Cahill on this project—bringing
to it his great knowledge of these Japanese artists and their work.

As the preparations for the exhibition and its catalogue have occupied a
number of years, we have often been in helpful communication with the
diplomatic world. In this connection, we wish to acknowledge the kind encour-
agement received from the Japanese Ambassador to the United States, His
Excellency Mr. Nobuhiko Ushiba, as well as that of our own Ambassador to
Japan, the Honorable Armin H. Meyer, together with Dr. James Hoyt, his Special
Assistant for Cultural Affairs. In New York, also, we have been most kindly
assisted by the Consul General of Japan, the Honorable Mr. Hiroshi Uchida, and
by Mr. Yasushi Kurokochi of the Japanese Information Service. In San Francisco,
similarly, we have enjoyed the support of the Honorable Mr. Seiichi Shima,
the Japanese Consul General in that city.

As may easily be surmised, there is no adequate way to acknowledge all the
generous help that comes to this institution on such occasions, as the officers
and trustees of The Asia Society fully comprehend and regret. Dr. Cahill, too,
who wishes to be included in these grateful acknowledgments, desires also to
mention his debt to Mrs. Yoko Woodson of Berkeley, California, who assisted
him so assiduously in his research on these Nanga painters. Generous help
has likewise come from old friends in other quarters in Japan, such as Mr.
Junkichi Mayuyama, the internationally renowned dealer, and Mr. Haruo Igaki
of his staff, without whose invaluable assistance we could never have under-
taken this project. We wish to add the name of Mr. James L. Stewart of The Asia
Foundation in Tokyo, to whom we are all grateful for his keen interest in our
problems and for the help he so generously supplied.

Nanga painting, we surmise, may be of special interest just at this moment
because it reflects another world of conflict and protest. As with our contemporary expression, Nanga embraces a wide variety of styles, there being no single
direction in it unless it be its strong opposition to the banal and commonplace.
The displacement of artists occurred in both worlds: in Japan because of the
rapid dissolution of the feudal world and the rise of a commercial middle-class,
and in our times because of the triumph of trade and commerce as a way of
life. The Nanga painters found refuge in a gentlemen's culture, one deriving
from Chinese models which had stressed amateurism and every sort of individual
freedom and originality. Our refuge, in contrast, seems sometimes to be in
the form of a sit-down strike and sometimes a howl of derision, but like that
of the Nanga artists, it always prizes eccentricity and non-conformance. It may
be helpful, just now, to be reminded that human beings have always been
brothers, whether born in Japan or America.

Gordon Bailey Washburn
Director, Asia House Gallery

Chapter I: Introduction

Of the major schools of later Japanese painting, Nanga has been least studied
and understood outside Japan. Ukiyo-e, the school of "pictures of the floating
world" which produced the universally popular woodblock prints, and which
was closely contemporary with Nanga (both having arisen in the early eighteenth
century and declined sharply in the mid-nineteenth), is familiar to almost
everyone who cares for art at all, and the Rimpa School of Sōtatsu, Kōrin and
their followers is nearly as well known. Nanga, with less of decorative appeal
than either, its expressive means more complex and its values less immediately
apparent, has been slower in winning admirers abroad. Just as early Western
writers on Chinese art regarded all later Chinese painting as degenerate, simply
because they were not able to see the point of it, pioneer students of Japanese
art gave their highest praise to some academic kinds of painting that we now
find much less interesting, and dismissed Nanga as trivial—Fenollosa, for
instance, pronounced it to be "hardly more than a joke."[1]

In recent years this situation has been largely reversed, and Nanga paintings,
along with the paintings of the Ming and Ch'ing dynasties in China, which were
the Nanga artists' chief models, appear in increasing numbers in our museums
and private collections, as well as in books and university courses on Japanese
art. But there has been no exhibition of Nanga in the United States, and there is
still no substantial book on the subject in any Western language[2]—this in contrast to, for instance, the extensive Western-language literature on such artists as
Hokusai and Hiroshige. The present exhibition is thus a first attempt in this
country to present Nanga painting as a whole, and to introduce its principal
artists at their best.

The name Nanga is not easy to define, nor are the school and its styles easy
to delimit. As a first working definition we can say that Nanga (or Bunjinga, a
term we will explain later, which is used more or less interchangeably with
Nanga) is the Japanese counterpart to the Chinese school of scholar-amateur
artists, or literati painters, which flourished in the Yüan, Ming, and Ch'ing
dynasties, that is from the fourteenth century onward. Most of the Nanga
painters had some competence also as scholars of Confucian and other Chinese
learning, as calligraphers, and as poets in the Chinese manner. They were inclined, like their Chinese predecessors, to individualism as artists and to a degree
of non-conformity as people. They were sometimes, although by no means
always, amateur painters rather than professionals.

1. Ernest F. Fenollosa, *Epochs of Chinese
and Japanese Art,* 2nd ed. (London and
New York, 1913), II, p. 165.

2. The only exception is a good little
paperback, now out of print, by Jon
Carter Covell, titled *Japanese Landscape
Painting* (New York, 1962), which, in
spite of its title, is actually devoted to
Nanga. An English translation by Betty
Iverson Monroe of *Bunjinga (Nihon no
Bijutsu* [Arts of Japan], Vol. 23 [Tokyo,
1966]),by Chū Yoshizawa and Yoshiho
Yonezawa, is in preparation, and will
make this excellent book, containing
much more information than can be
given here, available to an English-
reading audience.

Nanga means, literally, "Southern painting," and is an abbreviation of *Nanshū-ga* (Chinese *Nan-tsung hua*) or "Southern School painting." The Chinese concept of the Northern and Southern Schools (which are so named by analogy with two branches of Zen Buddhism, and have no geographical significance) originated with the Chinese painter-theorist Tung Ch'i-ch'ang (1555-1636). Tung equated the Southern School, loosely, with the tradition of the scholar-amateur artists, distinguishing them from—and elevating them above—the professional painters, whom he identified with the "Northern School." Although the terms are by no means clear-cut designations of style, in a general way "Northern School" painting was considered to be: skillful; detailed; relatively realistic; colorful; traditional; conservative. "Southern School" painting, by contrast, was supposed to be: less realistic; more spontaneous, intuitive, individualistic, even when it made use of earlier styles; often deliberately amateurish and quasi-awkward; done in ink monochrome or with a simple and formal (warm-cool) system of light colors; more dependent for its expressive force on distinctive, sometimes calligraphic brushwork, repetitions and distortions of form, and other essentially abstract means.

The latter was the kind of painting that was praised by, and practiced by, the Chinese literati of the Ming and Ch'ing dynasties, and it was the ideal behind the "Southern School" painting, or Nanga, of Japan. The Chinese Southern School remained virtually unknown, and so un-imitated, in Japan until the early eighteenth century. By that time, a group of people who formed a kind of Japanese equivalent to the Chinese scholars had come into existence in Japan. The Tokugawa government and the lords of the individual clans promoted the study of the Chinese doctrines of Confucianism among the feudal retainers (samurai) who served them. For the rulers, who were military men, such studies had practical value in their stabilizing effect on society and their benefits in education, administration, and personal ethics. But the interests of the scholars of Chinese learning (known as Kangakusha) did not stop there; they went on to read Chinese history, poetry and other literature, and theoretical works on many subjects including art. Chinese books were imported, some with woodblock pictures, and a few Chinese paintings by literati artists began to come to Japan, where a climate favorable to their appreciation had been created. These paintings were collected, studied, and in time imitated, by the Kangakusha.

Chinese literati painting thus came to Japan as one part of Chinese literati culture, and was admired there not only for its intrinsic artistic qualities, but also because it conveyed to the Japanese—as indeed it did to the Chinese, according to the whole theory of literati painting—some sense of the modes of thought, feeling, and being of the men who created it. The man and his work were considered to be indissolubly bound; the humanism, the broad learning and wisdom of the ideal Chinese *wen-jen* (Japanese *bunjin*) or literatus was seen or felt in the paintings, and gave to the best of these a depth of feeling and a flavor of cultural permeation which, while certainly not entirely new to Japanese art, had been absent from most of its recent painting. This quality, as well as more easily definable stylistic differences, distinguished Nanga from earlier Japanese schools of painting that had been, in one way or another, dependent on China. Yanagisawa Kien (1704-1758), one of the pioneers of Nanga in Japan, began as a follower of the very orthodox Kanō School, which, although it had sunk by this time to the routine production of hardened and stereotyped pictures, still monopolized most of the official patronage. But, as he wrote later, "when I turned twelve or thirteen, I suddenly realized that the professional artists of the

Kanō School, for all their exertions, never got below the skin (or surface); none of them reach the 'bones.' I realized deeply that one should rather take Ku, Lu, Chang and Wu [Chinese masters standing here for the whole Chinese tradition] as models in painting."[3]

Elsewhere Kien writes: "One must study painting from Chinese paintings. The reason is that the best Japanese artists have always imitated Chinese paintings. From the *Honchō Gashi* we can learn that [Kanō] Motonobu did so, imitating Ma Yüan, Hsia Kuei, and Mu-ch'i. . . . Besides him, Kose no Kanaoka [the ninth century reputed founder of the Yamato-e style], Ono no Takamura, Minchō Den, and others, all the famous artists, imitated the Chinese. Such non-specialists [?] as Yōtoku [Kanō Tsunenobu, 1636-1713] and [Kanō] Tanyū [1602-1674] liked to use rough and free ink styles [i.e., styles superficially like those of Nanga]; but their ink paintings lack maturity, and their use of color is beneath notice. This is because they are unacquainted with the origins [of these styles], due to their shallow approach."[4]

Kien's main point here is that earlier Japanese masters, including those of the Kanō School, had imitated Chinese painting, and that this practice was therefore not new with Nanga. There is no indication that he or other Kangakusha of the period were fully aware that, up to their time, most of the Chinese-derived styles in Japanese painting belonged in fact to the despised Northern School, and that the works of many revered artists, such as Shūbun and Sesshū, were based on just those "pernicious" academic styles of the Ming dynasty that Tung Ch'i-ch'ang had particularly castigated. Nanga, while not entirely free of influence from the Kanō School, represents in general a rejection of its techniques and values; the Nanga masters wanted it understood that theirs was a *new* mode of imitating China. At the same time, the Northern and Southern Schools distinction does not seem to have been very clear to the Japanese, especially in the early stages of Nanga. Styles that the Chinese would consider academic and irredeemably "Northern," such as the realistic and colorful bird-and-flower painting of the Nagasaki School, were freely practiced by artists who considered themselves Nanaga adherents.

Nakayama Kōyō (1717-1780), in his *Gatan Keiroku* (1775), made the first attempt in Nanga painting theory to distinguish clearly between the Northern and Southern Schools. But his ideas were taken without significant change from Chinese books, and there is no reason to think that the artists he listed as belonging to one or the other school were more than names to him.[5] The painter-theorist Kuwayama Gyokushū (1746-1799), writing around 1799 in his *Kaiji Higen,* had a more original view. It was his opinion that Sōtatsu and Kōrin, along with two less-known Japanese artists, should be considered as "the Southern School of our country."[6] The designation of these two decorative painters as "Southern" would have shocked a Chinese critic, but is really quite perceptive; a good argument could be made for Gyokushū's thesis, but this is not the place to do it. In any case, their greater openness to a variety of sources and styles is one of the ways in which the Nanga artists differ from their Chinese counterparts, and proved to be one of the strengths of Nanga.

The routes by which knowledge of Chinese literati painting reached Japan were several. As mentioned earlier, many books and some actual paintings were imported. Buddhist monks of the Ōbaku (Chinese Huang-po) sect of Zen Buddhism, which had been introduced to Japan in the seventeenth century, visited China and brought back paintings, or painted in Chinese-derived styles.[7] Also, a few Chinese painters visited Japan. All of these but one—Shen Ch'üan

3. *Fueki Ikkan-sho,* quoted by Yoshizawa and Yonezawa, *op. cit.* (n. 2 above), p. 15. The early Chinese masters to whom Kien refers (who were of course only names to him) are Ku K'ai-chih, Lu T'an-wei, Chang Seng-yu, and Wu Tao-tzu.

4. A somewhat free rendering. Quoted in Kisaku Tanaka, ''*Nanga Hasshōki no Sū-Kaji*'' [Some Artists in the Earliest Phase of Nanga], *Bijutsu Kenkyū* [The Journal of Art Studies], Vol. 138 (Tokyo, 1944), p. 19.

5. Quoted in Shizuka Sakazaki, ''*Nihon no Garon ni tsuite*'' [On Japanese Art Theory], II, *The Kokka,* No. 599 (Oct. 1940), p. 283.

6. Quoted by Yoshizawa and Yonezawa, *op. cit.* (n. 2 above), pp. 17, 18, 123, and Susumu Suzuki, ''*Nanga (Bunjinga),*'' in *Nihon: Edo II* [Japan, Edo Period II] (*Sekai Bijutsu Zenshū* [Arts of the World], Vol. 10, Tokyo, 1963), p. 154. See also Sakazaki, *loc. cit.* (n. 5 above), p. 284. Of the two other artists, one, Konoe Nobutada (1565-1614), was probably included because he was a courtier who painted simple pictures as an avocation (Gyokushū specifies his ''ink-plays''), and the other, Shōjō or Shōkadō (1584-1639), was a painter of flowers and birds in a Chinese-derived style.

7. For a good summary account of the impact of Obaku, see Aschwin Lippe, ''Ch'en Hsien, Painter of Lohans,'' *Ars Orientalis,* 5 (1963), pp. 255-258.

or Shen Nan-p'in (active 1725-1780), an academic bird-and-flower painter who was in Nagasaki from 1731 to 1733 and who left behind a whole school of imitators, the Nagasaki School which we have mentioned already—were minor artists, unknown in their homeland. Some were nonetheless admired and influential in Japan: for instance, the merchant named I Hai or I Fu-chiu, a decidedly amateurish landscapist, who came to Japan in 1720.

Influences from Occidental art reaching Japan through the Dutch traders at Nagasaki and the Japanese scholars of Dutch (or more broadly European) learning, called *Rangaku,* are also to be seen in Nanga, which thus reflects an age in which Japan began to be more aware of the outside world than it had been for centuries. In its diversity of subjects and styles, Nanga reflects also a new mobility and a new spirit of inquiry. In addition to these elements from foreign traditions, the Nanga masters often made use, as we will see, of elements of the Japanese painting tradition, such as the Sōtatsu—Kōrin School (Rimpa). Our evaluation of the achievements of the Nanga masters must be based in part on our judgment of the success with which they absorbed these various elements into their individual styles and put them to effective use in their paintings.

The question of influences and evaluation had best be faced head-on at this point, since the writer of this catalogue, a specialist in Chinese painting, will surely be suspected of favoring those artists who most closely approximate Chinese styles. In fact, as the reader will discover, he has tried to avoid at every point (out of real conviction as well as a sense of fairness) suggesting any such correlation between Chineseness and excellence. Influences from China or else- where do not, in themselves, make a painting either better or worse. The Chinese literati artists were always working "in old styles," with little or no real erosion of originality necessarily resulting; the Nanga artists' use of Chinese styles, as they understood them, is nothing but an extension of the same prac- tice, and should by no means be used as another occasion for the common (and usually misconceived) disparagement of Japanese art as less original because it imitates the Chinese. When the artist's knowledge of Chinese painting sup- plied him with new ideas and techniques, fresh material that enriched his own work, offering ways out of old and deadening habits, as it often did in Japan, then imitation was clearly of positive value. When, on the other hand, the artist made imitation a substitute for creation, working mechanically and with more concern for faithfulness to his model than for producing a good picture, then it was obviously negative in effect. For instance, if we charge some artists— Yanagisawa Kien, perhaps, or Noro Kaiseki—with following their models too closely, we may praise others, such as Hyakusen or Hankō, for having incorpor- ated the strengths of their Chinese models into the creative context of their own works, to their betterment. And we may be saying no more than that Hyakusen and Hankō are the better artists.

The impossibility of a clear stylistic definition of Southern School painting in Japan has led some recent writers to use for the school, instead of Nanga, the term Bunjinga (the Japanese pronunciation of the Chinese *wen-jen-hua,* "literati painting.") But this term, intended as a designation of the artist's social and intellectual status—just as Nanga designates the painting's style— in fact fits the reality no better. The identity of the "literati" in Japan is highly ambiguous,[8] and many of the Nanga artists painted for a living as the *wen-jen* or scholar-amateurs were not supposed to do. With no clear reason for choosing either term, we have retained the older one, which reflects the artists' own belief about their art-historical position, if not always their practice.

8. See Suzuki, *op. cit.* (n. 6 above), pp. 149, 150, and Yoshizawa and Yonezawa, *op. cit.* (n. 2 above), pp. 13, 14, for a discussion of this problem. A basic difference is that the Japanese *bunjin* were subordinate to feudal and military rulers, receiving low sal- aries and not owning their own land, or else were dependent on the patron- age of rich merchants and landowners. They had no such economic inde- pendence as the Chinese literati, who tended to come from the gentry class.

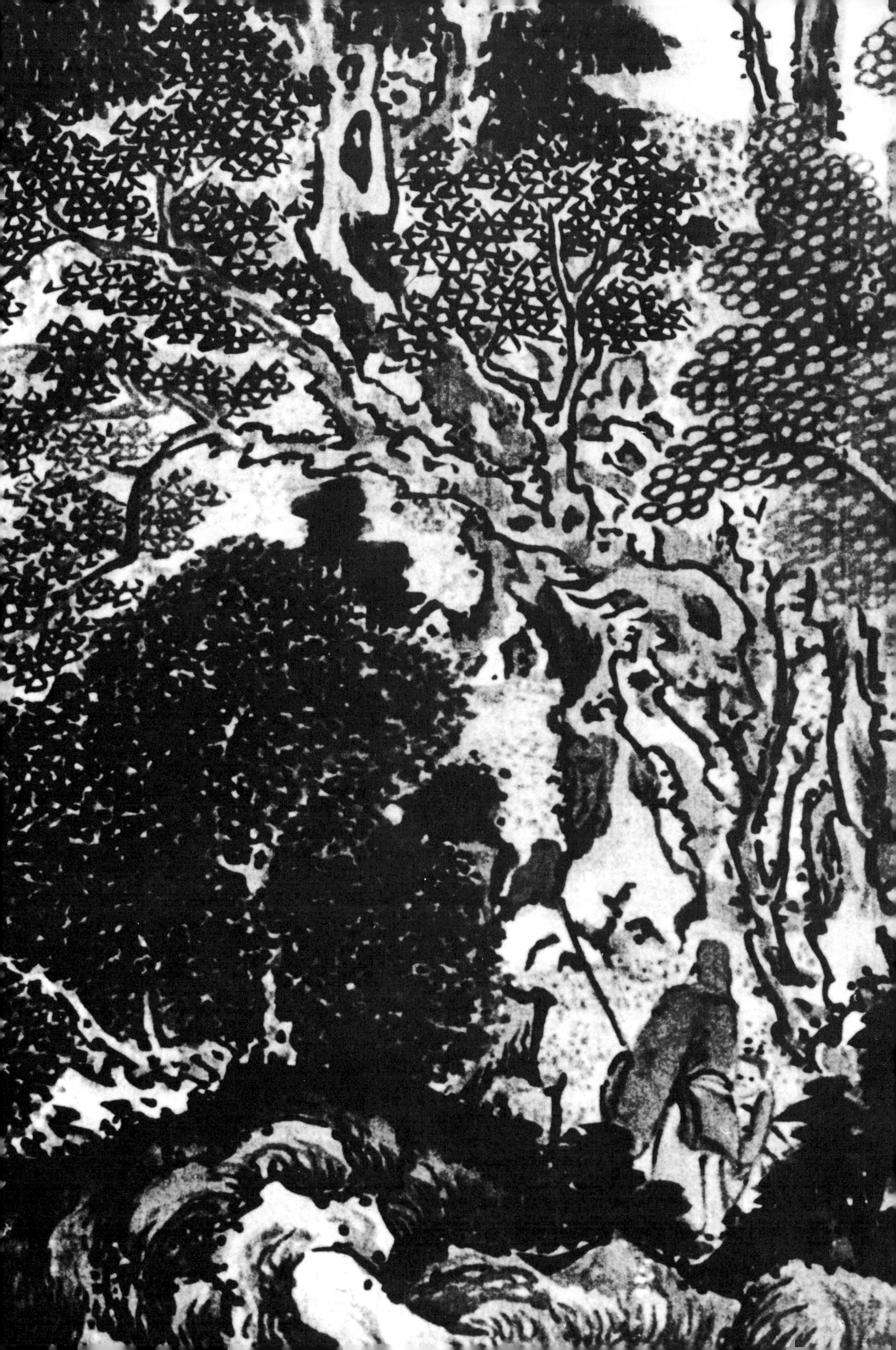

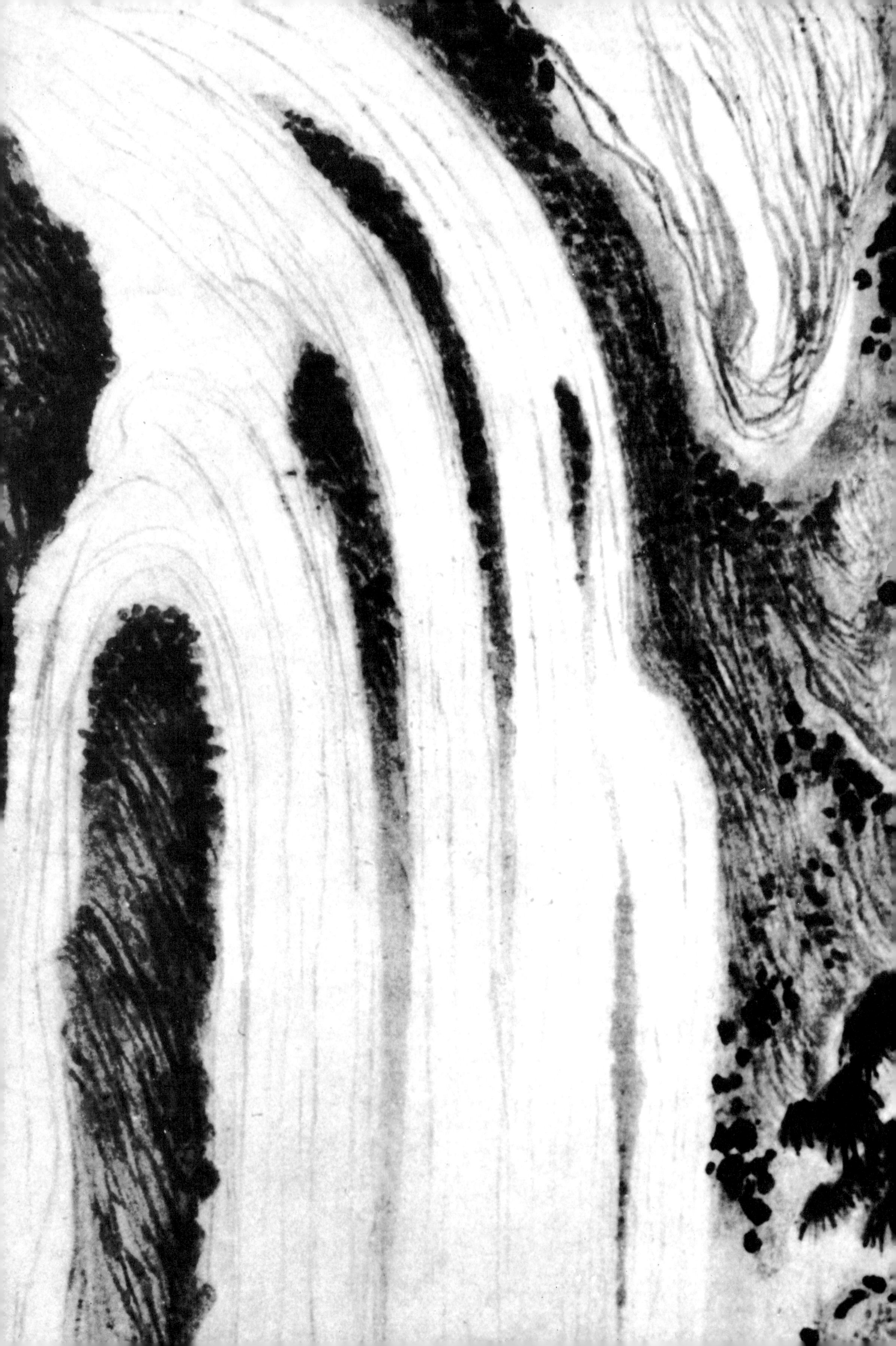

Chapter II: The Beginnings of Nanga

The first generation of Nanga painters is made up of those artists who were
active from the early decades of the eighteenth century into the 1750's. The three
outstanding figures among them were Gion Nankai, Yanagisawa Kien, and
Sakaki Hyakusen. The first two, although important as pioneers, were by training and temperament more properly scholars than painters; the third, Hyakusen,
was less scholarly, more wholeheartedly a painter.

The oldest of them, Gion Nankai (1676-1751), was the eldest son of the clan
physician of the Kishū clan in present-day Wakayama Prefecture. He studied
Confucianism and Chinese literature in Edo (modern Tokyo), and won some
renown for his calligraphy and his poems, which were composed not in
Japanese, but in Chinese. When he was twenty his father died, and Nankai
succeeded to his position as a Confucian clan official. In 1700, he was charged
with some misdemeanor, the nature of which is unknown, and banished from
the clan seat. He lived a wandering and impoverished life until 1710, when
he was pardoned and reinstated, eventually becoming a professor in the clan
school.

As a painter, he seems to have been self-taught. His only teachers were
Chinese paintings of the kinds he aspired to paint, and for the most part they
spoke to him in distant and distorted voices; he knew them chiefly through
woodblock reproductions, especially those in two multi-volume collections
that were popular among Japanese Sinophiles of this period. The first was a
group of eight albums of woodcut pictures gathered and published together in
China in the 1620's under the title *Pa-chung Hua-p'u,* or *Hasshū Gafu* in
Japanese, meaning simply "Eight Different Picture Albums." An excellent
Japanese reprint from recut blocks was issued in 1671. The second was the
famous *Chieh-tzu-yüan hua-chuan* or *Mustard Seed Garden Manual of Painting*
of which Part I, on landscape painting, appeared in China in 1679 and was
probably known in Japan by the end of the century. Parts II and III, treating
bamboo, blossoming plum, birds-and-flowers and similar subjects, appeared
in 1701 and reached Japan soon after. The first Japanese edition of the whole
was printed in Kyoto in 1748. The *Mustard Seed Garden Manual* was printed
partly in color, and used shaded (partially wiped) blocks to reproduce graded
washes. The *Hasshū Gafu,* by contrast, was printed entirely in black and white.
For subjects and styles in which tonal values and color were less important,
such as ink monochrome paintings of bamboo or branches of blossoming plum,

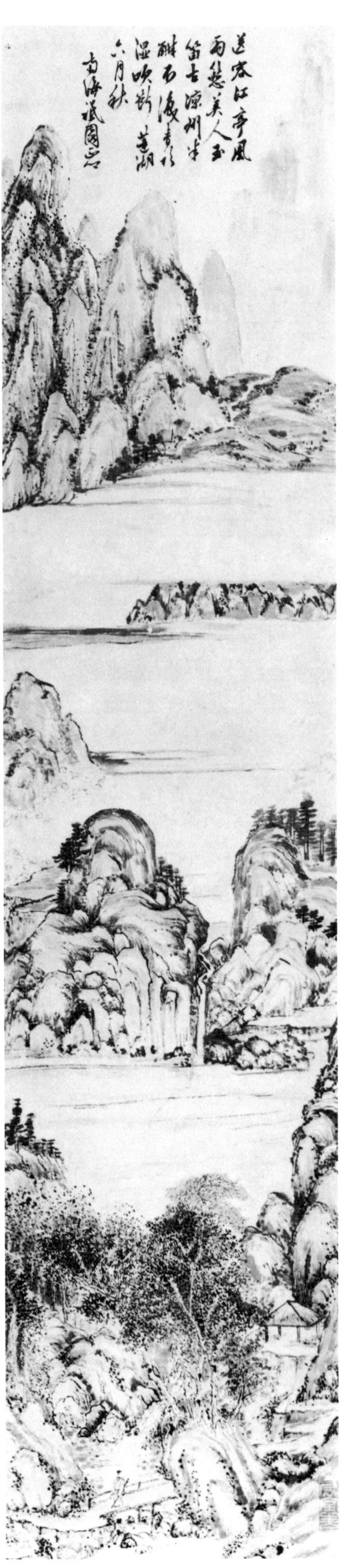

1 Gion Nankai Landscape
Hanging scroll, ink and light
colors on paper. H. 47½ in.
(120.6 cm.)

the products of the translation from (Chinese) painting into woodblock print
and back into (Japanese) painting could still be reasonably close approxima-
tions of the originals. For landscape, however, such crossing of media altered
the style more radically, in ways we shall see. How clearly the early Nanga
artists understood this discrepancy between the prints and the paintings on
which they were based is difficult to say; in any case, it appears to have been
the prints that they imitated, much of the time. Some of the qualities that
distinguish Nanga from Chinese painting—the prevalence of decorative abstrac-
tion and repeated patterns, a general flattening of the picture, a greater reliance
on heavy lineament—may be explained in large part by this circumstance.

Besides studying these and other books, Nankai was able to see a few actual
Chinese paintings when he was in Edo in 1711 and on other occasions. His
earliest dated work is from 1719; others date from 1732 and 1736. The landscape
in the Tokyo National Museum (No. 1) is undated. The composition seems to
represent a rather schematic application of the Chinese compositional device
of separating foreground, middle distance, and background, which are here
almost equally weighted. This was not an entirely new kind of composition in
Japan, but in this extreme form—tall, narrow, piling up stages of "distance"
with no real sense of recession—it was new. The materials of the landscape—
rocks, trees, buildings—are as conventionally Chinese as is the poem at the top.

More successful, because less taxing of limited artistic powers, is Nankai's
painting of a branch of blossoming plum (No. 2), painted in ink on paper, also
undated but probably from his late years, the 1740's. The artist's inscription in the
upper right is again a Chinese-style poem, written this time in the *li* or "clerical"
script. Blossoming plum, as one of the "Four Gentlemen" (plum, bamboo,
orchid, and chrysanthemum), was a specialty of the scholar-amateur artists,
and ink-monochrome renditions of these subjects had been painted by them
for centuries in China, usually without a great deal of stylistic variation, until they
had become a kind of conventional calligraphic exercise, more analagous,
perhaps, to the performance of a piece of music than to the creation of one.
The "Four Gentlemen" became favorite subjects of the amateurs in Japan for the
same reasons—their symbolic value and the ease with which anyone trained
in calligraphy could learn to paint them—as well as because of their close
association with the Chinese literati. Ink paintings of plum branches had been
brought to Japan quite early, even before the rise of Nanga, and Nankai seems
here to have had an original painting as his model, rather than a woodcut
picture, since he imitates not only the composition but the brushwork, including
the "flying white" technique in which the brush tip is allowed to split and
leave streaks of white within the stroke, for an effect of swift movement.

Yanagisawa Kien (1704-1758), who also used the Chinese-sounding name
Ryū Rikyō, had a similar background. He was born in Edo as the younger son in
a family of feudal retainers. After the retirement of his father in 1710, he was
brought up by his older brother. In 1788 Kien, like Nankai, was accused of some
"misdemeanor"—again of unknown nature, but perhaps some quite pardon-
able infringement of the strict clan rules, such as anyone of an independent turn
of mind might commit—and was prevented from assuming his proper rank
in the family. Two years later he was reinstated. He was a man of many talents,
rich, learned, and versatile, a dilettante in the best sense. It was Kien whom we
quoted above, telling how he began by studying painting in the Kanō School
style, but became dissatisfied with this and turned to Chinese models. He
learned bird-and-flower painting in the style of the Chinese artist Shen Ch'üan

曾飄東閣夢虛竇復上壽陽
鏡裏妝今日江南知己少清香
乱入誰家篴　深琯詩画併隸

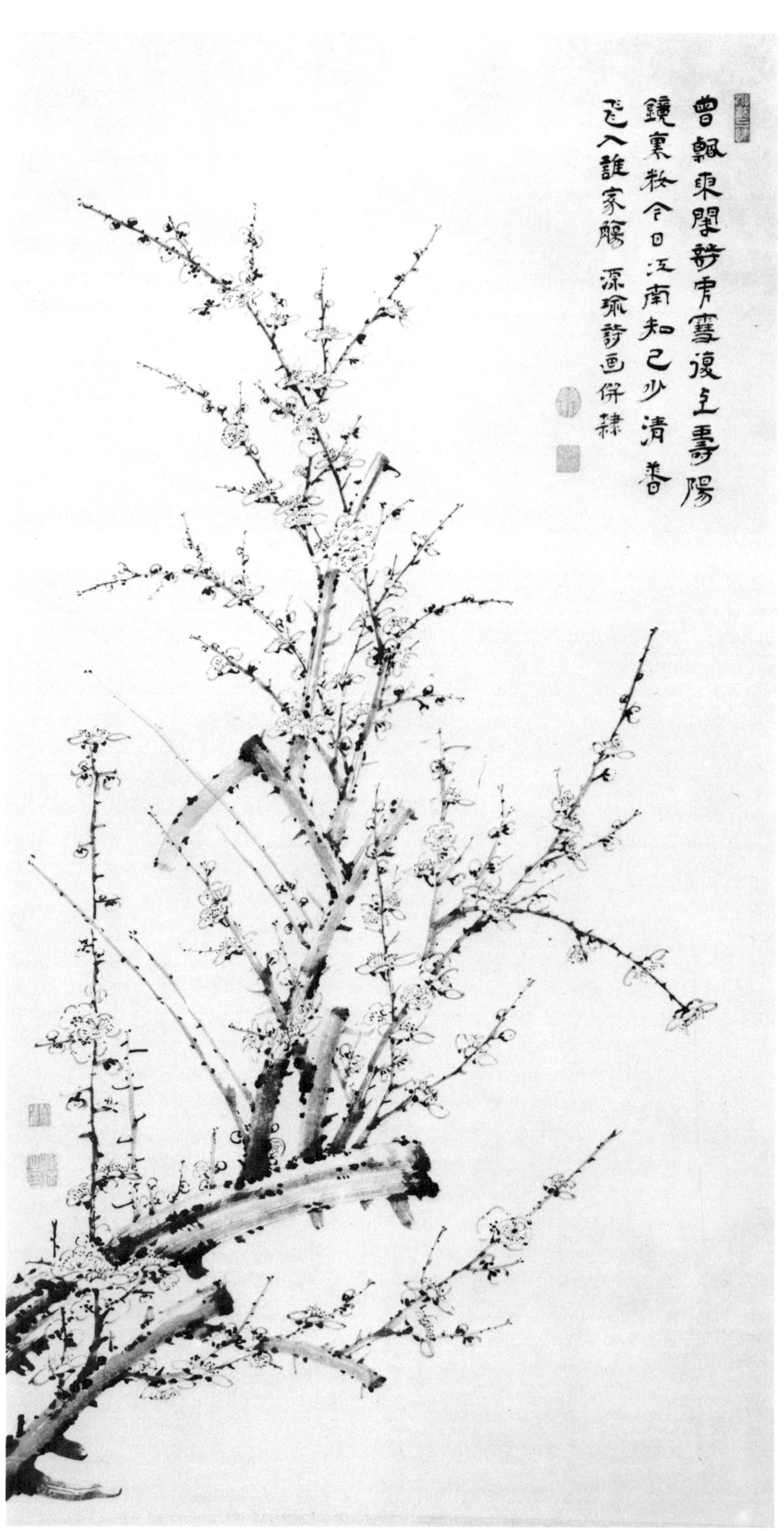

2 Gion Nankai A branch of Blossoming Plum. Hanging scroll, ink on paper. H. 38³/₈ in. (97.6 cm.)

3a, b, c Yanagisawa Kien Flowers of the First, Fifth, and Ninth Months. Three hanging scrolls, colors on silk. Each, H. 38⁷/₈ in. (98.8 cm.)

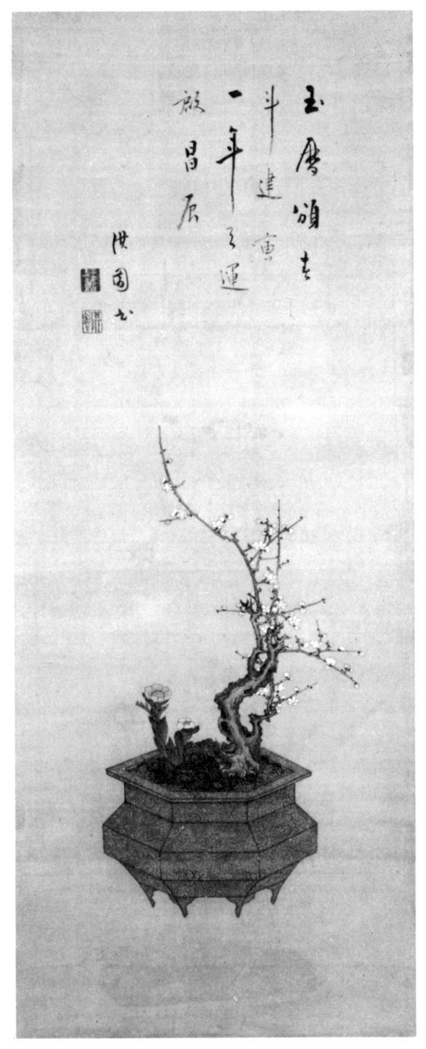

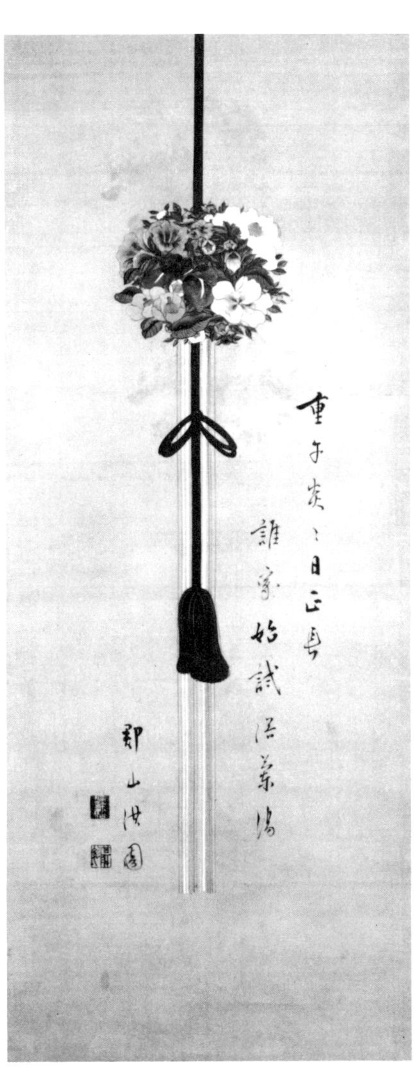

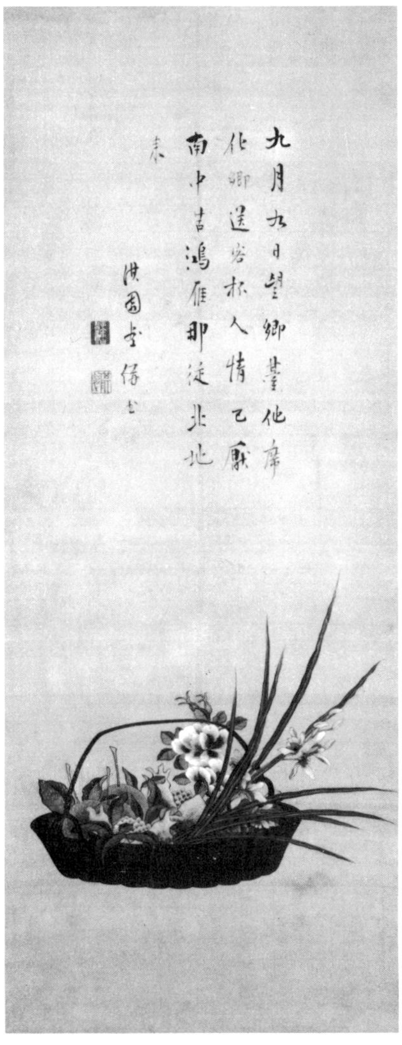

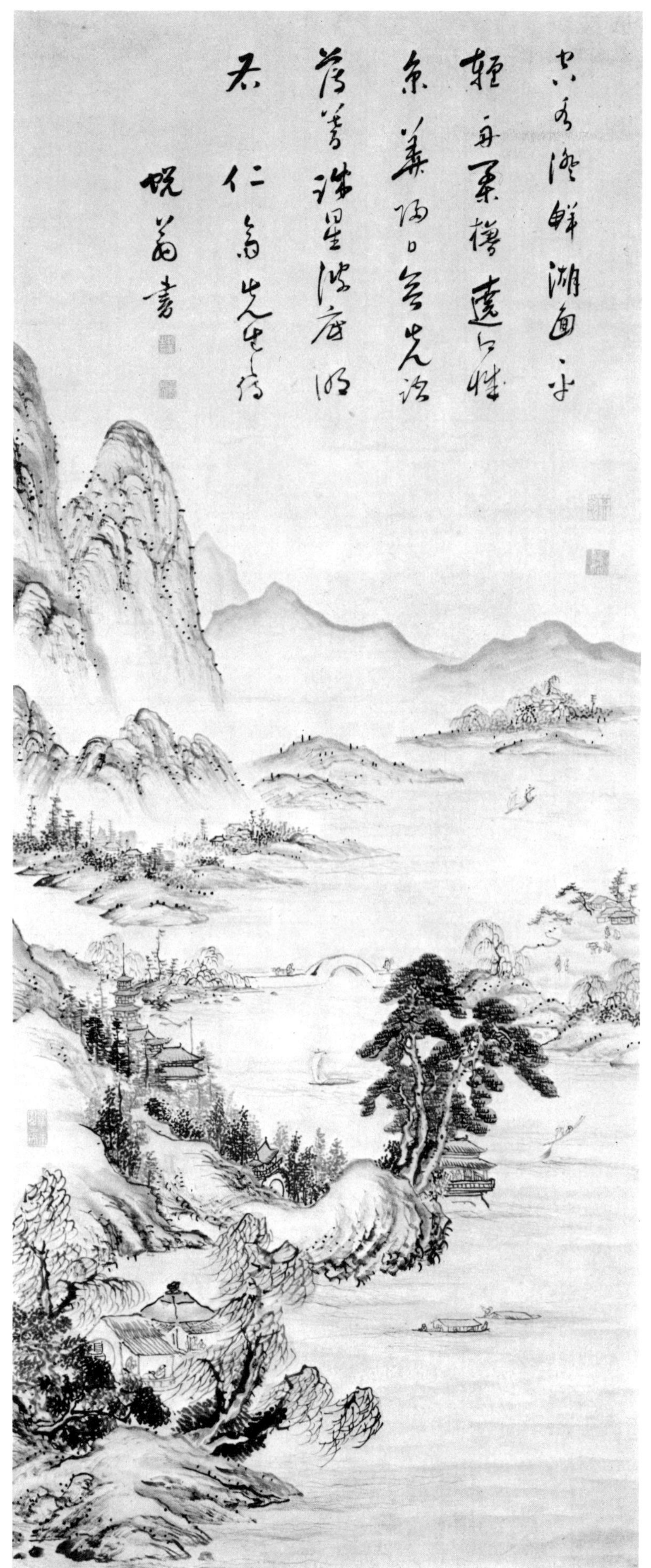

4a, b Yanagisawa Kien Landscape of the West Lake at Hangchow. Pair of hanging scrolls, ink and light colors on paper. Each, H. 53³/₄ in. (136.6 cm.)

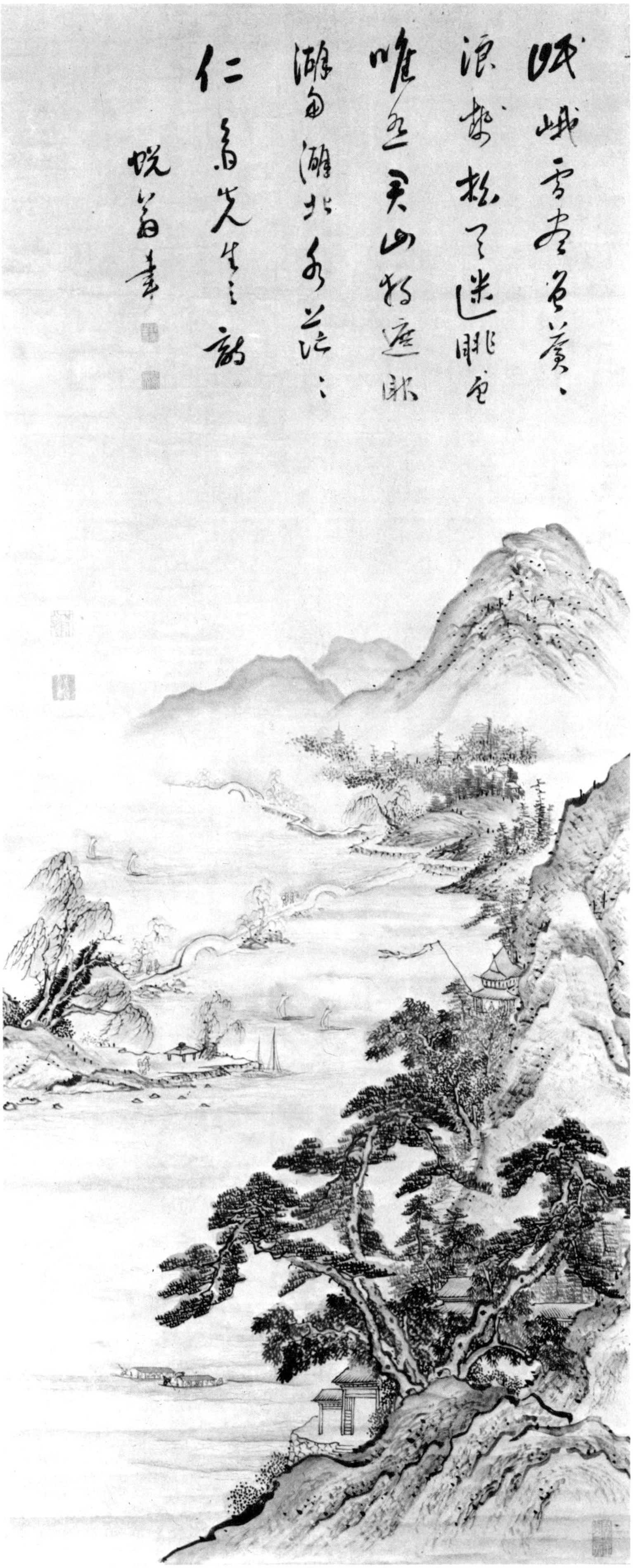

峨峨雪嶺為奇觀、
浪捲松濤了迷眺色
唯至天山物遮晾
游魚澥北香蘭
仁翁先生之韻
晚笛書

from a Nagasaki School artist named Ei Genshō, and landscape painting from
the same second-hand sources that Nankai used, chiefly the *Mustard Seed
Garden Manual.*

His triptych representing "Flowers of the First, Fifth and Ninth Months"
(Nos. 3a-c) in the Japanese Imperial Household Collection is the best known of
his flower compositions. The paintings are in heavy colors on silk, and are
undated. The compositions are very formal and static; they might have been
based on academic Chinese pictures of such subjects that had long been preserved in Japan, ascribed to such early artists as Ch'ien Hsüan but actually the
productions of anonymous minor masters. The hard line drawing presumably
imitates woodblock pictures.

The two landscapes representing "The West Lake at Hangchow" (Nos. 4a-b)
reveal more of the new Southern School spirit in subject as well as style. The
West Lake, rich in historical associations as well as in scenic beauty, had been the
subject of innumerable Chinese paintings and poems, and so was regarded by
Japanese Sinophiles as part of the literati culture to which they felt so drawn.
Their paintings of it were based partly on Chinese pictures, partly on literary
descriptions, partly on imagination. Kien's picture includes the features that
identify the scene immediately, the dikes with arched bridges that connect
islands in the lake with the shore, where temples and villas were located at the
foot of wooded hills. He uses softer, more fluid brushstrokes here, and enriches
the surfaces of the banks and hills with applications of the texture strokes
(ts'un) and dots *(tien)* of the Chinese literati styles. There is little that is distinctive
in the pictures, however, which seem remote from any truly visual involvement
with the scene they represent.

Sakaki Hyakusen (or Bō Hyakusen, 1697-1752) was born in Nagoya, the son of
a druggist, possibly of Chinese ancestry. Unlike Nankai and Kien—and contrary
to the status of the "literati painter" strictly defined—he was not a Confucian
scholar-amateur at all, but a trained professional artist. He learned, and used, the
styles of both the Kanō and Tosa Schools, the two orthodox traditions of
Japanese painting prevalent at this time. He was also an accomplished *haiku*
poet, and a pioneer in the art of *haiga,* simple pictures drawn to accompany
haiku poems. In these as in other kinds of painting he was followed by Buson,
whose achievements in *haiga* we will encounter later. Like Taiga and Buson after
him, he painted screens and *fusuma* (sliding door) compositions, which,
because they are functional in nature and require skill in organizing large areas,
were normally the province of the professional painter. He worked in such
a variety of styles and manners that it appears to be very difficult to find any
coherence or development within his *oeuvre.*

Those of his works that can properly be called Nanga were based on his studies
of Chinese paintings, of which he appears to have seen more—or which he
understood more deeply—than either Nankai or Kien. Certain of his works, for
example the pair of screens now in the Tokyo National Museum, reveal
unmistakably a first-hand contact with the works of late Ming artists such as
Sheng Mao-yeh. He compiled a book of biographical information about Chinese
artists of the Yüan and Ming periods, the *Gen-Min Gajin Kō,* published in 1751.
His contribution to the development of Nanga was twofold: he captured in
his pictures positive qualities of the Chinese styles that escaped Nankai and Kien
(sensitivity and variety of brushwork, nuances of tonal gradation, greater
complexity combined with clarity of organization); and he also began the
process of assimilating these styles into the Japanese tradition of painting,

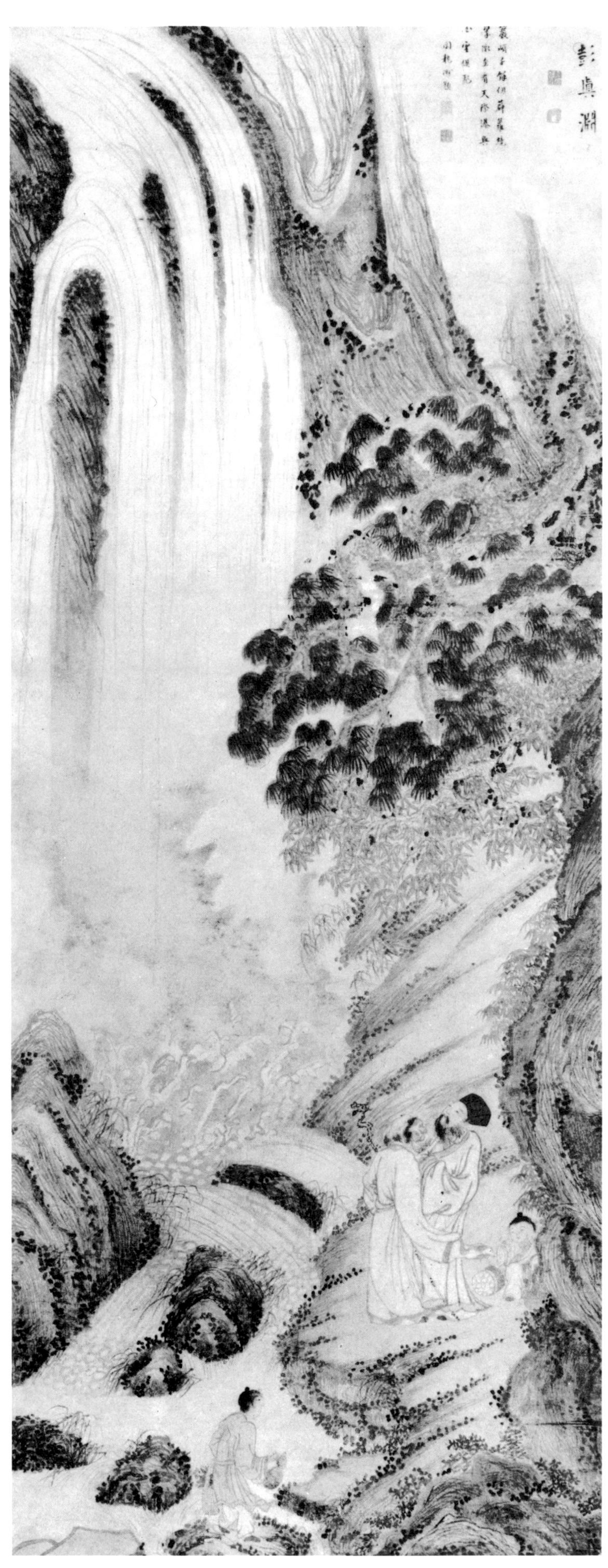

6 Sakaki Hyakusen Li Po Gazing at a Waterfall. Hanging scroll, ink and light colors on paper. H. 53¹/₂ in. (135.9 cm.)

a process that, eventually, Taiga and Buson were to complete.

Hyakusen's landscapes with figures convey, like their Chinese models, ideal moments in the lives of ideal scholars. In one, which he painted in 1745 (No. 5), an elegant gentleman leans over the railing of a riverside pavilion, where he is spending a hot summer day in the green shade of willows, to consider gravely a fish offered for sale by a local fisherman. The composition follows a plan developed in China during the fourteenth century, in which the sharply slanted recession of an expanse of water is demarcated by the placement of widely separated land masses, in foreground and distance. The picture of "Li Po Gazing at a Waterfall" (No. 6) may be based on some late Ming Chinese model; similar pictures by Sheng Mao-yeh and others are known. It is drawn in fluid, supple brushstrokes that serve to enliven the forms, which are also given a feeling of surging motion in their shapes. Both pictures are imbued with particularized moods—and realize the expressive capacities of the Chinese styles in a way that makes the works of Nankai and Kien seem by comparison rather cold. A conventional explanation of this quality in Hyakusen would be that he, like Buson, was a poet of the subtle and evocative *haiku*. We would prefer to say simply that he was a man of less severe temperament, and a better painter.

Other works of Hyakusen which could not be included in this exhibition bring us still closer to the world of Taiga and Buson, showing even less of doctrinary adherence to Chinese conventions and more of the Japanese fondness for color, for decorative surface, for anecdotal detail. The direction to be taken in the best of Nanga painting was already set in these works; significantly, it was a direction quite opposed to the stated ideals and standard practice of the Chinese literati painters. Nanga was already moving toward independence.

A lesser master of this early period was Nakayama Kōyō (1717-1780). He was a native of Tosa, Kōchi Prefecture, in Shikoku. His father was from a samurai family, but had become a merchant. Kōyō studied Confucianism in his early years, and may have studied painting also, under Hyakusen, although he seems to have learned most of what he knew about painting from books. In 1759 he moved to Edo (modern Tokyo) and was active in scholarly circles there. He is the author of the *Gatan Keiroku,* a book on painting to which we referred in the previous chapter as containing the first attempt to distinguish clearly between the Northern and Southern Schools. In 1772 he made a seven-month trip to the Tōhoku region, after his house had been burned in a great fire in Edo. It was probably on this trip that he painted landscapes of Matsushima and Hisagata, of which we include the former (No. 7). According to his diary, these were painted in the styles of two early Chinese masters: the scene of Matsushima after Li Ssu-hsün (651-716), and the scene of Hisagata after Tung Yüan (d. 962). These two were regarded in Chinese writings as the founding fathers, respectively, of the Northern and Southern Schools[1]; the pictures thus might be seen as demonstrations in pictorial form of the same distinction that Kōyō was later (1775) to discuss in his book. Little if anything is to be seen of Li Ssu-hsün's style, however, in the landscape of Matsushima, which is, like Kōyō's other work, pleasant and rather amateurish. The long inscription at the top adds to the literary flavor.

5 Sakaki Hyakusen River Landscape with Willows, 1745. Hanking scroll, ink and light colors on paper. H. 52 in. (132.2 cm.)

7 Nakayama Kōyō Landscape of Matsushima, probably painted in 1772. Hanging scroll, ink and light colors on paper. H. 38¼ in. (97.1 cm.)

1. It was, of course, Wang Wei who was called the founder of the Southern School by Tung Ch'i-ch'ang and others; but this was largely for reasons of symmetry, to place the origins of both schools in the T'ang period, and in order to contrast the court painter Li Ssu-hsün with the poet-artist Wang Wei. Tung Yüan is the proper founder of the landscape tradition that made up the main line of development in the literati school.

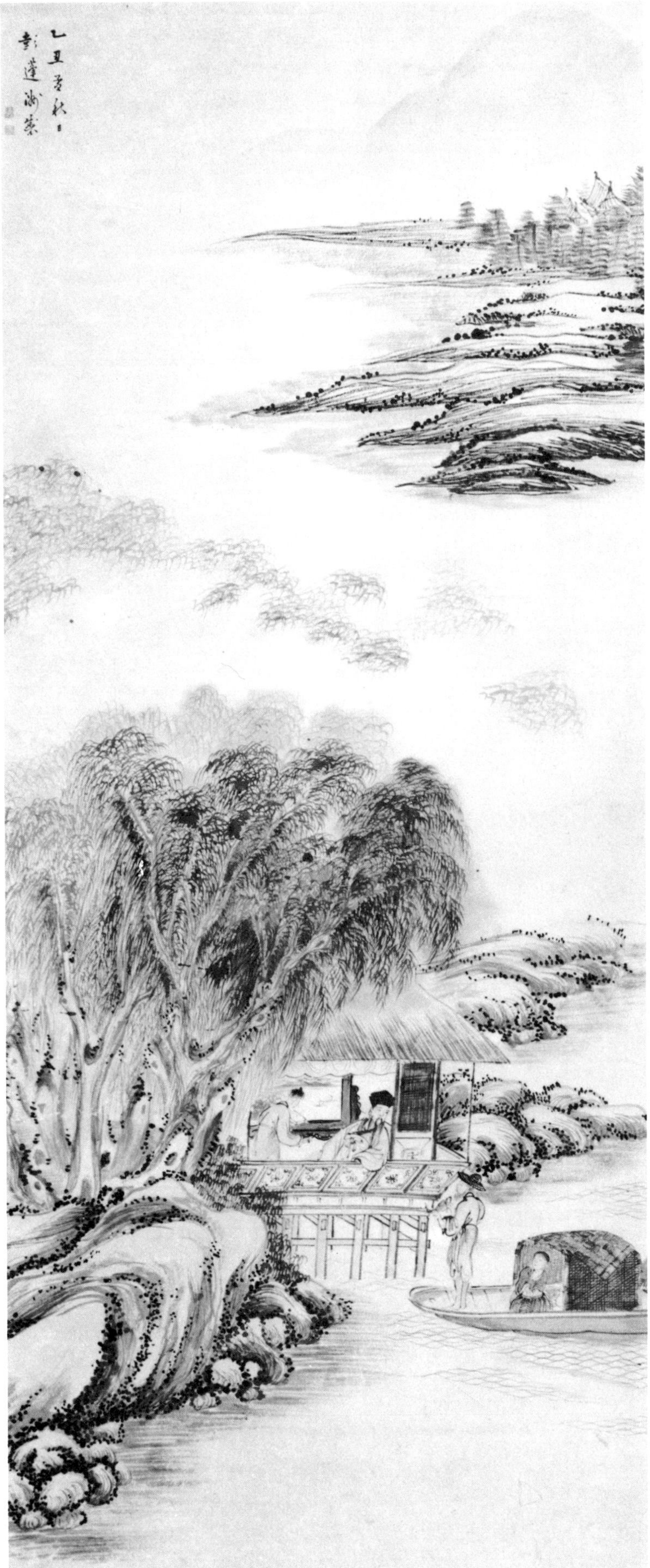

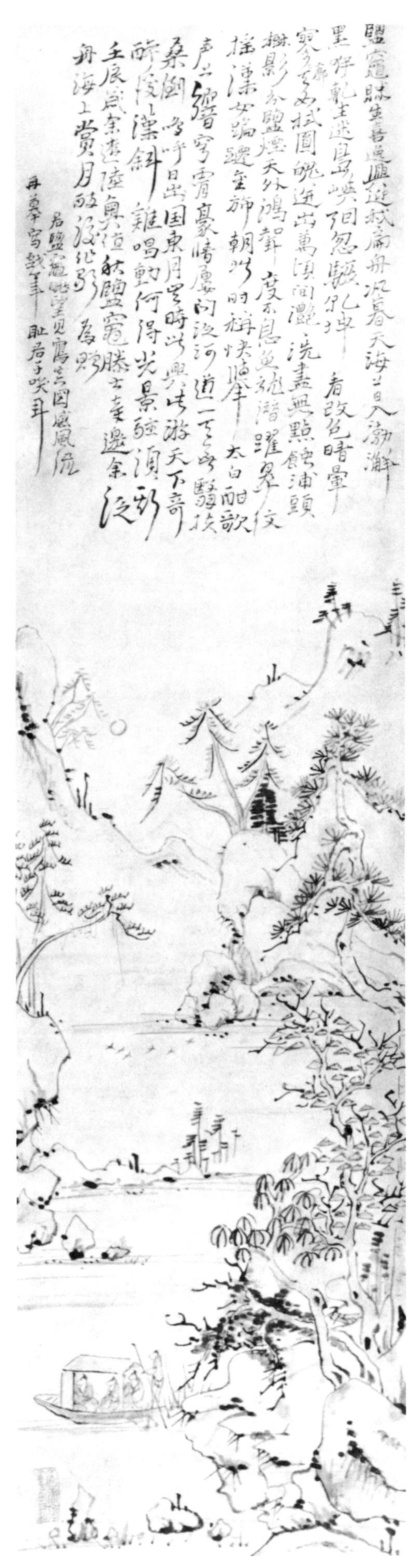

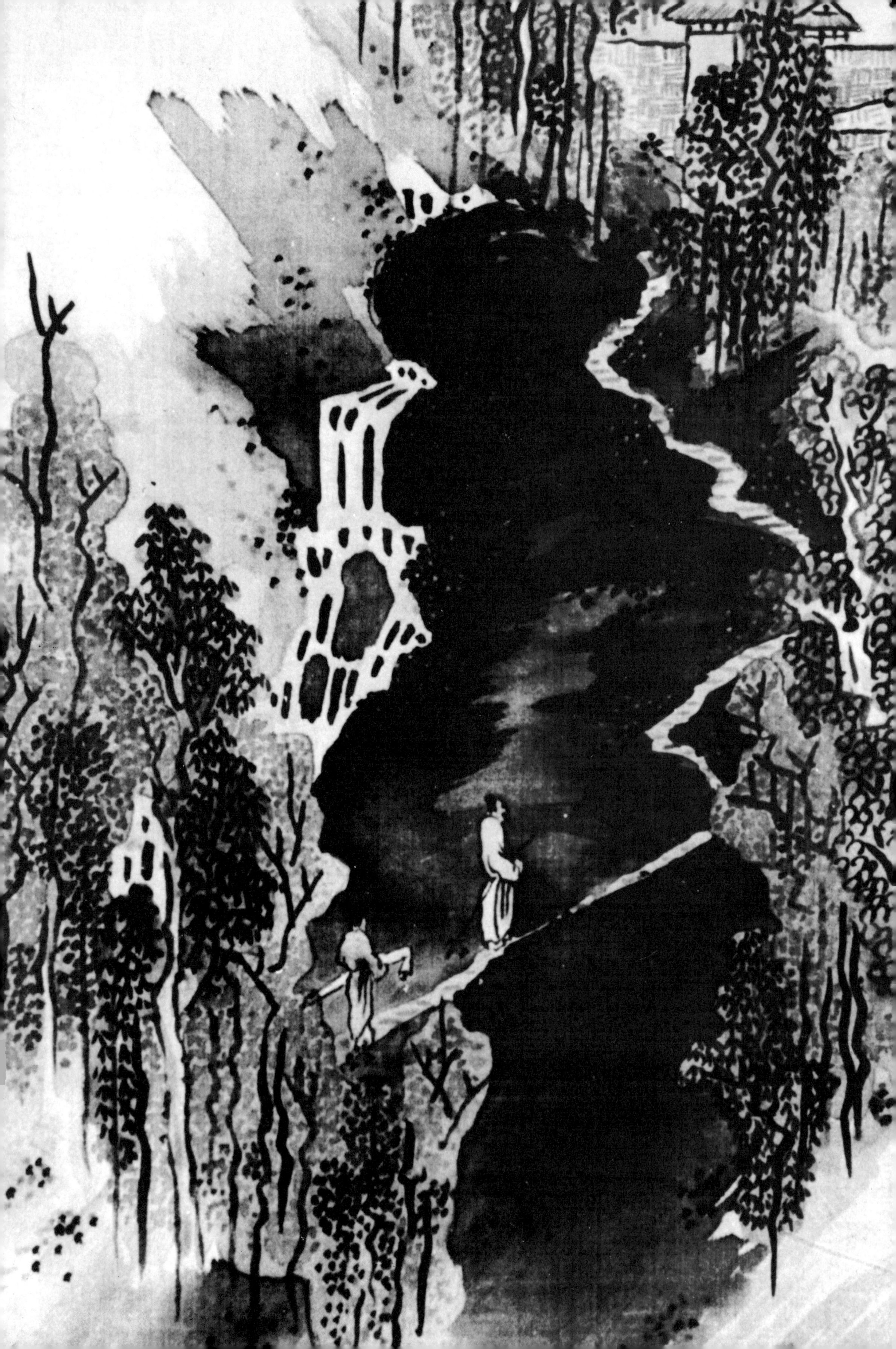

Chapter III: Ikeno Taiga and His Followers

18 Kuwayama Gyokushū
Landscape with Figures, 1798
(detail)

The Nanga School reaches full maturity with the period of Taiga and Buson, beginning in the third quarter of the eighteenth century. Borrowings from China have by this time been assimilated into an independent, Japanese school of painting with new and viable styles of its own.

Ikeno Taiga (1723-1776) is one of the prodigious figures of Japanese art. Considering his relatively short span of activity, about four decades, he produced an amazing quantity of paintings and calligraphy—a recent compilation of surviving, authenticated works included over eight hundred pieces,[1] and many more were left out. Moreover, an impressive number of these are large compositions, screens and sliding doors. Most impressive of all, perhaps, is the versatility and endless inventiveness of Taiga. He was forever trying new compositions and new techniques. Many of these did not prove very successful, at least in his hands, and there is a great deal that is odd and awkward in his works. But there is much more that is fully realized and brilliantly original. Taiga created a world of forms that is as rich in its scenery, as entertainingly peopled, as any in Japanese painting.

Taiga was born into a farmer's family in a village in the hills north of Kyoto. His father had come to Kyoto to work in the silver mint. The man under whom he worked may have been the same Nakamura Kuranosuke who was a friend and patron of Kōrin. The father died when Taiga was four. Taiga had mastered the art of calligraphy and was already painting by the age of seven; by the time he was fifteen, he was supporting himself and his mother with the income from a fan shop he had opened in Kyoto. The designs for the fans he adapted from the *Hasshū Gafu,* a Chinese book of woodcut pictures mentioned earlier. Thus Taiga was, from the beginning, a professional artist, as we know also from other evidence, such as a reference to him in the diary of a contemporary, written when he was twenty-two, which calls him a *gakō* or "artisan painter."

We know very little about Taiga's training as a painter. He is said to have learned the Tosa style from Tosa Mitsuyoshi (1700-1772). He also, however, associated with scholars of the area, and from them absorbed the Nanga styles and taste. From 1738 he lived for two or three years with Yanagisawa Kien, and studied painting under him. One of Kien's specialties was finger-painting, in which the ink was applied to paper with the fingernails, fingers, and hand; quite a number of Taiga's early works are done in this technique. When Taiga visited Edo in 1748, after climbing Mt. Fuji and visiting other scenic places, he

1. Susumu Suzuki *et al., Ikeno Taiga Sakuhin-shū* [Collection of Works by Ikeno Taiga] (Tokyo, 1960).

was invited everywhere to do "performances" of finger painting. In 1750,
through Kien's introduction, he met Gion Nankai, who was impressed by his
finger paintings, but even more by his buoyant and unconventional personality.
Taiga reportedly asked Nankai for instruction in painting, and was told that
he should study the works of the scholar-artists of China—advice which Taiga,
by this time, scarcely needed. Nankai presented the young artist with an album
of woodcut pictures after paintings by Hsiao Yün-ts'ung (1596-1673), probably
his *T'ai-p'ing shan-shui.*

In Edo, Taiga was able to see European pictures, probably engravings, at the
house of the herbalist Noro Genjō. He was fascinated by them, and later used in
his own paintings some of their techniques, particularly in the ways of rendering
distance in landscapes. Taiga also studied Japanese styles of painting, especially
the Rimpa (Sōtatsu—Kōrin School.) He sometimes painted screens and *fusuma*
pictures on a gold ground, in styles that were in some part derived from
Rimpa. Most of all, however, he studied Chinese paintings, any that he could
see—genuine works, copies, forgeries—and books such as the *Mustard Seed
Garden Manual.* Certain of his compositions are based on pictures in that book.
All these elements were adopted, and more or less absorbed into his personal
style. In his early works, the borrowings are often obvious; in works of his middle
and late periods, the assimilation is more complete and one is less conscious
of the diversity of sources.

The handscroll titled *"Rakushi-ron"* ("Lo-chih lun," or "Essay on Enjoying
One's Will," No. 8) illustrates an essay by a Chinese scholar of the later Han
period, Chung-ch'ang T'ung (A.D. 179-220), in praise of living in retirement. In
the picture Chung-ch'ang is seen in his house in the mountains, seated at a desk,
with a *ch'in* (zither) on the table in front of him, along with books and brushes.
A servant in an adjoining library is preparing tea. The title preceding the painting
is in the calligraphy of Yanagisawa Kien, and mounted after it is the entire text
of the essay, copied out by Gion Nankai. The scroll is thus a record of Taiga's
association with these two older Nanga masters. It was painted in 1750, when
Taiga was twenty-eight (by Japanese count), and is in the relatively tight and
unadventurous style of his early years. The conventions used for rocks and trees
are taken fairly directly from the *Mustard Seed Garden Manual* and other
Chinese books; the sloping ground surfaces are covered with stringy lines
imitating the woodblock renderings of the Chinese painters' *ts'un,* or texture
strokes, and the repeated patterns of dots and leaf groups used in the tree
foliage are similarly based on printed pictures of trees. Such conventions served
as important sources of Taiga's style. The picture is not very strongly organized;
transitions are masked or handled in the most perfunctory way. The pastiche-
like character of the composition is seen, for instance, in the awkward dispro-
portion between the large figure at the beginning, a visitor about to cross a
bridge in the middle ground, and the smaller figures in the house in the foreground. It is apparent that Taiga is still in the process of mastering his art, but is
already capable of working in a lively and entertaining manner.

Along with such idealized scenes of China and the lives of its literati, Taiga
began quite early to paint landscapes representing scenes in Japan that he knew
first-hand. The series of scrolls representing "Six Sights in Kyoto" (Nos. 9a, b)
painted when he was in his early thirties,[2] two of which are shown here, are of
this kind. Even these, however, are not entirely independent of Chinese models;
they are painted, according to Taiga's inscriptions, in the manners of six great
Chinese masters of the Sung dynasty. The picture of the Daibutsu-kaku

2. Accompanying the paintings is a set of
six poems written by Gion Nankai; but
since Nankai died when Taiga was only
29, while the paintings appear from their
style to have been executed somewhat
later, it is assumed by Japanese scholars
that the paintings were done after
Nankai's death to match already existing
poems. The paintings may originally
have been panels of a screen.

"imitates" Mi Fu (1051-1107), a landscapist who (judging from the works
ascribed to him) built up his mountains and trees in heavy dots of ink. Taiga
follows this technique in using large, evenly-applied touches of ink for most of
the forms, but the effect is very different from that of any Chinese "Mi-style"
works. Ink values are distributed decoratively, as in ink-monochrome paintings
of the Rimpa School, and no real sense of depth results, except perhaps on
the peak, where the dots are used as stippling to distinguish light and shadow,
a technique that Taiga was to use more effectively later in such works as the
"Real View of Kojima Bay" (No. 14). The Daibutsu-kaku or Great Buddha Pavilion
once stood in southeastern Kyoto; it was built in 1598, and burned in 1798. In
Taiga's picture, it is viewed across the Kamo River, against the eastern hills.

The other scroll we include represents the Tōfukuji, a Zen Buddhist temple
also located in the southeast section of Kyoto. This picture is inscribed as being
in the manner of Hsia Kuei, the great Chinese landscapist of the late twelfth and
early thirteenth centuries. It is difficult to discern anything of Hsia Kuei in
Taiga's picture, which uses colors as Hsia never did, avoids the graded washes
that Hsia employed so brilliantly, disperses detail and interest where Hsia
concentrated them, and otherwise belongs at an opposite pole from the Southern
Sung master's style. Within Taiga's *oeuvre,* however, it represents a great
advance over the *"Rakushi-ron"* handscroll in its tighter interlocking of parts
and firmness of drawing.

Taiga's individual style was not fully formed and under control until he had
reached his late thirties. A new assurance, a harmony of technique and intent, is
revealed in his screen representing the "Poetical Gathering at the Orchid
Pavilion" (*"Rantei,"* or in Chinese *"Lan-t'ing"),* which belongs to this period of
his life (No. 10). The event depicted took place in southern China in the year
353, when a group of poets and scholars, led by the great calligrapher Wang
Hsi-chih, met at the Orchid Pavilion to compose poems while seated on the
banks of a winding stream, drinking wine from cups floated to them on the
water. Such scenes of scholarly gatherings were favorite Nanga themes. The
round and oval areas of foliage, varied decoratively according to the type of tree
and backed with graded washes of green and blue color, form a unifying
motif, set against the more substantial rocks. With the groups of poets, drawn
in fluid lines and seen sometimes through convenient openings in the rocks, we
encounter Taiga's favorite figure types, genial old gentlemen in flowing robes.
The marked contrast in manner of drawing between broadly treated areas and
fine-line patterns, heavy and light, works against any convincing sense of space
and mass, but is a very effective abstract device for combining lively detail
with a bold design.

The reduction of some of these textures to flat, decorative patterns represents
(and this is the key to much of Taiga's style) a reconversion to brush painting
technique of the necessary flatness of woodblock color prints. For example, the
brush-textures of areas of tree foliage in the original Chinese paintings had
been reproduced in the prints by using ink-blocks for a dotted pattern, with flat
or evenly shaded areas of color superimposed. Just such flat areas of dotted
pattern overlaid with flat or shaded color wash appear in the trees in Taiga's
paintings. The texture-strokes on the rocks in Taiga's picture for the most part do
not overlap to produce richly matted surfaces, as they do in Chinese paintings—
such overlapping is of course impossible in woodblock—but are applied as
separate lines. The prominence of the linear drawing is probably due in large
part to its source in the same technique. It would certainly be wrong, however,

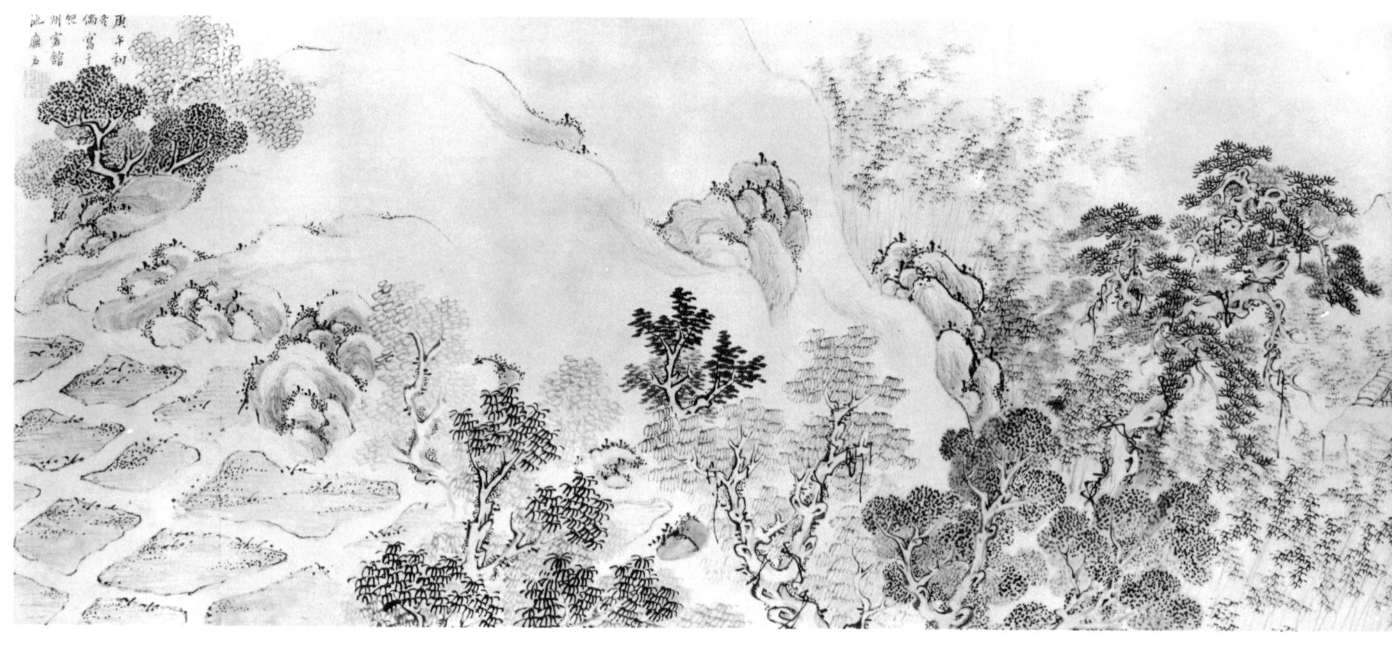

8 Ikeno Taiga Essay on Enjoying
One's Will *(Rakushi-ron* or
Lo-chih lun), 1750. Handscroll,
ink and light colors on paper.
H. 11⅛ in. (28.3 cm.)

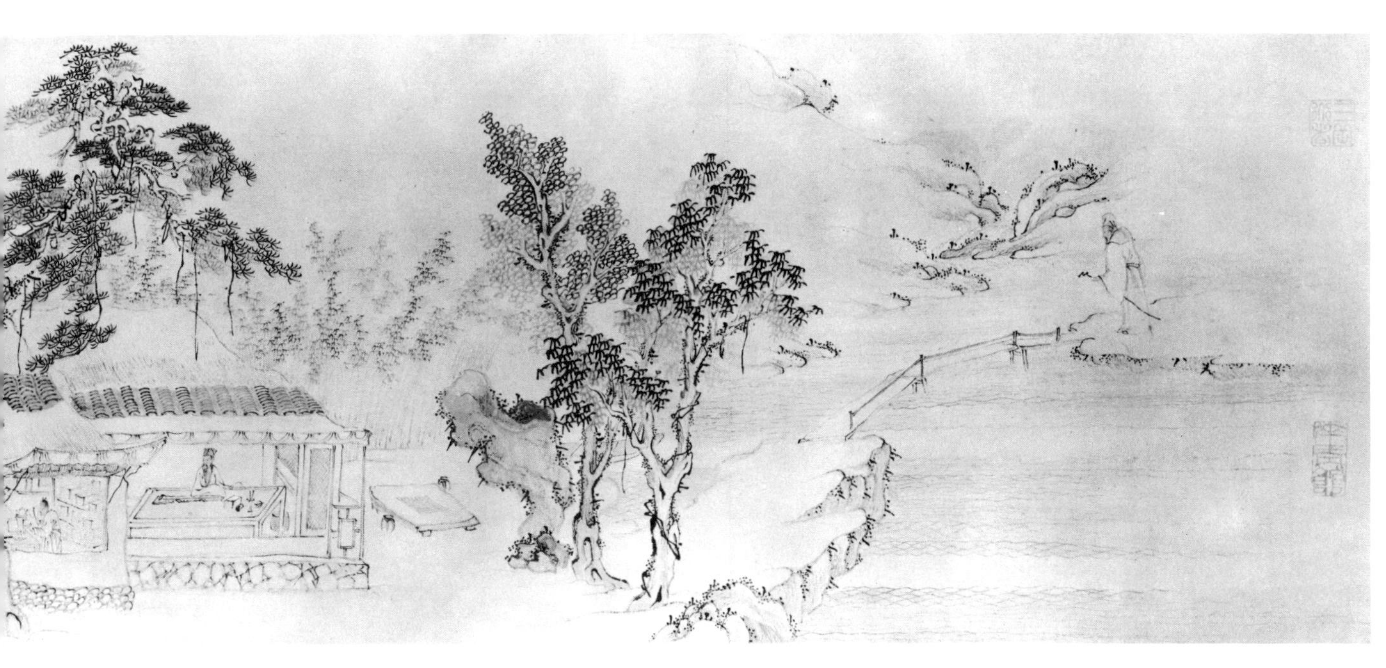

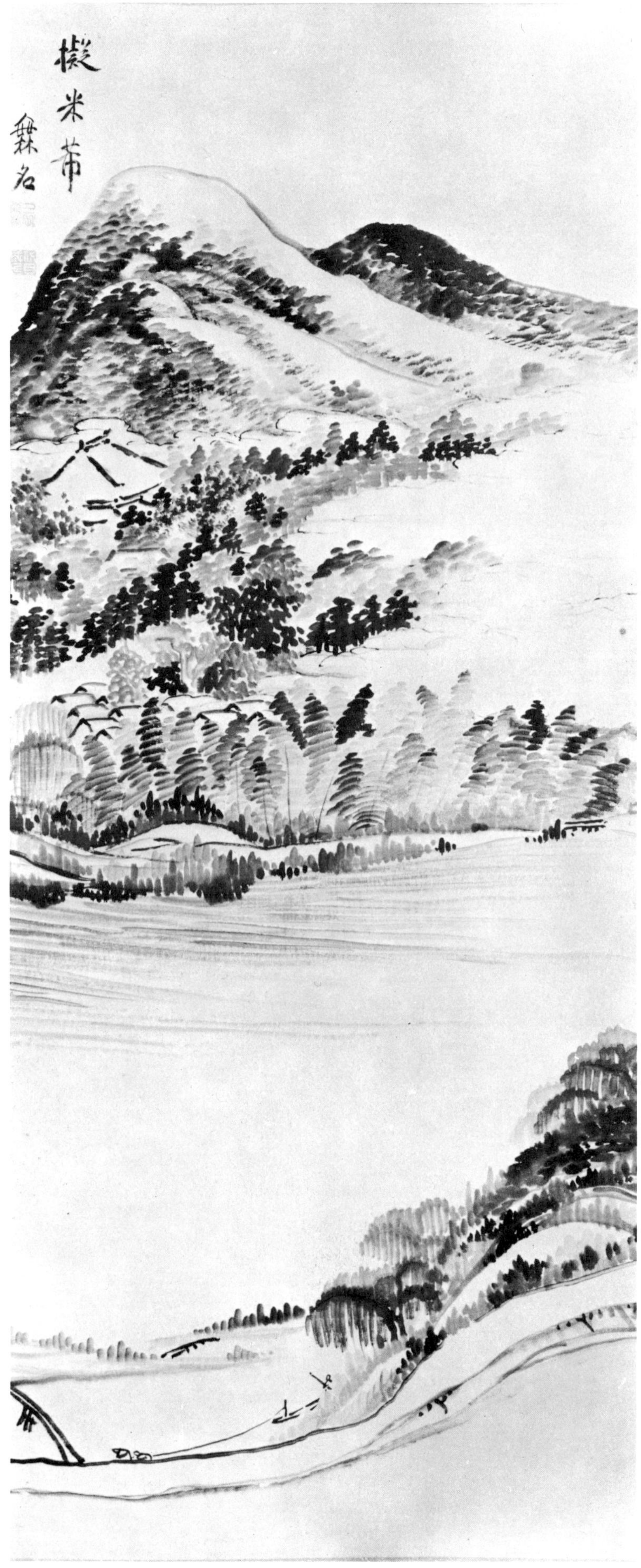

9a, b Ikeno Taiga The Daibutsu-kaku and Tōfukuji, from Six Sights in Kyoto. Two hanging scrolls from a series of six. a. Daibutsu-kaku: ink on paper. H. 51½ in. (130.9 cm.), b. Tōfukuji: ink and light colors on paper. H. 50½ in. (128.2 cm.)

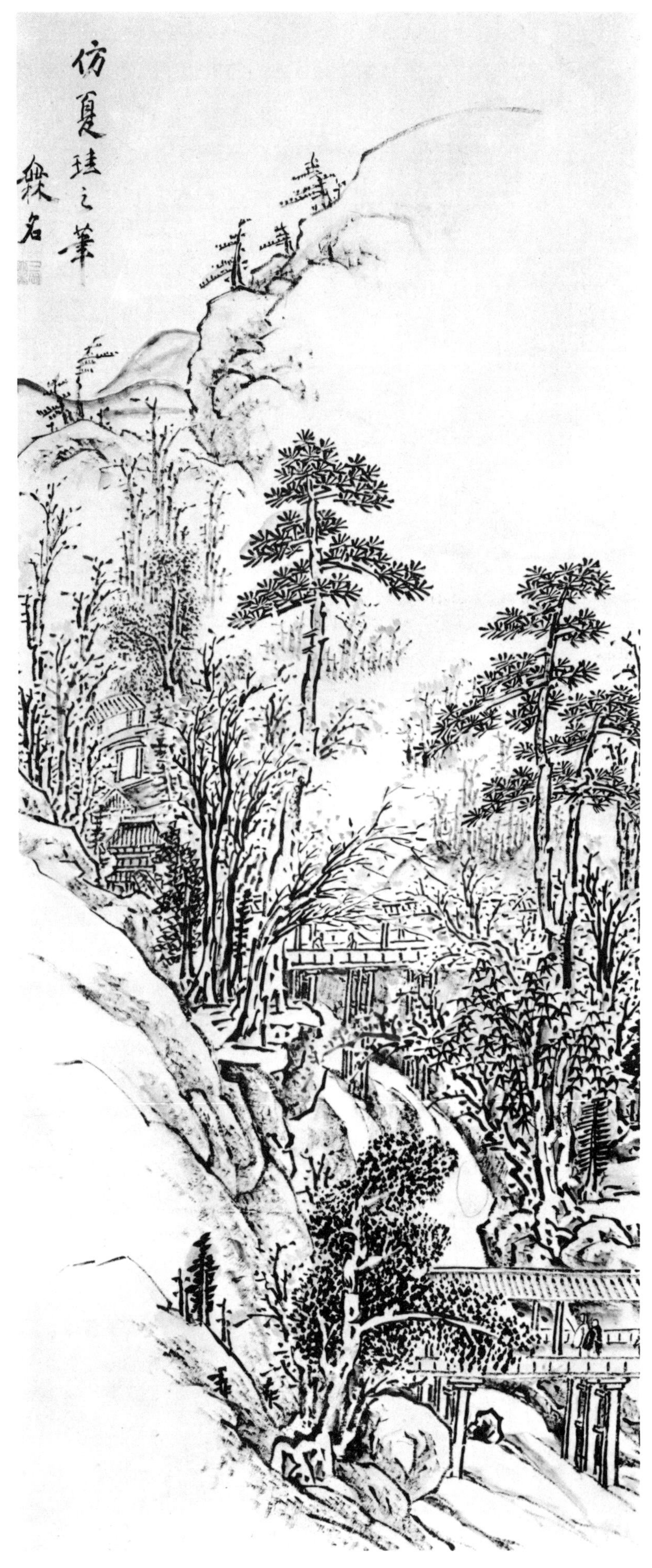

仿夏珪之筆
狨名

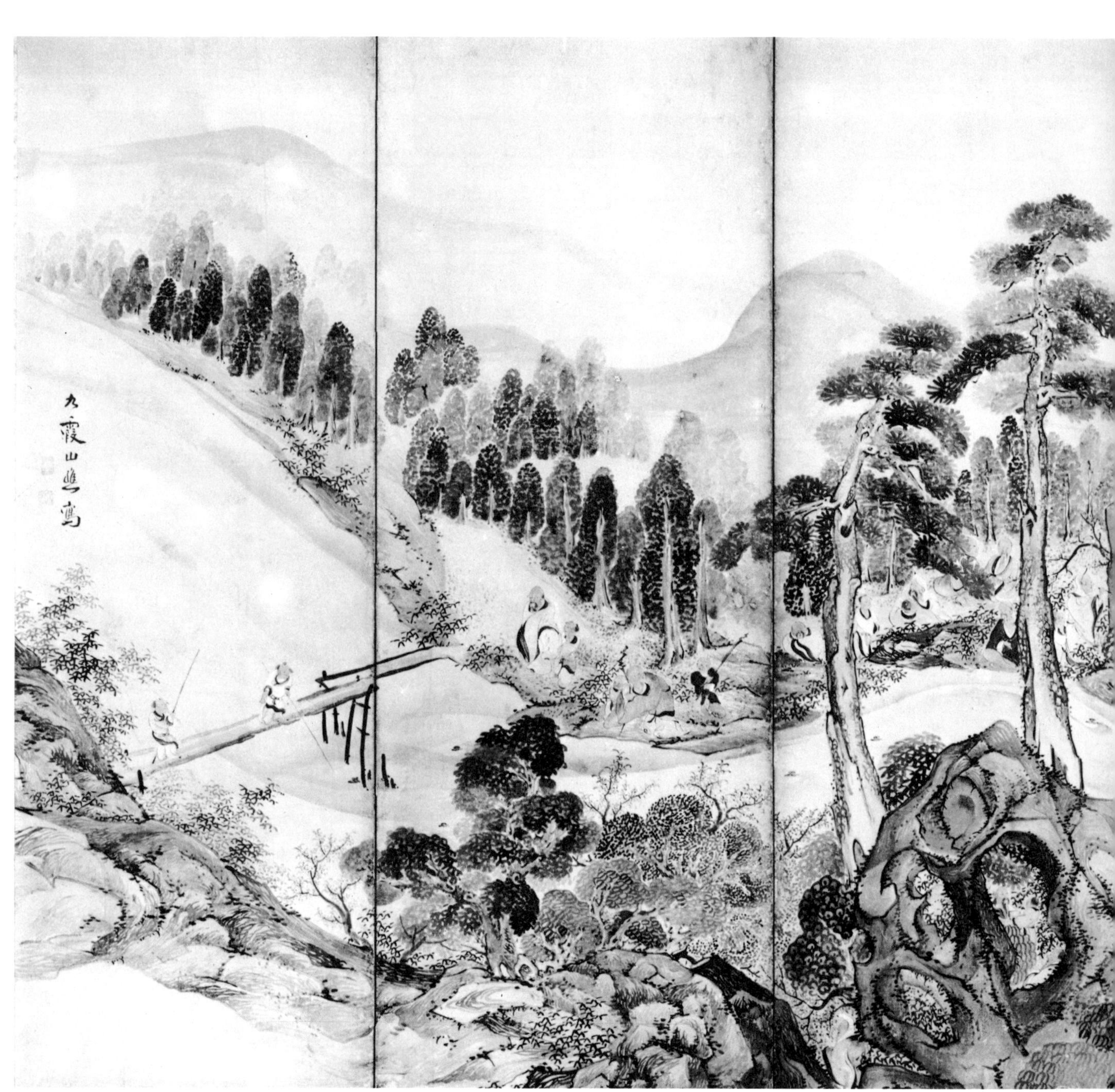

10 Ikeno Taiga The Poetical Gathering at the Orchid Pavilion (*Lan-t'ing*). Six-fold screen, ink and colors on paper. H. 64¹/₈ in. (162.8 cm.)

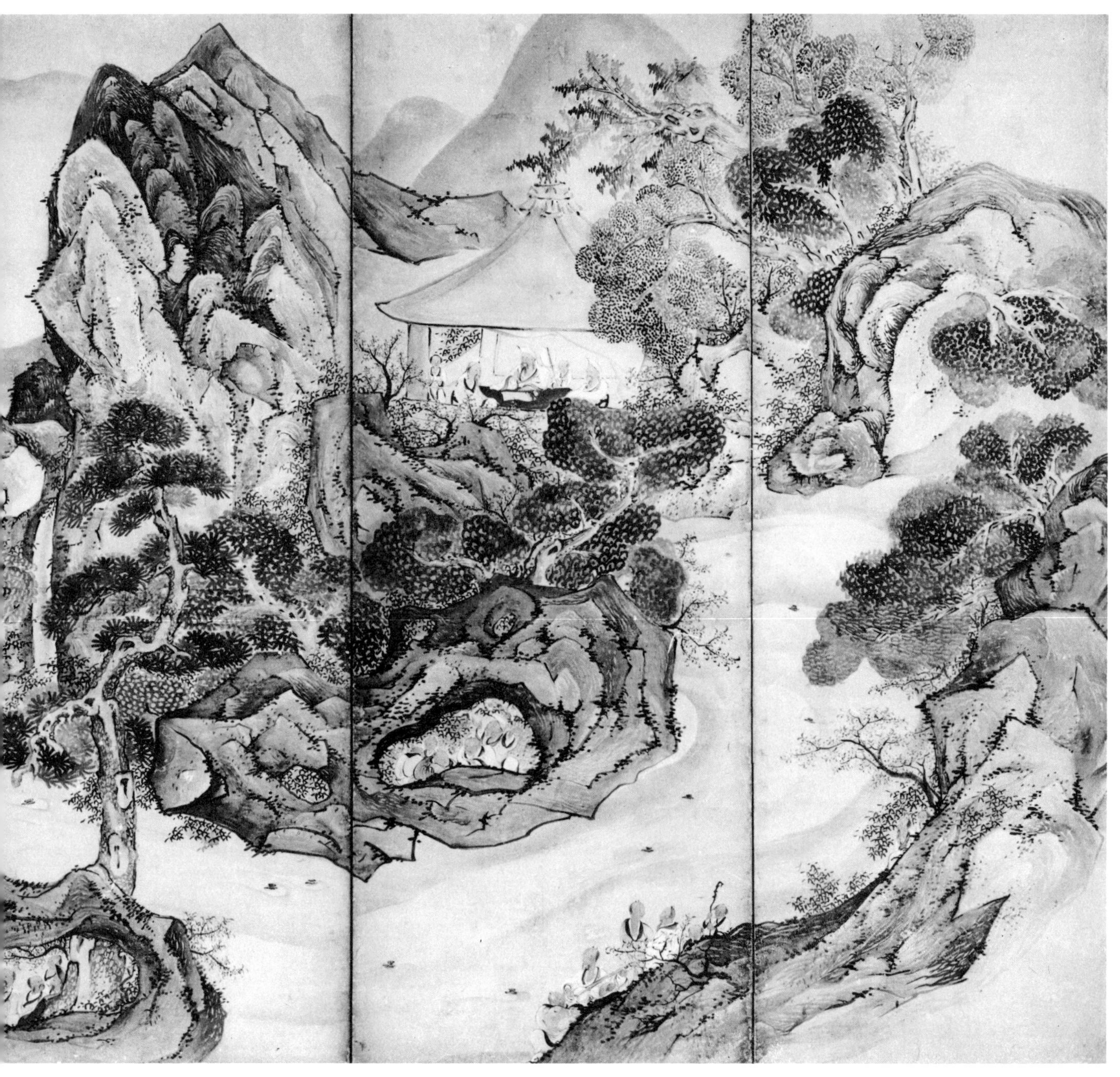

to regard these features purely as the outcome of Taiga's misunderstanding
of Chinese styles; they are elements of a new style, based in part, to be sure, on
an imperfect knowledge of Chinese painting, but already assimilated into
an original and pleasing manner of his own.

This derivation does not, however, account for the composition as a whole.
The distortion of ground and water planes, seen most radically in the way the
river flows deeply uphill at the far left, may recall similar decorative flattening in
screen compositions by artists of the Rimpa and other schools of Japanese
painting; nothing quite like it could be found in China. Taiga's style, then, adapts
elements of Chinese painting, imperfectly apprehended, into the more decorative and playful mode that characterizes so much of later Japanese painting.
Perhaps the temporal and cultural remoteness of the classical Chinese subjects
released Taiga from any obligation to take them very seriously.

In paintings such as this that are devoted to Chinese themes, Taiga's display
of learning gives to his paintings a special flavor, a bit bookish, devoted to the
past, and to culture more than to everyday experience. In others, however, even
where the theme is ostensibly classical, the artist in Taiga overcomes the scholar,
and supposed exercises in archaic idioms turn into perceptive interpretations
of Japanese scenery. This is the case in the album of "Landscapes in the Blue,
Green, and Gold Style," painted in 1763 (No. 11). The ten leaves are painted on
silk with heavy mineral colors, and in outline drawing augmented with strokes of
gold. The model for this style appeared long before, in eighth century China,
when T'ang dynasty masters such as Li Ssu-hsün inaugurated this mode of
decorative landscape. As practiced by their followers in China, it was an
academic style, featuring outline drawing in fine line, bright colors, minute
detail, precision rather than spontaneity. It belonged in fact to the rejected
Northern School, and thus was not properly to be practiced by a Southern School
(or Nanga) artist at all. Taiga, however, for whom such distinctions were unclear
and perhaps ultimately unimportant, uses variants of this mode for softer and
more pictorial effects: evening mists floating through a forest of leafy trees,
the wind blowing over the reeds and sandbanks where wild geese are alighting,
a waterfall in a rocky gorge, a view over a river seen through willows. These
pictures are probably meant to represent the scenery of China, but have the
freshness of scenes observed in nature. Where Taiga's depictions of Chinese
scenery differ from earlier ones, such as those of the ink-monochrome land-
scapists of the Muromachi Period, is that although they were similarly based on
imported Chinese pictures, as modified by the Japanese artists' imaginations,
Taiga (at least in his best works) fills out the given formulae more with the substance of observed appearances. We are told by his friend Kuwayama Gyokushū
that before Taiga painted his famous handscroll of 1771 representing the
scenery of Lake T'ung-t'ing and the Red Cliff on the Yangtze River, he went several times to the shores of Lake Biwa, near Kyoto, to gaze at its surface and
study the phenomena of waves and water.[3]

Taiga shares with his contemporary and friend Buson a love for grassy and
leafy surfaces depicted by patient accumulation of many small strokes, backed
with washes of color. In some of his paintings he depicts foliage in masses of
dots of varied colors, a technique that reminds Western viewers of the pointil-
lism of Seurat and Signac, invented over a century later. Although Taiga arrived
at this device by quite a different route—it is, of course, another form of the
woodblock-derived dotted foliage technique seen in his earlier works—the
effect is sometimes surprisingly similar, and it would be unjust to Taiga not to

3. Tokyo National Museum, *Nihon no
Bunjinga* [Japanese Literati Painting]
(Tokyo, 1966), pl. 44, note on p. 166.

credit him with having realized, however intuitively and unscientifically, the visual effect of such separation of dots of pure color. Through this technique Taiga achieves a lightness and vibrancy that catches the shimmering surface of spring greenery, although it must be admitted that he, like Seurat and Signac, uses the technique a bit schematically—none of them were so sensitive to natural textures as, for instance, Buson.

From this middle period of Taiga's life we have a number of complex and ambitious landscape compositions, among which the "White Clouds and Red Trees" (No. 12), a work of his forties, is outstanding in the consistent sureness of execution and the beauty of its colors. With washes of the standard red ochre and indigo (*taisha* and *ai*) as a basis, Taiga adds brighter reds in the trees and green-white dots on the rocks for an unusually rich coloring. The leaves on some of the more distant trees are painted in touches of pure color, instead of the more usual combination of ink dots and color washes. Two figures, an old scholar with a staff and his boy servant, enter the picture in the lower right corner and stand in a hollow typically enclosed by trees and rocks. Before them is a valley with a rushing stream; a cliff rises at left, cut by bands of mist, and far in the distance is a waterfall. One could observe generally of Taiga's landscapes, and this is no exception, that they are not easy to find one's way through, visually; they invite disinterested aesthetic contemplation more than imaginary involvement. But if we think of the earlier history of Japanese landscape painting, whether by Sesshū or the Kanō masters or Kōrin, we realize that this is more a Japanese trait than a peculiarity of Taiga's; it is part of what we mean when we speak of decorative tendencies in Japanese painting.

Taiga continued throughout his life to learn from all he saw and to experiment with new techniques and modes of composition. Often his explorations of Chinese styles and conventions seem intellectually oriented, aimed more at meeting some poorly-understood classical norm than at painting a better picture. In a series of six paintings which were done in 1766 (Nos. 13 a-f), originally mounted on a screen, he demonstrated the "Six Distances" of Chinese painting theory—six ways of achieving effects of distance in one's compositions. Three of these "distances" had been described by the eleventh century landscapist Kuo Hsi: "high distance," "deep distance," and "level distance." The other three, the "broad," "shrouded," and "dark" distances, were added in the early twelfth century by Han Cho.[4] Taiga did not indicate on the pictures which "distance" was used in each, and the poetical inscriptions by six scholarly contemporaries give no clue; there is some difference of opinion among modern scholars as to how they should be identified.

As in the "Six Sights in Kyoto" (Nos. 9 a, b), he paints each picture in a different "brush-manner"—one employs the ink-dots of Mi Fu, another uses the angular rock structures and "axe-cut" texture-strokes of Li T'ang, and so forth—but these are not identified in the inscriptions either. Since paintings of the literati school were all, in theory, intended for the enjoyment of men with similar backgrounds of learning, the artist was supposed to be able to make such stylistic allusions as these in the confidence that they would be understood. In Taiga's time this was not a safe assumption; his own understanding of Chinese painting was shaky, and less assiduous students of the subject probably saw these pictures only as performances in novel and entertaining styles. They strike us now as rather dry and didactic, as Taiga sometimes is when making scholarly points instead of simply painting pictures.

We include also two landscapes from Taiga's late years that represent actual

4. See Robert Maeda, *Two Twelfth Century Texts on Chinese Painting,* (Ann Arbor, 1970), p. 16.

11 Ikeno Taiga Landscapes in the
Blue, Green, and Gold Style,
1763. Leaf H from an album of
ten leaves, ink, colors, and gold
on silk. Each leaf, H. 8⅝ in.
(22 cm.)

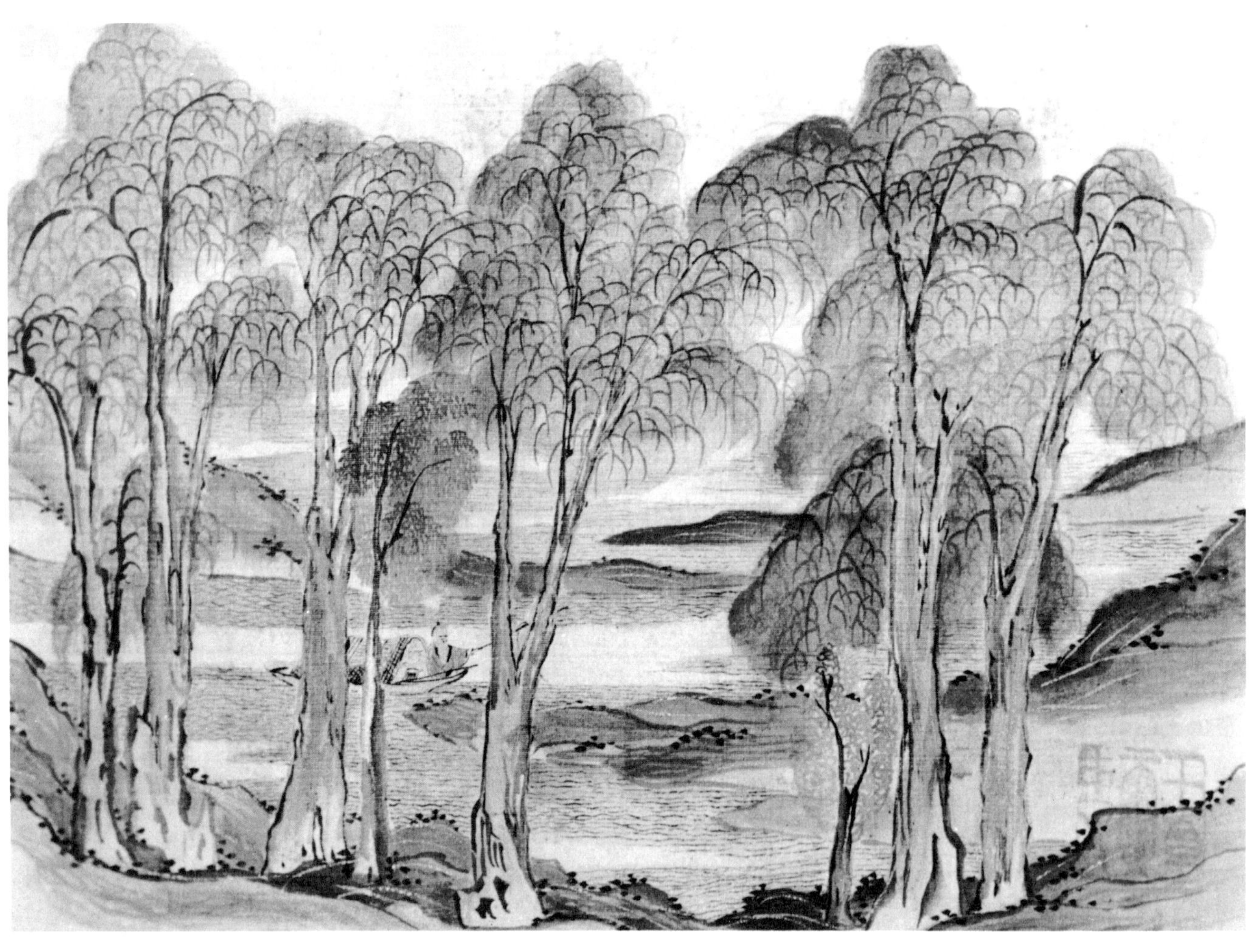

12 Ikeno Taiga White Clouds and Red Trees. Hanging scroll, ink and colors on silk. H. 47⅞ in. (121.5 cm.)

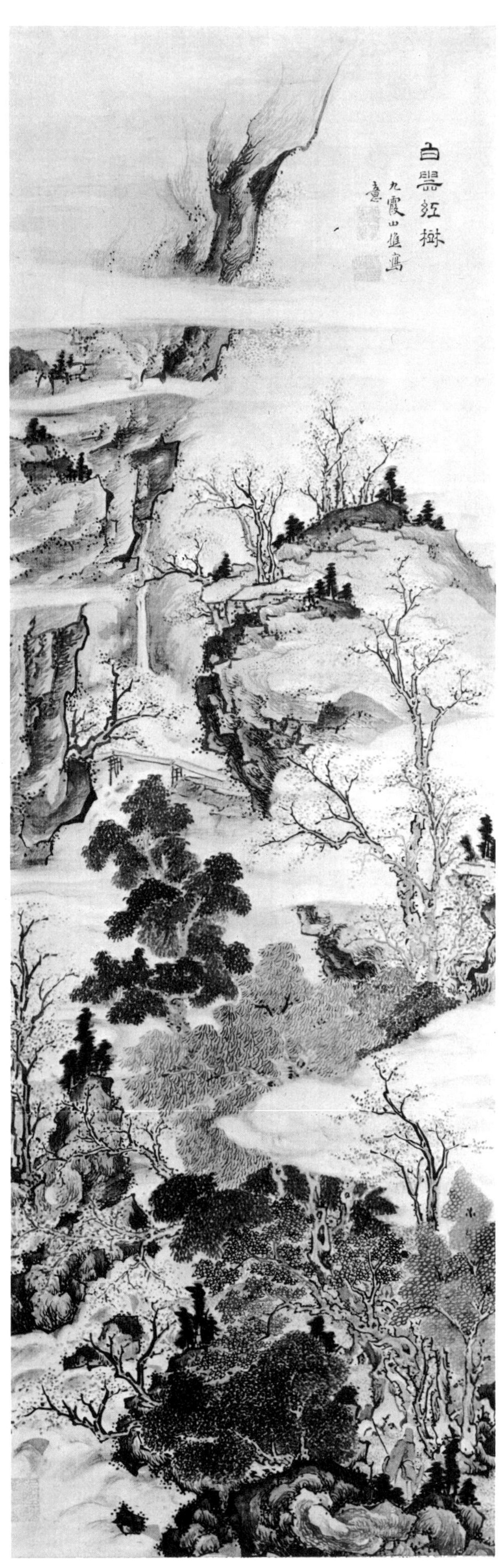

places. The "Real View of Kojima Bay" ("*Kojima-wan Shinkei,*" No. 14) was painted in Taiga's mid-forties. The bay is on the Inland Sea, in Okayama Prefecture. The composition, with distant hills viewed above nearer ones, is of a type the artist had used several times before. Such a picture plan had no precedents in Japan, and few in China, although something similar may be seen in works of seventeenth century individualists such as Kung Hsien and K'un-ts'an. The slopes of the hills are painted in a technique distantly derived from the "Mi dots" of Mi Fu (cf. Nos. 9 a, b), but the addition of color and the size and prominence of the dots produces here the same kind of vibrant effect as does Taiga's "pointillist" tree foliage, although with more sense of mass. Such features as rendering of sunlight on the nearer hills and the naturalistic shading of the distant ones, the fairly convincing deep recession, and the sudden diminution (from figures on the path to boats on the bay) are very probably the outcome of Taiga's interest in Occidental painting.

"The Nachi Waterfall" (No. 15), painted when Taiga was around fifty, seems much less naturalistically conceived. This is not because it was based on imagination, like his Chinese scenes; Taiga had probably traveled to this famous place in Wakayama Prefecture. The unreal quality of the picture is rather a matter of intent. Any representation of the Nachi Waterfall invites comparison with the great painting of the Kamakura Period now in the Nezu Museum,[5] and comparison with that far more sober and noble work immediately reveals the essentially decorative nature of Taiga's. There is nothing of the aura of mystery and religious feeling that inspires the Kamakura painting. The composition interested Taiga more than the subject; trees and rocks occupy a major portion of the painting, and the waterfall is removed to middle distance, where it is unnaturally broadened—to compensate, perhaps, for its shortness. The interplay of deep and dilute ink tones, and of warm and cool color, is similarly decorative. But we must remember once more that "decorative" is scarcely a disparaging term when applied to Japanese painting; much of the best of it had always been that.

From all the foregoing, we may begin to assess the strengths of Taiga as an artist. They are not primarily in monumental or otherwise impressive scenery, although he painted many landscapes in which a kind of monumentality is achieved. Neither are they primarily in decorative beauty, although a great many of his paintings have that. The particular values of Taiga's paintings derive rather from a subtlety of taste and poetic sensitivity, and so offer us a highly special, in fact rather rarefied, visual experience. We could broaden this statement to say that these are just the qualities that distinguish the finest painting of the eighteenth century in China (the works of the Yangchow masters and others), as well as the best of Taiga's contemporaries in Japan, whether of the Nanga school, as with Buson or Gyokushū, or of other schools such as Ukiyo-e—as in the color prints of Harunobu, perhaps. It is in this context that Taiga may be seen as one of the greatest masters of his age, and in this context two of his late works, both albums of modest size, can be placed among his highest achievements. They are the ten-leaf album titled Jūben or "Ten Conveniences" painted in 1771, which could not be included in this exhibition, and the album of eight fan paintings representing the "Eight Views of the Hsiao-Hsiang Region" (No. 16).

This album is undated, but is surely a work of Taiga's last years. The fans, whatever the artist's intention may have been, were never mounted on frames for actual use, but have been preserved as an album. Accompanying the

5. See Yukio Yashiro, ed., *Art Treasures of Japan* (Tokyo, 1960), II, pl. 293.

13a **Ikeno Taiga** The Six Distances, 1766. One from a set of six hanging scrolls, ink on paper. Each, H. 53½ in. (136 cm.)

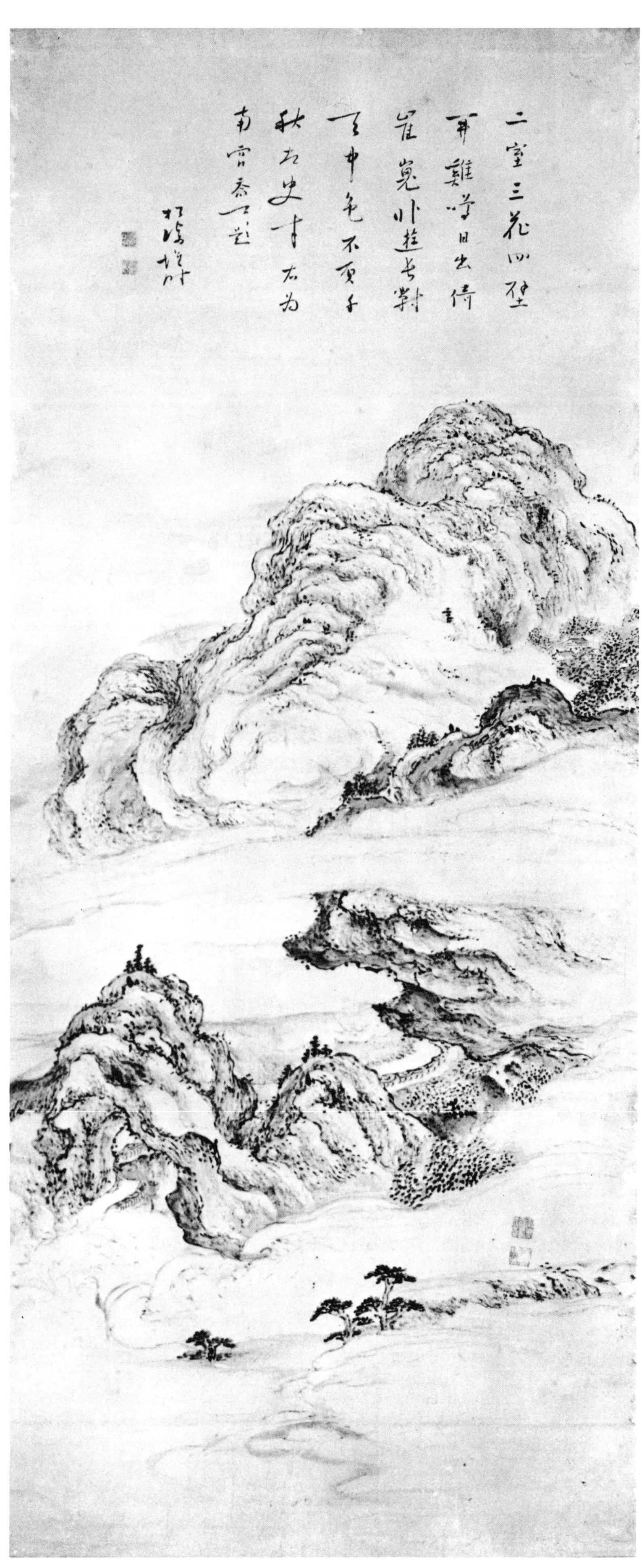

41

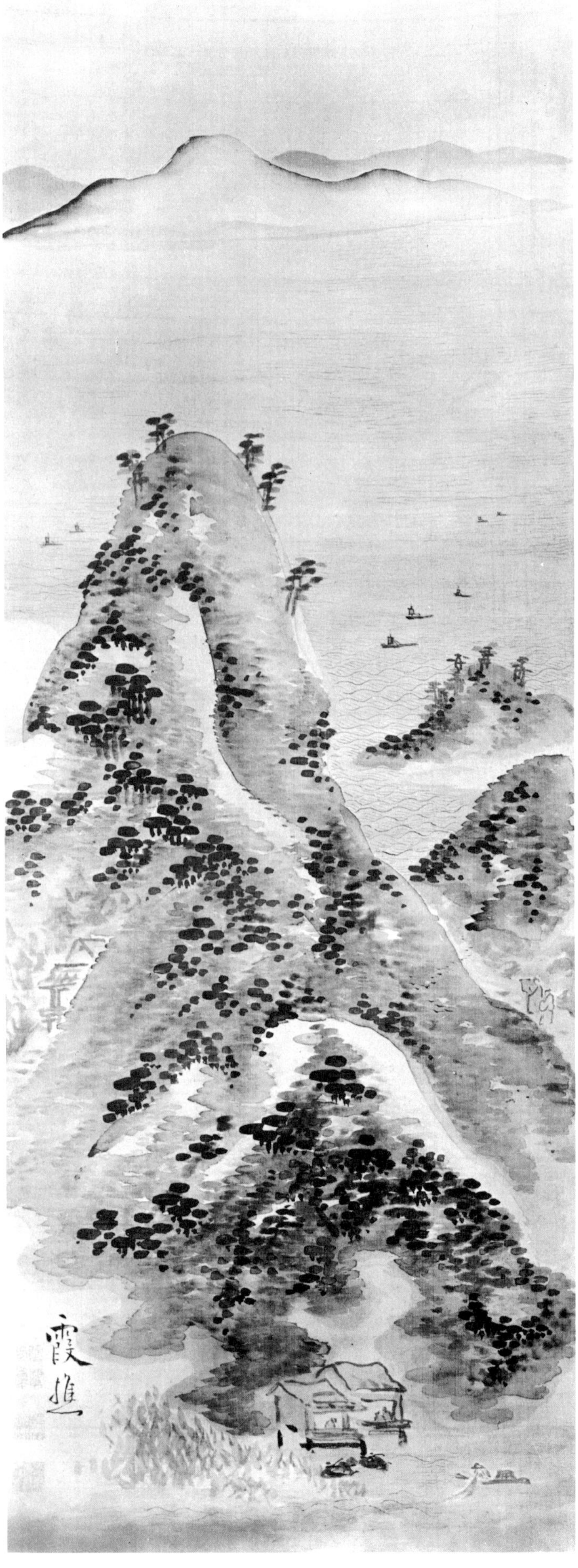

14 Ikeno Taiga A Real View of Kojima Bay. Hanging scroll, ink and colors on silk. H. 39¼ in. (99.6 cm.)

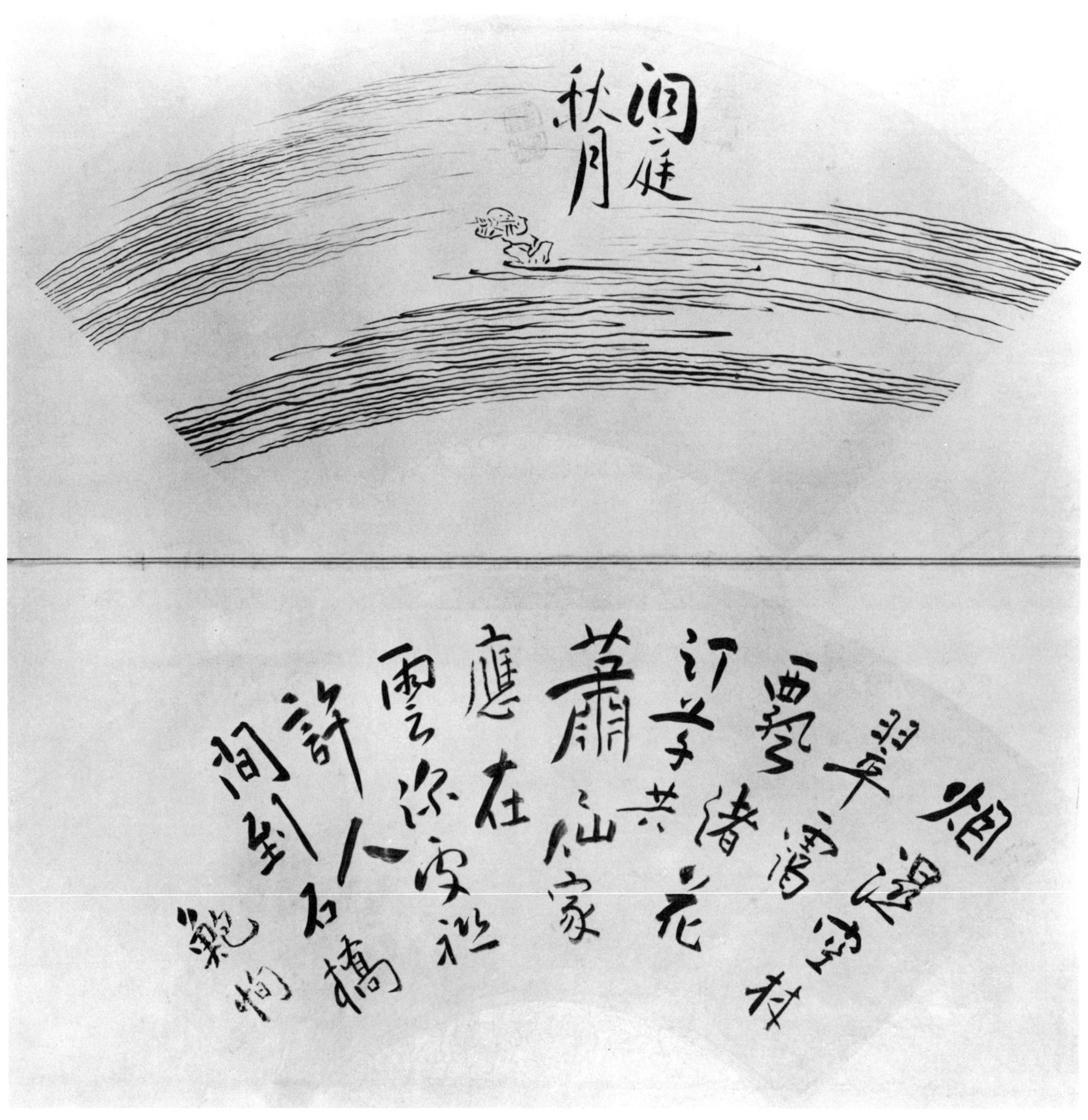

16 Ikeno Taiga Eight Views of the Hsiao-Hsiang Region. Leaf E from an album of eight fan-shaped paintings, ink on paper, accompanied by eight fan-shaped leaves of calligraphy. Each, H. 7⁷/₈ in. (20 cm.)

paintings are leaves of calligraphy, likewise fan-shaped, which Taiga copied from
different Chinese masters. The paintings, however, are entirely original. Earlier
Japanese depictions of the "Eight Views," notably those of the Muromachi
Period, had generally followed the late Sung Chinese examples in allotting most
of the compositions to mist and space, in the midst of which patches of scenery
appeared as if glimpsed through rifts in the fog. By this means, a minimum of
solid matter was made to evoke a landscape of vast extension. Taiga's evocative
means are rather those of the Japanese *haiku* poet: a few carefully selected
objects and items of scenery occupy the entire space of the picture and the
entire attention of the artist; they stand for much more, but are all we are given.
Through a consummate control of broad, sometimes shaded brush-strokes and
ink gradations, a sense of space and substance is created in each picture in
spite of its extreme simplicity. A variety of techniques has been used to apply the
ink to paper: the Rimpa School techniques of *tarashikomi,* dropping water into
a still-wet area of ink for a puddly effect; *katabokashi,* uneven inking of the
brush (picking up dense ink with the brush-tip while the remainder is loaded
with water or dilute ink) which produces a shaded stroke, dark along one edge
and light on the other. In the last leaf, representing snowy mountains (No. 16H),
Taiga uses this latter device in an unusual and brilliant manner, with the stroke
shading outward into space (as Liang K'ai had done five centuries earlier, in
his famous portrait of Li Po) instead of, as commonly, inward.

Also brilliant is the utilization of the fan shape, for instance, in the marvelous
"Autumn Moon on Lake T'ung-t'ing" scene (No. 16E) of the fisherman in his
boat playing a flute, with wave lines subtly curving in partial accommodation to
the curve of the shape and somehow echoing the sound of the flute. The
titles are written very large, relative to the sizes of the paintings, and are integral
to the compositions, even to the meaning—in this one, for instance, no moon
is shown, but the presence of the moon is clear from the title. In "Evening Rain
on the Hsiao and Hsiang" (these were two rivers that flowed together near
Lake T'ung-t'ing in Hupei Province) the feeling of rain is caught by wetness of
brushwork, and by dimming of ink tone in the bamboo groves and other areas
of the picture (No. 16F).

Taiga had a number of direct disciples, all of whom were painters of pleasant
but on the whole not very original pictures. One of the better of them was
Aoki Shukuya (d. 1789), a native of Ise who may have been of Korean extraction.
He lived in Taiga's house after the master's death. His "Autumn Landscape
with Mt. Fuji" (No. 17) uses the convention of clearly separated fore, middle,
and distant grounds, with a slanting land mass in the middle ground, a Taigaesque
feature here used to balance the slope of Fuji. Apart from some difference in
brushwork—the hand or "touch" of the artist—this could be mistaken for a
lesser work by Taiga, and the same could be said of much of the work of other
followers.

More independent and interesting by far is Kuwayama Gyokushū (1746-1799),
who was an intimate friend of Taiga. He was born in Kishū, Wakayama
Prefecture, of a rich family, but is said to have squandered all his patrimony on
paintings and calligraphy. He visited Edo a number of times, but was
unimpressed with the painting being done there; it was only after he had come
to know Taiga and other artists of the Kyoto area that he found his own style
as a painter. He composed two books of theoretical discussions on painting, in
one of which he offered the opinion, quoted earlier, that Sōtatsu and Kōrin
should be numbered among the "Southern School artists of Japan." His paintings

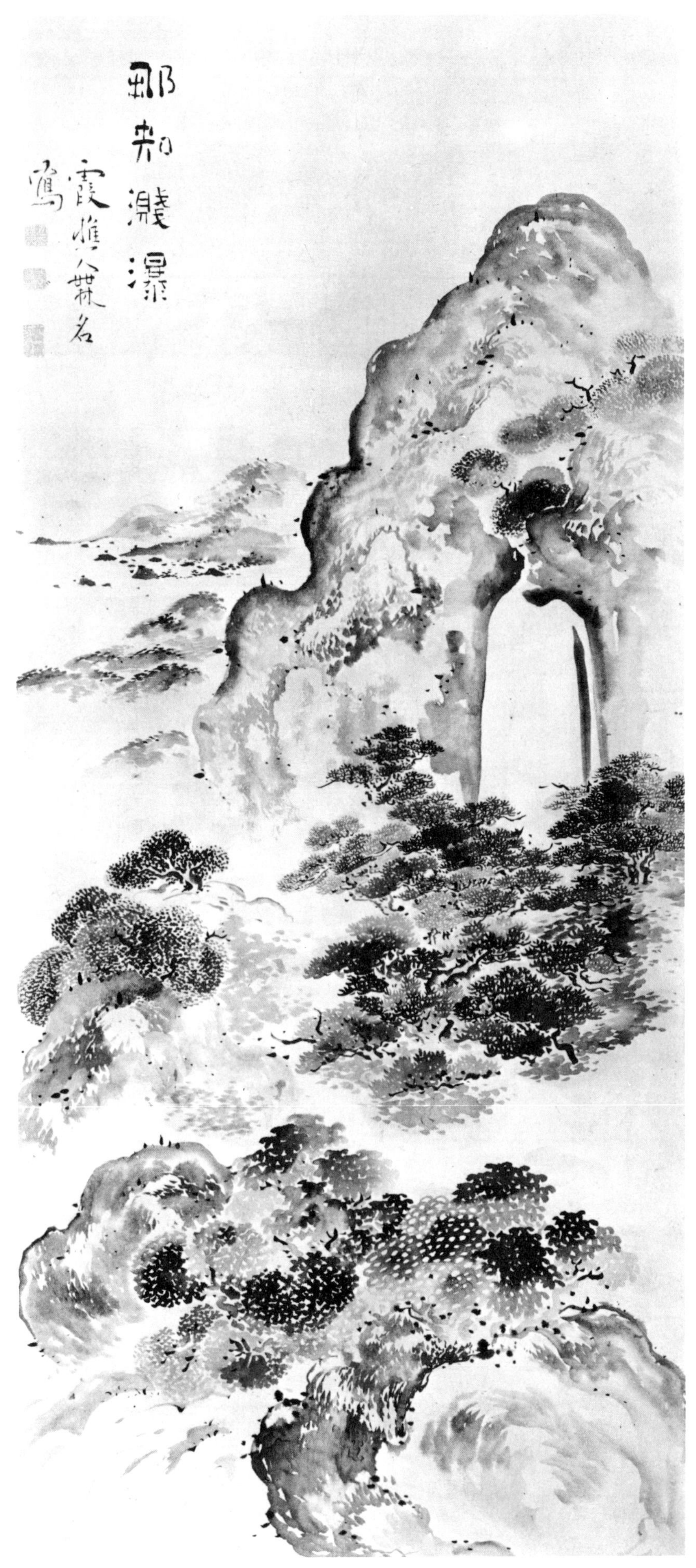

15 Ikeno Taiga The Nachi Waterfall. Hanging scroll, ink and light colors on paper. H. 49½ in. (125.7 cm.)

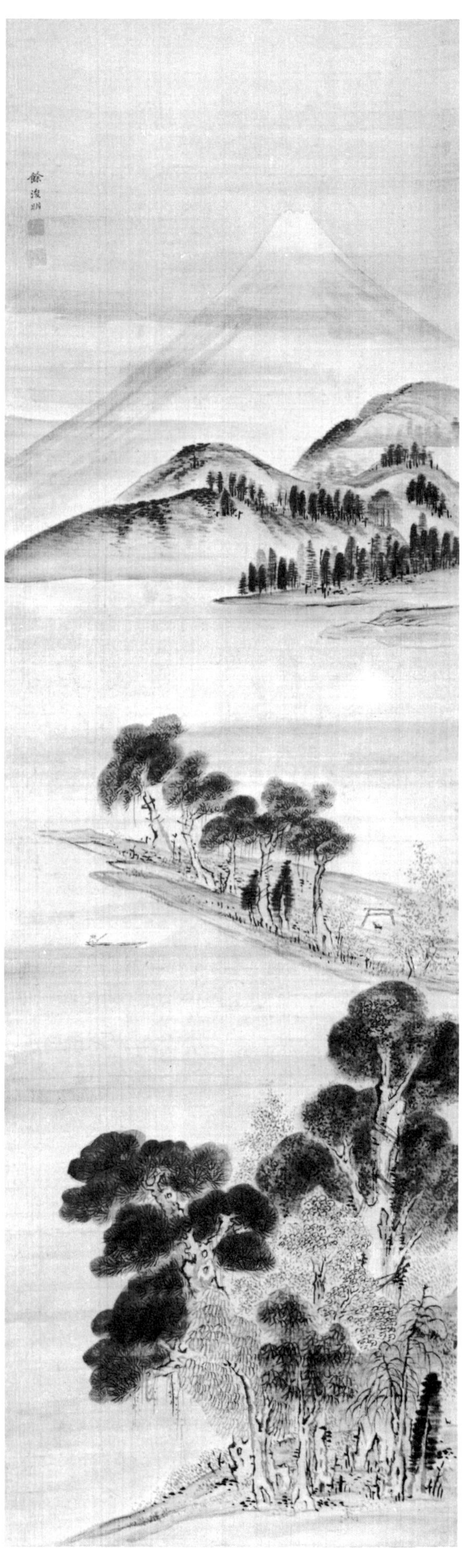

17 Aoki Shukuya Autumn Landscape with Mount Fuji. Hanging scroll, ink and colors on paper. H. 45¼ in. (114.9 cm.)

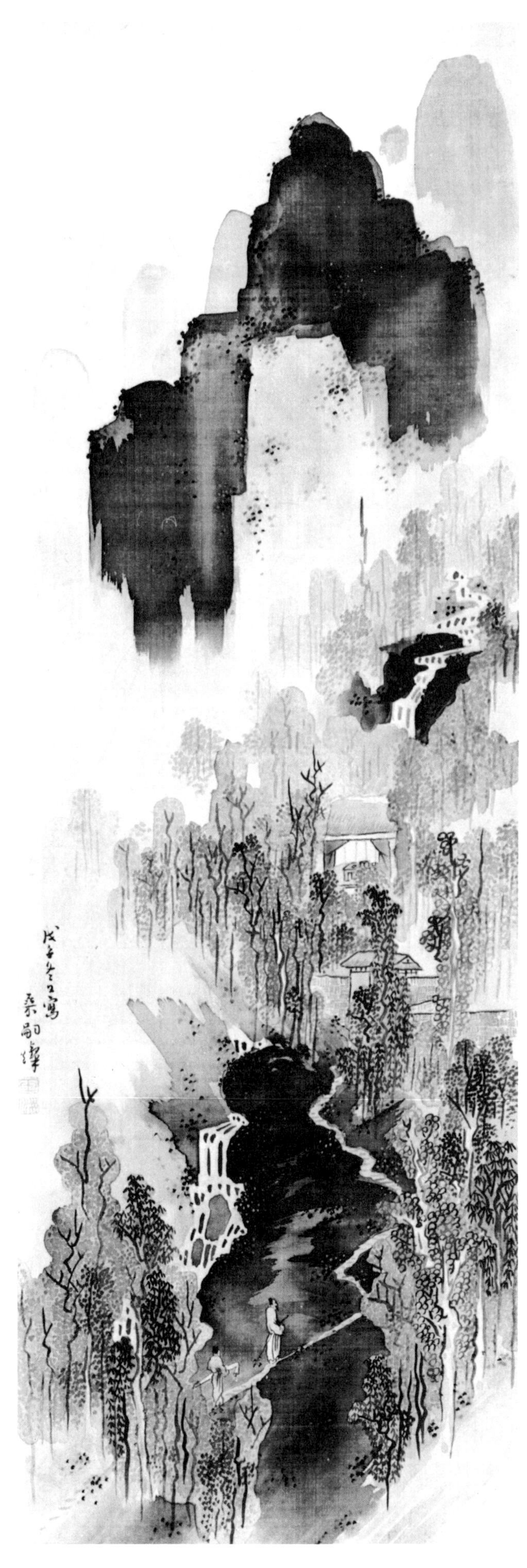

18 Kuwayama Gyokushū
Landscape with Figures, 1798.
Hanging scroll, ink and colors on
silk. H. 37³/₈ in. (94.9 cm.)

reveal the same leaning; like Taiga, he reconciles the Chinese-derived landscape styles with a Japanese taste for decorative pattern. The landscape we have
chosen (No. 18), painted in 1798, the year before his death, is a brilliant example
of this synthesis. He works in nervous, wavering lines and flat washes of ink
and color which often take curious shapes. He thus unifies his compositions by
reducing them to a highly restricted system of static and active forms. Once
more we must see the influence of colored woodblock prints as crucial in the
formation of his style, but the paintings stand on their own as products of a
very special taste and temperament.

Noro Kaiseki (1747-1828) was born in Wakayama, and began to study painting
there with Gyokushū when he was fourteen years old. In 1767 he went to
Kyoto, where he may have been a student of Taiga. He returned to his native
place in 1793, summoned back by the lord of the Kishū clan, and went into
the service of that lord. In 1799 and again in 1801 he made trips to Edo, where he
was able to see many more Chinese paintings. During his late years he was
highly regarded and praised. Tanomura Chikuden visited him in 1811, and
reportedly learned much from him.

A turning point in his development as a painter was in 1810, when he copied
some version of the famous *"T'ien-ch'ih shih-pi"* ("Heavenly Lake and Stone
Cliff") composition of Huang Kung-wang (1296-1354),[6] and through this experience reached a deeper understanding of Chinese literati painting. His "Autumn
Landscape" (No. 19) dates from the following year, 1811, and presumably
reflects this new influence. It is to be seen in the composition, which presents a
mountainside built up systematically of squared, repeated forms in a manner
distantly derived from Huang Kung-wang. The brushwork still retains some trace
of Gyokushū's wavering-line drawing, but is more repetitive and restrained.
Rows of horizontal strokes are applied evenly to the vertical contours. Other
works by Kaiseki confirm what this one suggests: the Orthodox landscape style
of Ch'ing dynasty China, in its later and dryer form, had reached Japan. By
Kaiseki's generation, Chinese painting styles could be studied in many more
originals and were much better understood by the Japanese artists. The effect on
Nanga of this closer acquaintance was not all for the good.

6. The original of this famous composition does not appear to have survived.
The best of several extant copies is the
one reproduced in Hsieh Chih-liu, *T'ang
Wu-tai Sung Yüan ming-chi* (Shanghai,
1957), pl. 99.

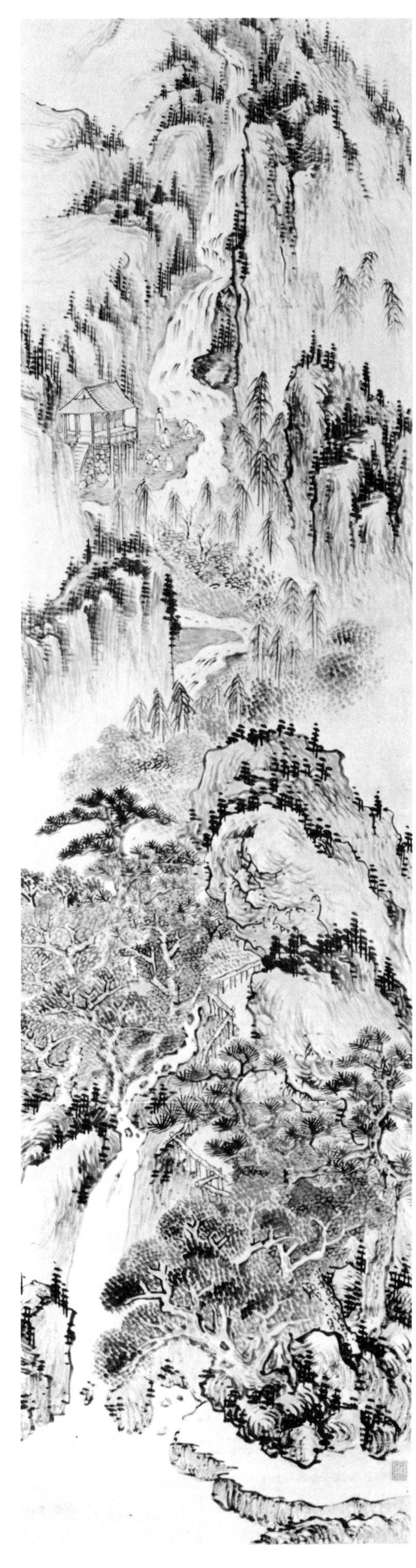

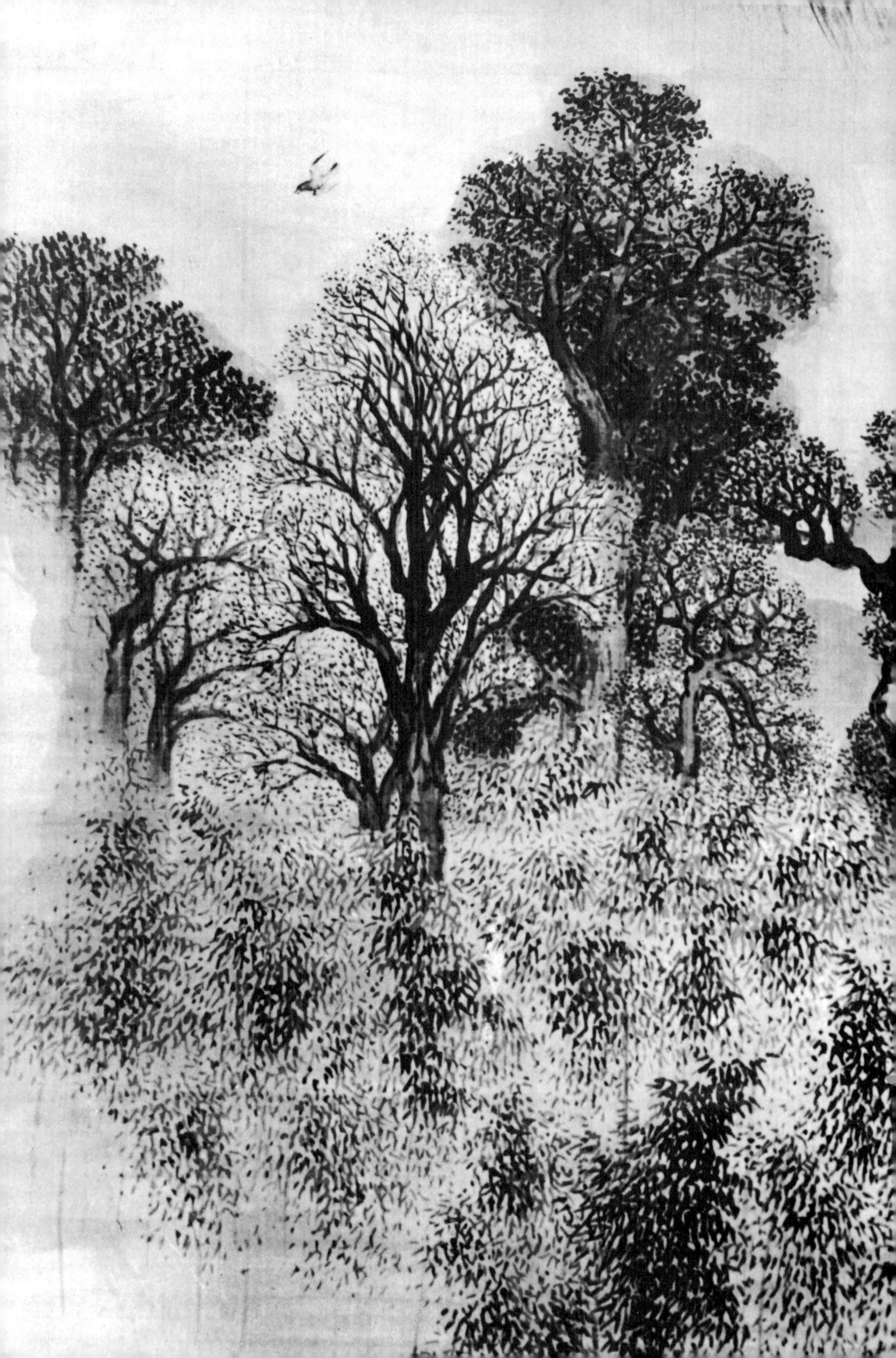

Chapter IV: Yosa Buson and His Followers

The second major master of Nanga, usually ranked as equal with Taiga, is
Yosa Buson (1716-1783). Buson has the added distinction of being considered
one of Japan's three best *haiku* poets.

He was born near Osaka, the son of a farmer.[1] Little is known about his early
life. He went to Edo when he was twenty, and there became a disciple of Hayano
Hajin, a famous *haiku* poet and a follower of Bashō (1644-1694), the greatest
master of that seventeen-syllable verse form. In 1742, upon the death of Hajin,
Buson set off on a series of wandering journeys, which ended finally in 1751
when he settled in Kyoto. He remained there for the rest of his life, except for a
three-year period from 1754 in the nearby province of Tango, and several trips.

Buson had painted in a variety of styles from the time of his stay in Edo, but it
was only after he came to Kyoto that he decided to make his living as a professional painter instead of as a poet. He may have known Hyakusen briefly
before the older master's death in 1752, and was certainly influenced by him,
both in painting and in *haiku* composition. Besides the Nanga styles, he studied
bird, flower, and animal painting in the realistic manner of Shen Nan-p'in, and
figure painting after the rather academic models of the Che School in China;
some of his middle-period works are of those kinds. Gradually, however, he left
behind the more academic manners, and by the 1760's had developed the
sensitive and fluent style of his finest works.

As an example of his early style we include the "Landscape" of 1758 (No. 20)
done after his return from Yosa in Tango Province where he had lived in a temple
and concentrated on learning painting. This work cannot be regarded as one
of his most attractive—the drawing is relatively heavy-handed, the forms
ponderous—but it is valuable in understanding the development of his style.
Already Buson shows a predilection for fluid treatment of surfaces, accomplished with long, ravelled brushstrokes, and for forms that play rounded
convexities against concavities; it is easy to see the influence of Hyakusen (cf.
No. 6) in these features, which will persist in Buson's works, variously trans-
formed and softened. The composition follows a type common in Ming dynasty
landscape painting in China, especially in the Che School, in which the
principal mass is built vertically up one side, incorporating whatever buildings
and figures provide the focus of interest, and horizontal elements in the
foreground and middle distance stabilize this on the other side, which is otherwise given over to an expanse of river. Although the Che School is another

1. The following summary of Buson's life
is based on the information in Susumu
Suzuki, *Buson* (Tokyo, 1958), to which
the reader is referred for a fuller account
(English text pp. 3-7). See also William
Watson, *Yosa no Buson* (London, 1960).

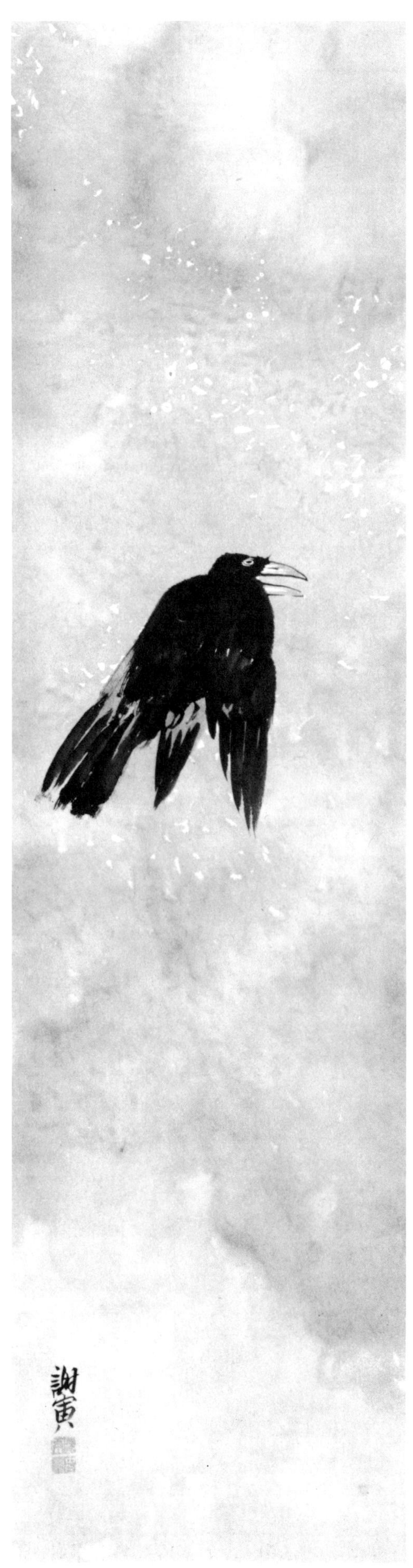

21 Yosa Buson A Crow in a Wintry Sky. Hanging scroll, ink on paper. H. 43⅞ in. (111.5 cm.)

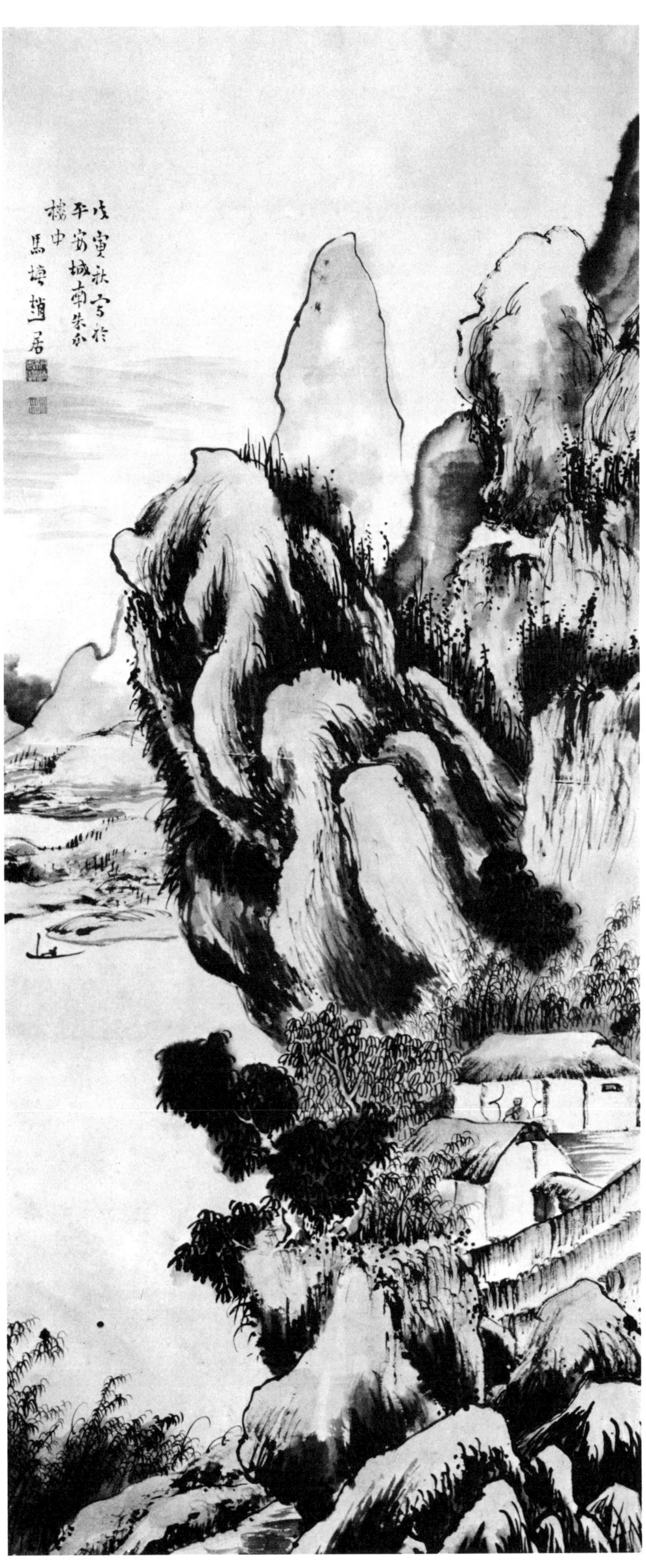

20 Yosa Buson Landscape, 1758. Hanging scroll, ink and light colors on paper. H. 50½ in. (128.2 cm.)

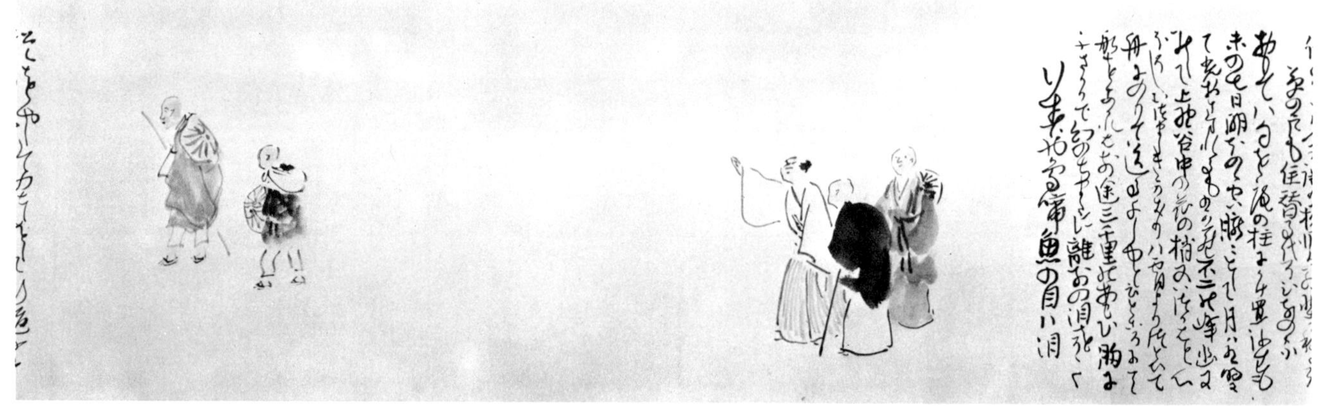

22a Yosa Buson The Narow Road to the Deep North *(Oku no Hosomichi),* 1778. One of two handscrolls, ink and light colors on paper. H. 11-5/16 in. (29 cm.)

of the "Northern" traditions that properly lie outside the range of Nanga, Buson
takes many of the elements of his early and middle period style from it, in
both landscapes and figure paintings.

Buson also painted a number of pictures of birds, of which the finest are a pair
representing "A Kite" and "Two Crows on a Snowy Branch."[2] Another work
of the same kind is "A Crow in a Wintry Sky" (No. 21). It was painted as one of a
triptych representing "Snow, Moon, and Flowers" for a collector in Tango
who asked three famous painters of the time to depict these subjects. Buson
painted "A Crow in a Wintry Sky" to represent "Snow", Maruyama Ōkyo
(1733-1795) painted a "Bird and Moon" and Buson's pupil Matsumura Goshun
(1752-1811) painted "Cherry Blossoms." Ōkyo's painting is dated 1774, and
Buson's is probably from the same year. Japanese depictions of strong, aggressive
birds must always evoke comparisons with the works of Miyamoto Niten,
the seventeenth century master of such subjects. Buson's bird is similarly
executed in swift, telling strokes, but is less serious than those of Niten, more
dashing and witty. The crow appears against a sky rendered in a manner
that was probably Buson's own invention: along with some use of the *tarashikomi* technique of the Rimpa School (dropping water into a still-wet area of
ink wash, seen here notably in the upper right corner) he criss-crosses broad,
curling strokes of dilute ink so as to leave between them, in reserve, randomly
shaped areas of white to represent falling snowflakes. The bird is caught in
mid-motion, as if by a high-speed camera's shutter, its wings downswept, its
beak open to indicate that it is cawing. The whole effect is of a momentary
impression quickly captured.

This quality in Buson's paintings is commonly attributed to, or at least related
to, his greatness as a poet, and although the suggestion of such interdependence
among an artist's activities in different spheres is generally facile and dangerous,
and so to be regarded with suspicion (the idea, for instance, that Miyamoto Niten
painted with bold, thrusting brush strokes *because* he was a great swordsman),
the connection is difficult to deny in the case of Buson. He himself combined and
interrelated poetry and painting in every way that he could. The man he
most revered was the great *haiku* poet Bashō, and his homages to Bashō were in
paintings as well as in words; he did portraits of him, pictures to accompany
his poems, illustrations to his poetical narratives. During his own period of wandering Buson had attempted to retrace the course of one of Bashō's poetical
journeys, the "Narrow Road to the Deep North" (Oku no Hosomichi").[3] Buson
twice copied this text, a travel record interspersed with poems composed
on the road, and added simple illustrations in the sketchy *haiga* style. One version is in screen form and the other consists of two handscrolls; we include
the latter, which were painted in 1778 (No. 22).

The scrolls are composed with blocks of text as compositional units and
simple pictures occupying intervening spaces. In the "Parting at Senju" scene
(No. 22a),[4] Bashō is seen setting off on foot, an old and bent figure with straw
rainhat and staff, accompanied by his traveling companion Sora. Behind, set
apart from them by an interval that already conveys the feeling of separation, are
three friends who have come to see them off. Bashō and Sora are smaller
in scale and placed higher, moving into the distance. The figures are painted in a
loose, abbreviated style—a few broad strokes for a coat, several dots and a
hook for a face. The depth of characterization achieved by these simple means,
and by posture and placement, is remarkable.

Another scene (No. 22b) portrays two young prostitutes, whom Bashō hears

2. Tokyo National Museum, *Nihon no
Bunjinga* [Japanese Literati Painting]
(Tokyo, 1966), pl. 68; also reproduced in
many other books.

3. See Yuasa Nobuyuki, trans., *Bashō:
The Narrow Road to the Deep North and
Other Travel Sketches* (Harmondsworth,
Middlesex, 1966). Bashō's journey was
made from 1689 to 1691, but the famous
travel record interspersed with *haiku*
poems covers only the first six months.

4. *Ibid.*, p. 98.

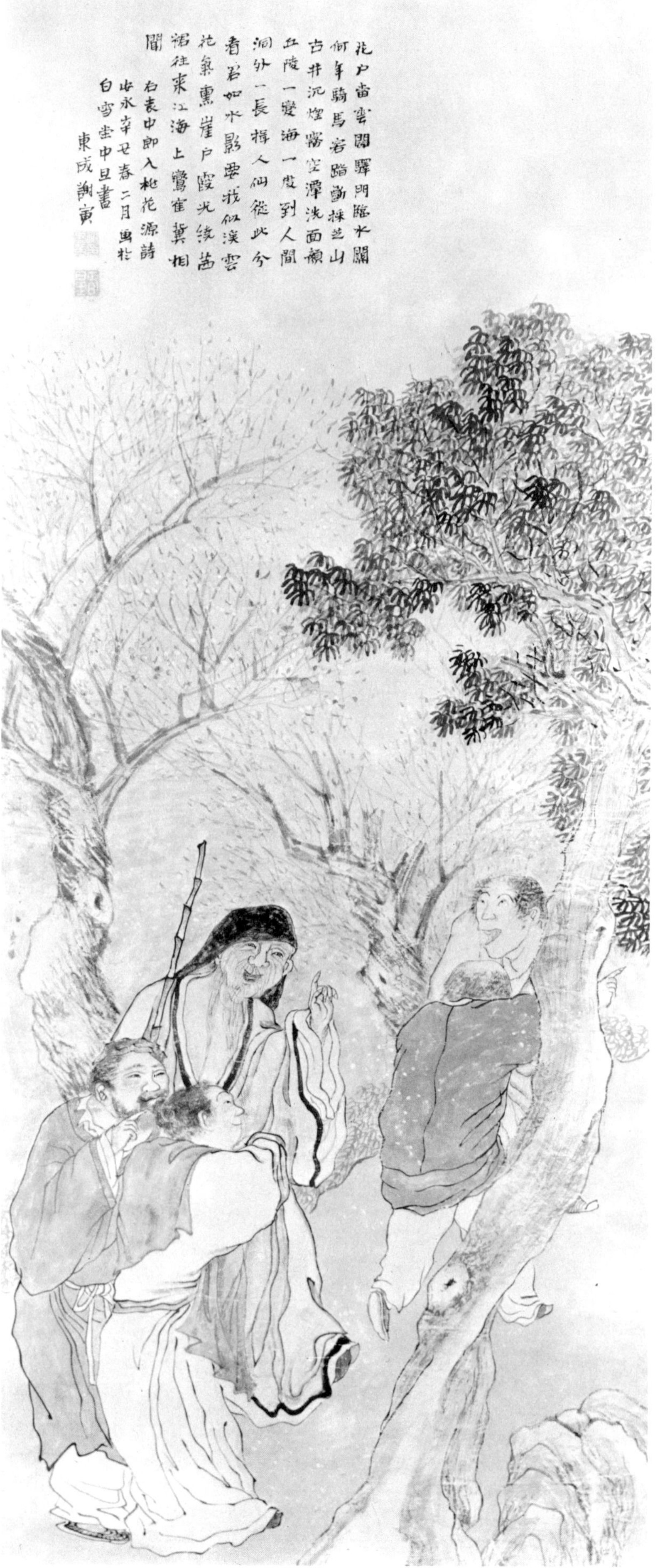

23a, b Yosa Buson The Elysium of the Peach Blossom Spring, 1781. Pair of hanging scrolls, ink and colors on paper. Each, H. 54³/₈ in. (138 cm.)

溪雨濯雲根花林水氣溫晴鷺
常守月仙犬欲迎門緣壁紅霞
宅丹砂石髓村人中幾甲子洞
裏一黃昏
白頭丁醫子托裏去如仙島
嗅雲霞柵人耕之水田庚年
看紅葉生死在蒼煙認著
爐香去瞿童火尚然
日本東成謝寅畫采書

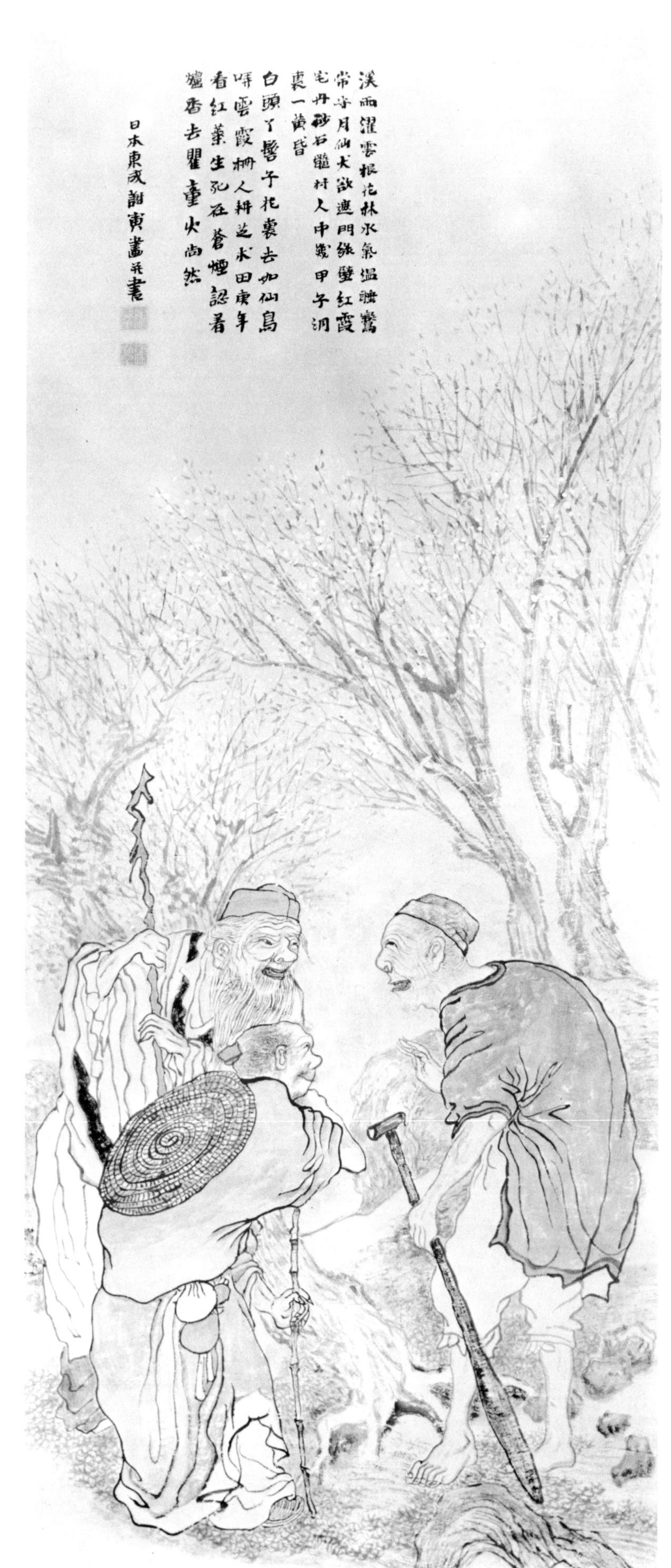

in the room next to his at an inn; they are giving messages to an old man from their home village, to be delivered to relatives and friends. The next morning they ask Bashō if they may accompany him; he refuses, while giving them his blessing, and composes a *haiku* as he continues on his way: "Under the same roof/We all slept together,/Courtesans and I—/Bush clovers and the moon."[5] At every stage from the original occurrence through Bashō's aesthetic (rather than some other) response to it in composing a *haiku,* and thence to his literary account of the event and finally to Buson's picture, the raw stuff of experience is transfigured into the stuff of poetry—simplified, withdrawn from reality, intensified as art and diluted as human emotion. On this level, the somewhat removed, Buson again catches moods and relationships skillfully.

Haiga is a form of painting somewhat peripheral to Nanga, not properly to be included in it at all; like *haiku,* it is purely a Japanese invention, with no Chinese model or equivalent. When Buson turned to a Chinese subject, he was likely to use a Chinese-derived style, although never really imitatively. His pair of paintings representing scenes from "The Elysium of the Peach Blossom Spring" (Nos. 23a, b), painted in 1781, illustrate a story that was originally told by the Chinese poet T'ao Yüan-ming (365-427). It concerns a fisherman who strayed into a hidden valley in the deep mountains, reached through a cave behind a grove of blossoming peach trees. There he found people living in perfect peace, isolated from the rest of the world. After staying with them for several days, he returned to his home, thinking to remember the way back to the valley, but neither he nor other searchers could ever find it again. The poems written above Buson's paintings are by a Ming poet, and follow T'ao's theme. The figure holding the oar in the right painting is the fisherman, who is talking with two old men, inhabitants of the secluded valley. Another old man and two younger ones are led up a path by excited boys in the left picture; they have just heard of the arrival of the visitor from a forgotten outside world, and are hurrying to see him. The origin of the style seen here is, again, in the Che School of the Ming dynasty, in figure painters such as Chang Lu; characteristic are the active postures, the intense facial expressions and narrowed eyes, the drawing of the robes in continuous, restless line. In the hands of Buson, however, this style relaxes from tension into poetic fancy; the forced urgency of the later Che masters does not fit Buson's taste or mood, but echoes of it reinforce his sub-theme, which is the preservation of youthful vigor into old age. Buson bends his figures so that each group fits into an enclosed, oval shape, and curves his trees so as to enclose these in turn; in the left picture, particularly, this device leads to an interesting warping of space.

Another figure composition by Buson, a recent discovery that is as yet little known, represents a legendary wonder-worker of the seventh century named En no Gyōja with two of his attendants (No. 24). A cult called Shugendō, an offshoot of Esoteric Buddhism, claimed him as its founder. Monks of this sect would retire in large groups to sacred mountains and live for weeks on the slopes, meditating and praying as they climbed slowly to the peak, with each stage of the ascent representing symbolically a stage in the progress toward spiritual enlightenment.[6] En no Gyōja appears at the top of Buson's picture, an old man carrying a monk's rattle-staff and standing on the rocks on tall *geta,* his legs spread in a striding stance. Of the two demonic attendants below, one carries a pilgrim bottle, perhaps containing some magical elixir, and the other the axe that is an identifying attribute of En no Gyōja. The style of the painting appears to be an extension of the sketchy linear drawing and loosely applied

5. *Ibid.,* pp. 131, 132. Since it is not mentioned in Sora's diary, there is some suspicion that this encounter with the two prostitutes was invented by Bashō.

6. This information is taken from John Rosenfield's excellent discussion of a self-portrait by Buson's follower Yokoi Kinkoku, who represented himself as a Shugendū monk. See *Japanese Art in the John and Kimiko Powers Collection* (Cambridge, Mass., 1970), no. 123, p. 307

24 Yosa Buson En no Gyōja.
Hanging scroll, ink and light
colors on paper. H. 51 in.
(129.5 cm.)

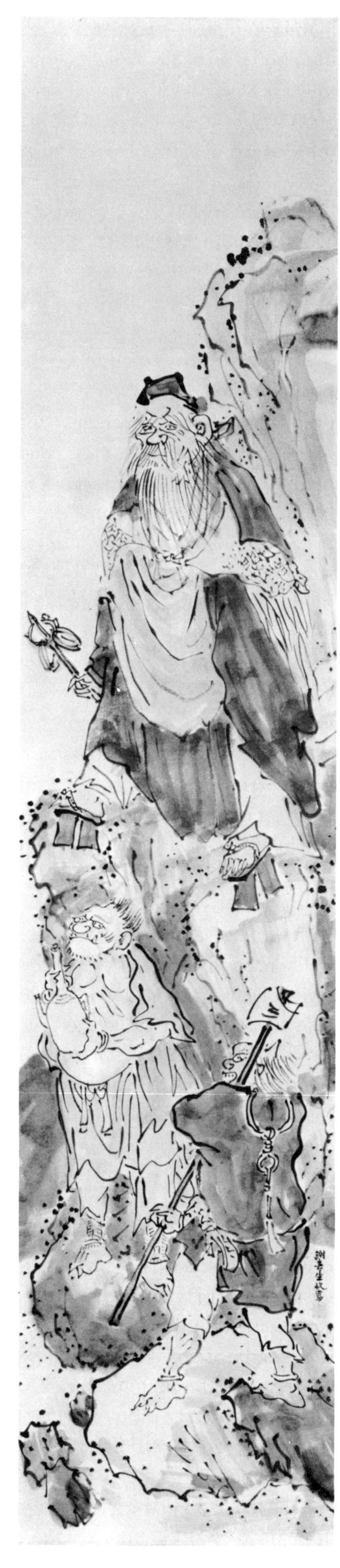

25 **Yosa Buson** Clearing after Rain in Spring. Hanging scroll, ink and colors on satin. H. 11¼ in. (28.5 cm.)

26 **Yosa Buson** Cuckoo in Flight over New Verdure. Hanging scroll, ink and colors on silk. H. 60-9/16 in. (153.8 cm.)

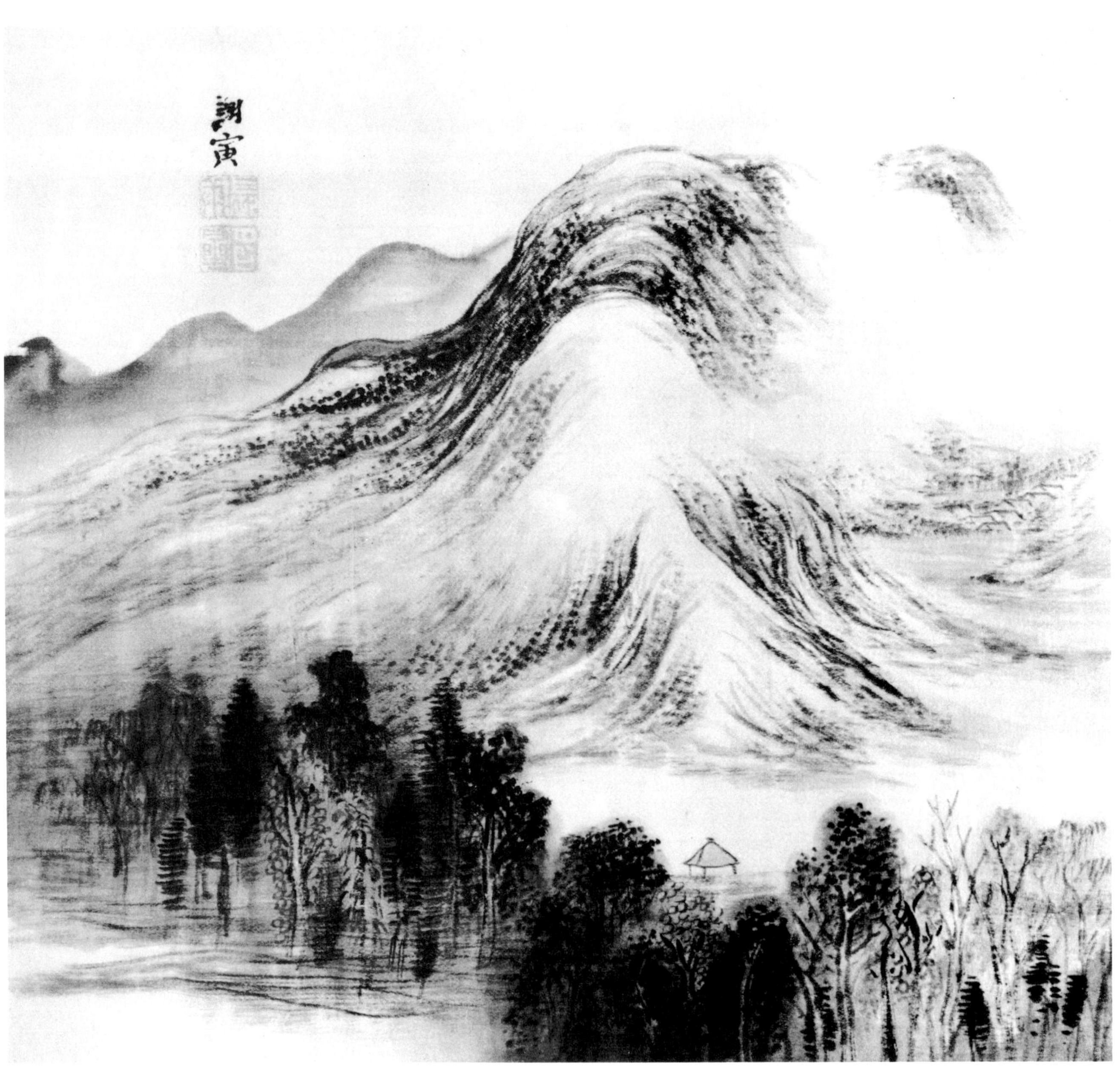

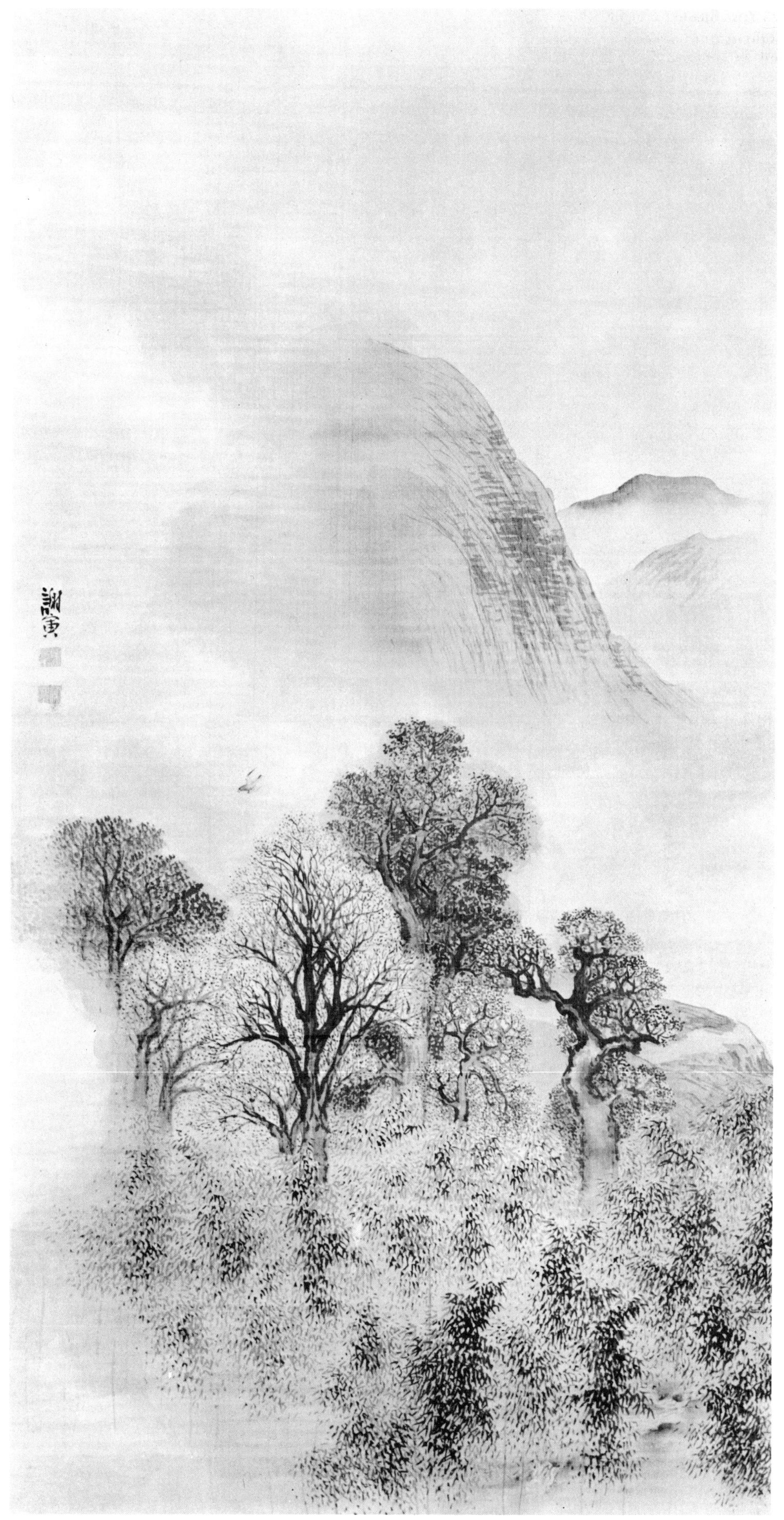

謝寅

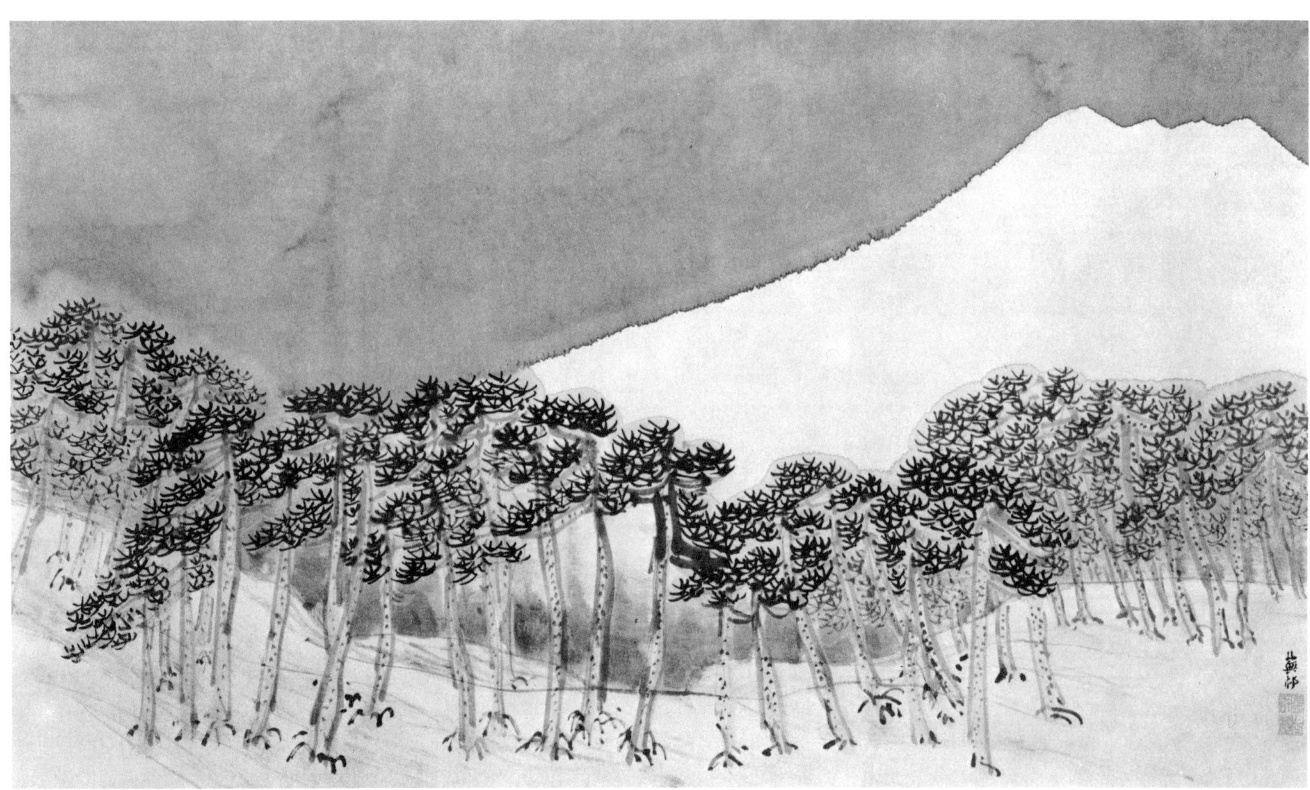

27 **Yosa Buson** Mount Fuji. Hanging scroll, ink and light colors on paper. H. 20^1/$_8$ in. (51.1 cm.)

washes of Buson's *haiga* manner to a larger and more complex composition; here again, Buson has chosen a Japanese style to depict a Japanese subject. The line is in constant dancing motion, and the energetic aspect of the figures depends as much on this quality of line as on their postures. The scattered dotting and the prevalence of steep diagonals add to the effect of agitation. The signature that Buson uses on this painting, Shunsei, is one that he used during the fifteen-year period 1763-1778, and allows us to date the picture to that part of his life.

Sensitive as he was to nuances of human feeling, Buson as a painter is at his best (and most Japanese) when revealing transient aspects of natural scenery. Nothing could be further from the timelessness and universality of typical Chinese landscape than such Buson paintings as the lovely little "Clearing After Rain in Spring" (No. 25) in which the sun breaking through clouds after rain lights up the area to the right of the hill, where patches of yellow suggest fields of spring flowers, while the left side and the trees in the foreground are still dark under an overcast sky. Buson has chosen to paint on satin, which has a glossy surface ideally suited to the rendering of effects of light. It also gives a cool tone to the ink, and permits a special kind of diffuse brushwork that here adds to the impression of dampness.

Buson shares Taiga's love for soft foliage, which often occupies larges areas of his compositions. His treatment of it is less schematic than Taiga's, more devoted to reproducing visual impressions. This is in accord with a more general difference in approach between the two. Taiga puts old conventions to new use in a way that is somewhat intellectual, revealing an attachment to the history of painting as well as to the act of painting, and perhaps a greater attachment to both than to nature itself. With Buson, the bond between the artist and his subject seems more intimate, and the painter's immediate impressions and feelings are more decisive in determining the character of the painting. In this sense, Buson seems closer in spirit to the Sung painters of China than to the Ming-Ch'ing masters who were closer to him in time, and whom he imitated.

In the "Cuckoo in Flight over New Verdure" (No. 26) the whole lower part of the picture is filled with lush greenery—trees, a grove of bamboo—forming a sensuous surface that is broken only by the tree trunks, a few bamboo stalks faintly seen, and an opening at the bottom through which a stream is glimpsed. The hills above are revealed only partially above the fog, as a Sung artist might have painted them, the furthest hill in blue wash; and as in a Sung painting, the focus of the composition is on one spot, the flying bird. The *hototogisu* or cuckoo, a bird that sings as it flies, is always associated with spring in Japanese poems and paintings. Buson's special fondness and aptitude for seasonal themes in his landscapes may relate to his study and practice of *haiku* poems, in which there is always some clue to the season.

The landscapes by Buson that have the closest affinities with *haiku*, however, are those done in another manner, in thick brushstrokes and broad washes. They are simple in plan and ingenuous in feeling. Finest of all is the superb "Night Over the City," in which a single motif, the rooftops of Kyoto, is repeated almost to the point of being read as an all-over pattern, but varied in form and arrangement just enough to avoid monotony.[7] This is a typically Japanese mode of composition, much used by artists of the Rimpa School, which plays between picture and decorative design as alternate readings. Buson's rendering of that most Japanese of all landscape themes, Mount Fuji, of which he did several versions, is of this same type (No. 27). Here it is the pine trees, drawn as a child might

7. An especially good reproduction in Chū Yoshizawa and Takeshi Yamakawa, *Nanga to Shasei-ga* [Nanga and Realistic Painting], *(Genshoku Nihon no Bijutsu* [Japanese Art in Original Color], Vol. 18 [Tokyo, 1969]), pl. 30.

28 Yosa Buson Bare Peaks of
Mount Gabi *(O-mei)*. Handscroll,
ink and light colors on paper.
H. 11³/₈ in. (28.9 cm.)

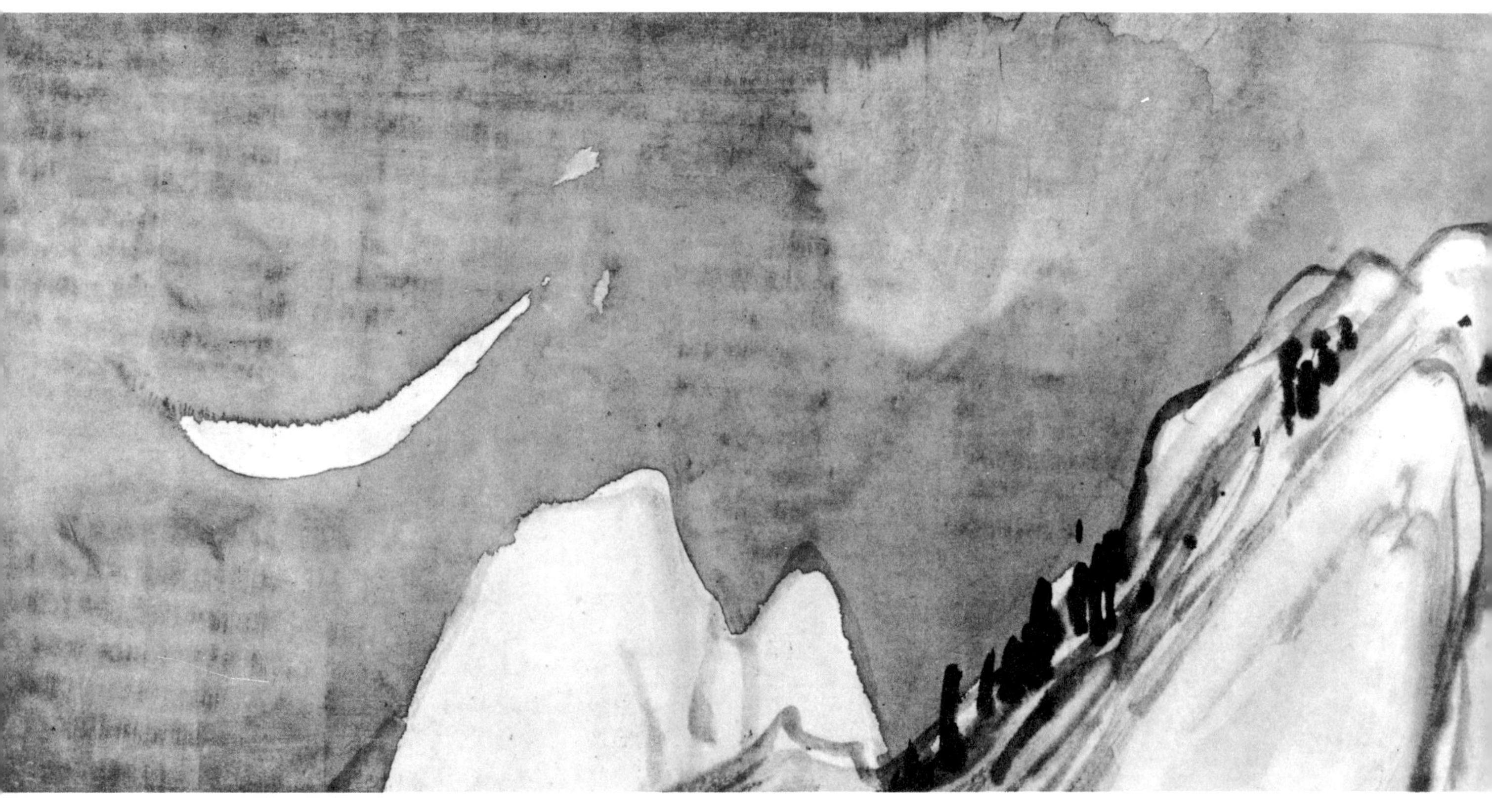

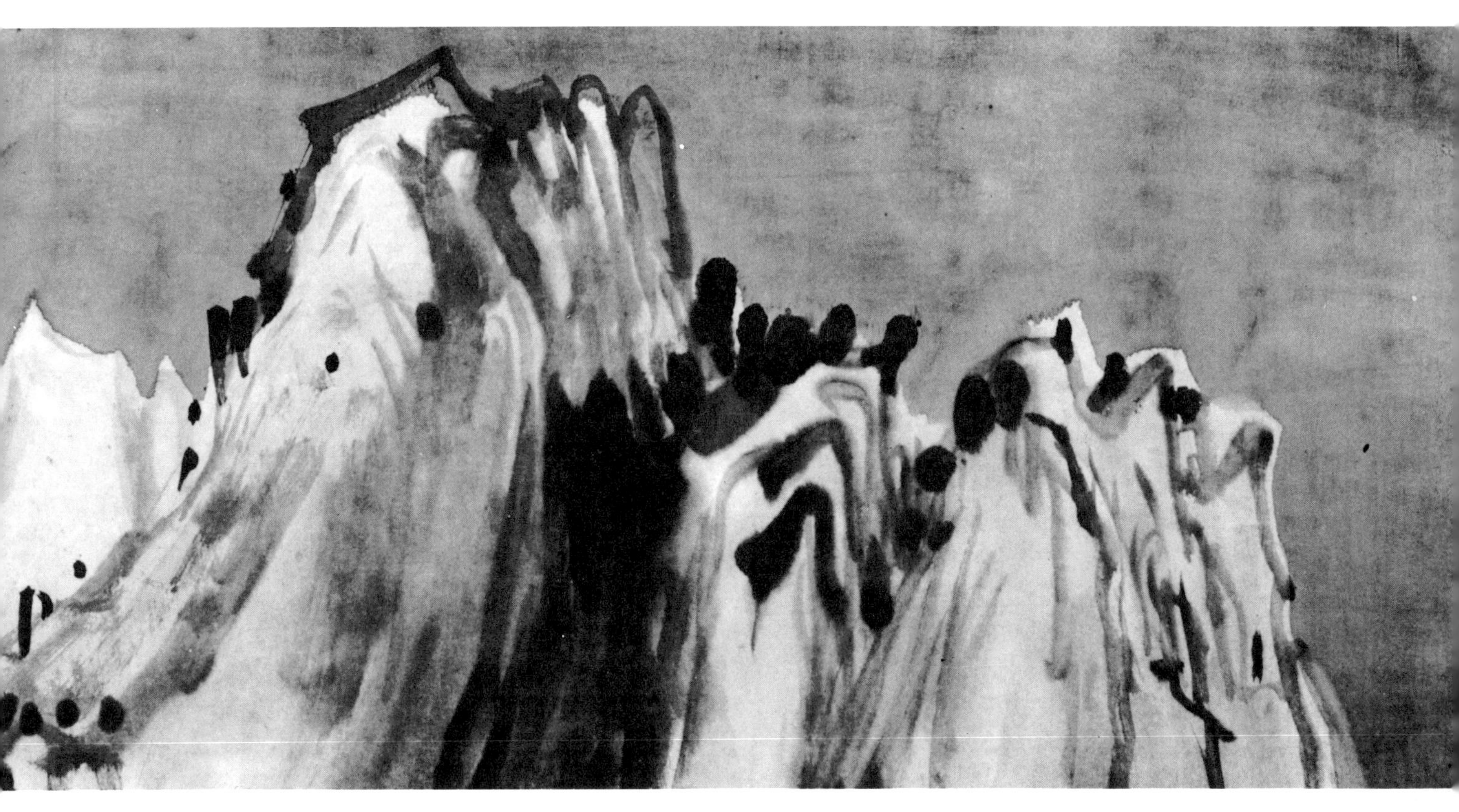

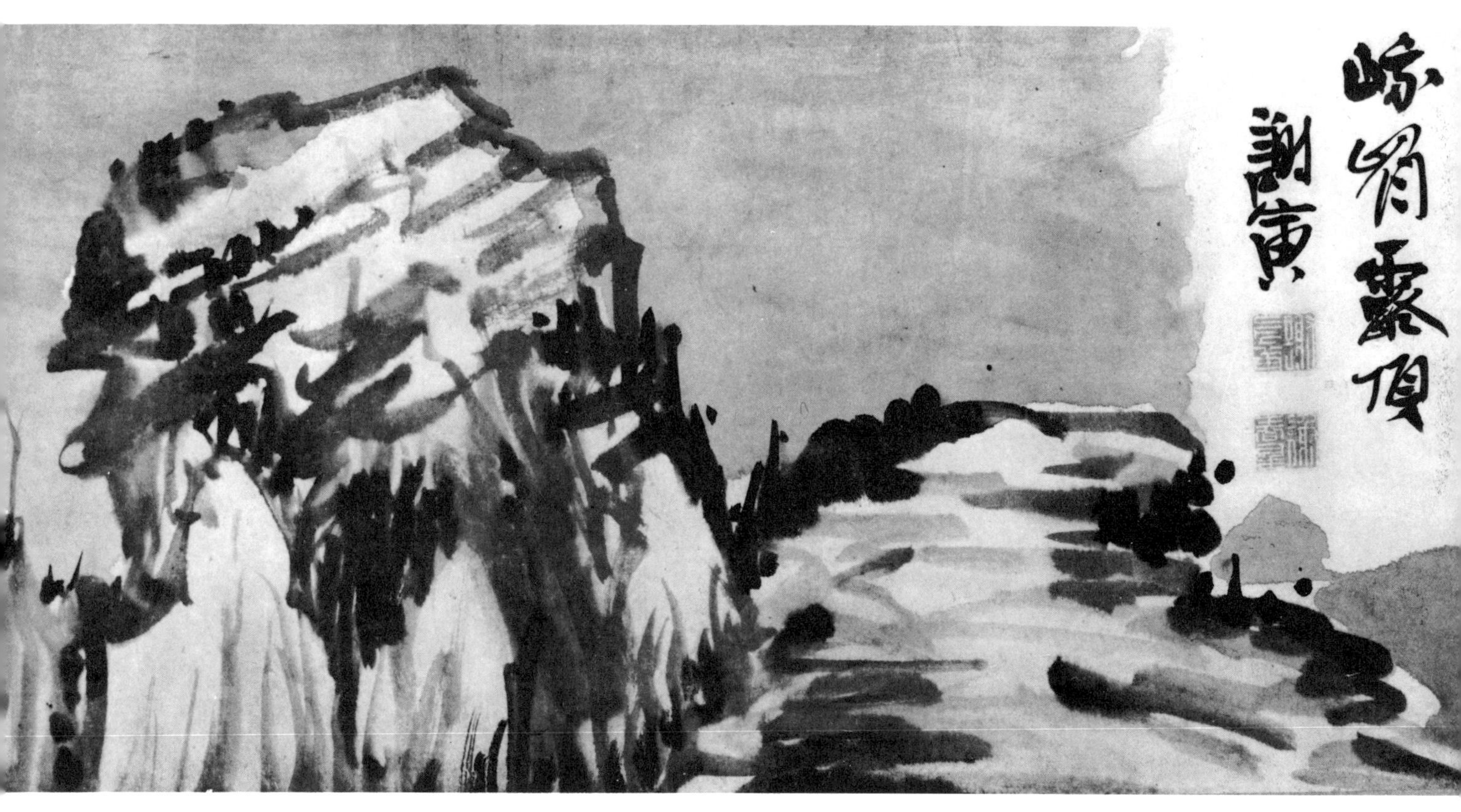

draw them—with their trunks bounded by thick lines, dots for scales, and large clumps of needles—that are repeated to make up the pattern. Groups of trees at each end are set back into the middle distance, and dimmed slightly in tone without disturbing the essential flatness of the whole expanse. Above the busy, prickly area of the pines, Mount Fuji rises majestically, a simple white silhouette against a darkened sky. Nothing more is given, or needed; only Fuji, pines, and sky: a precise pictorial equivalent of the *haiku*.

Buson's handscroll painting titled "Bare Peaks of Mount Gabi" (i.e., Mount O-mei, a mountain in Szechwan Province in southwest China), unknown and unpublished until a few years ago, has become one of his best known works (No. 28). It is based on a poem by the T'ang dynasty poet Li Po titled "Moon on Mount O-mei." The peaks are drawn boldly in broad, lax strokes, without detail, and colored lightly with *taisha* (red ochre), all but a single moonlit one at the end, over which the crescent moon hangs, a white shape in reserve in an ink-wash night sky. Representing mountain peaks in a painting of horizontal shape might seem to present a challenge to the painter, but Buson uses the form effectively to present the peaks looming mysteriously out of an undefined depth.

Among Buson's followers was Yokoi Kinkoku (1761-1832), another artist who has only recently come into prominence. He was born in Ōtsu, near Lake Biwa, and is said to have studied painting under Buson in Kyoto from the age of thirteen, imitating him even to the style of his calligraphy. In later years he was a wandering Buddhist priest, reportedly given to drinking and dissipation as well as asceticism. He was extremely prolific, even excessively so, as many of his works seem to have been produced hastily and rather carelessly. Implicit in the ideals of Nanga—spontaneity, individualism, amateurism—were dangers to which lesser artists of the school frequently succumbed, as even the major ones sometimes did. Kinkoku's painting of the "Road to Shu" (No. 29) is a good representative of his more successful works. Snow scenes and night scenes were specialties of Kinkoku, who follows in them Buson's manner of working in fluid lineament and extensive washes. Here he uses the material, silk, to good effect, soaking the washes of ink into it with rich gradations of tone to render sky, mountain slopes, dark masses of tree foliage, and shadowy hollows. Shu is the old name for Szechwan Province, and the road through the mountains by which is was reached was famous for its precarious passages along sheer cliffs, where the road was built out on poles from the faces of the cliffs. Parties of travelers are seen at intervals on this road, climbing toward a pass, wearing heavy coats against the cold, which is conveyed by a light spattering of white pigment to represent falling snow.

29 Yokoi Kinkoku The Road to
Shu. Hanging scroll, ink and
colors on silk. H. 43-7/16 in.
(110.3 cm.)

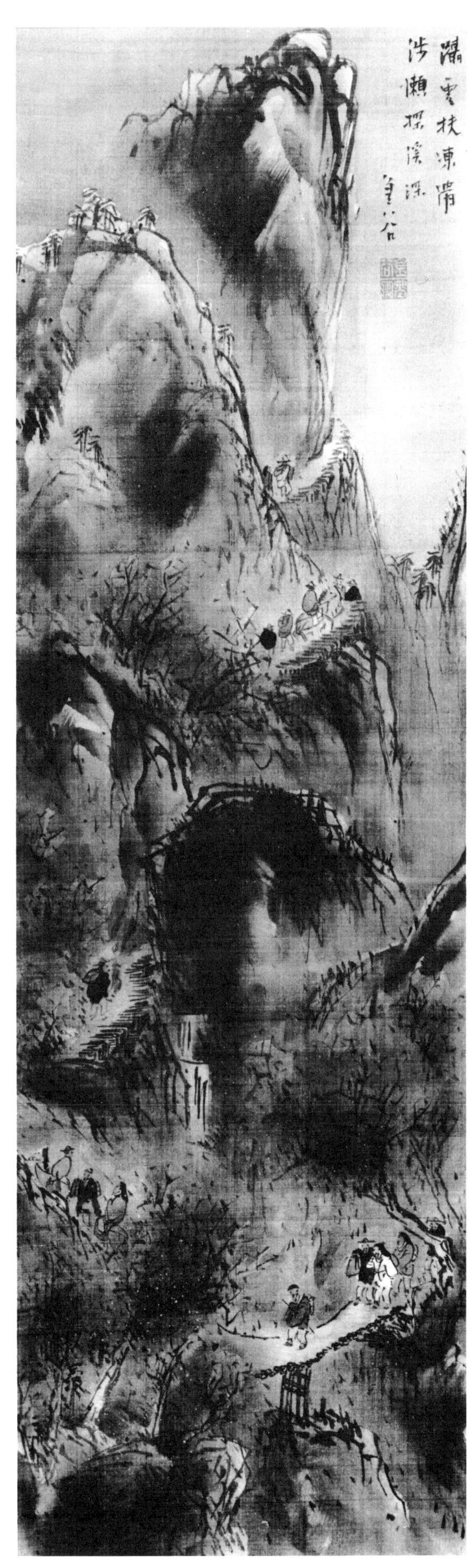

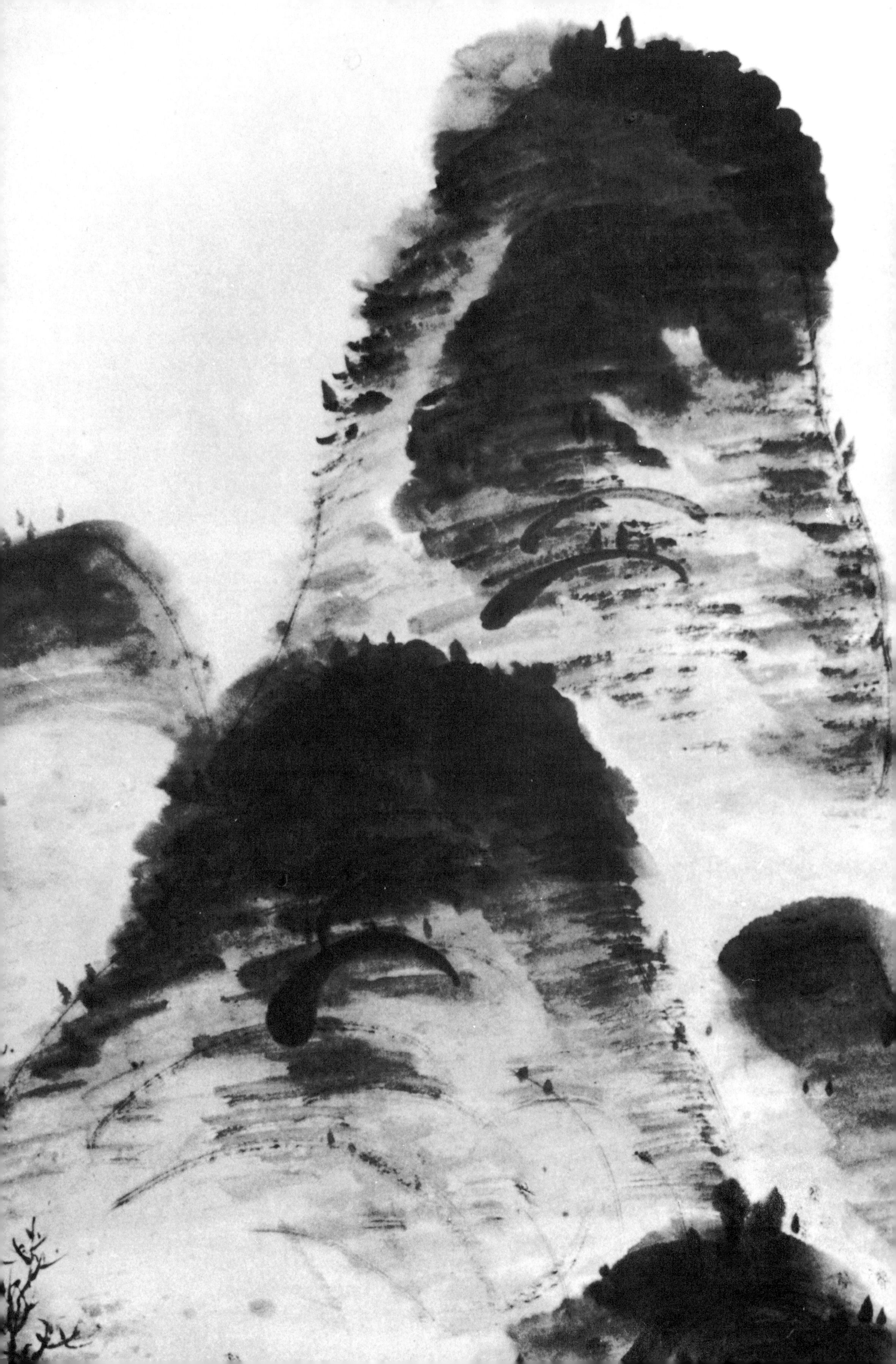

Chapter V: Uragami Gyokudō

The third of the major masters of Nanga, Uragami Gyokudō (1745-1820), was
not until recently ranked on the same level with Taiga, Buson, and Chikuden. His
reputation has risen spectacularly over the past thirty years, and now his paintings are probably more in demand by museums and private collectors than those
of any of the others. Gyokudō's paintings appeal powerfully to the twentieth
century eye and sensibility because, like the works of some Chinese individualist
painters with which they have strong affinities, they are satisfying and exciting
in two ways: as pure form, in their ink-and-paper existence, and as profoundly
moving visions of nature. These two aesthetic modes of being are so perfectly
fused in Gyokudō that the fairly few writers who have tried to deal with his
paintings at all have seemed uncertain whether to treat them as abstractions
or as landscapes; they have been called objective, subjective, impressionistic
and expressionistic.[1]

The facts of his life are known in some detail, thanks to recent research.[2] He
was born into a family of feudal retainers (samurai) serving the lord of the Ikeda
clan in Bizen Province, modern Okayama Prefecture. He became the titular head
of his family at the age of six, on the death of his father. Later he studied
Confucianism, and was given a post as personal attendant to the lord of the
Ikeda clan. On ten trips to Edo, he studied poetry, painting, and playing the
zither (*ch'in*). The name "Gyokudō" (Jade Hall) he took from an inscription on
a Chinese zither that he owned, and he called himself Gyokudō Kinshi, "The
Jade Hall Zither Master."

The lord whom he served died in 1768, and Gyokudō's interests turned more
toward scholarship and poetry, music and painting. The death of his wife in
1792, and the prohibition by the Tokugawa government of the study of certain
"heterodox" doctrines, including the form of Neo-Confucianism expounded by
the Ming dynasty Chinese philosopher Wang Yang-ming, to which Gyokudō
evidently subscribed, led him to resolve at last to withdraw from feudal service.
He made the break in 1794, setting off with his two sons on a series of journeys
all over Japan. He made his living chiefly as a musician; he does not seem to
have been a professional painter. He drank heavily, and some of his pictures are
inscribed as having been painted "while inebriated." He was evidently not much
appreciated as a painter in his lifetime; we are told that his son Shunkin (1779-
1846), who can now be seen as a pleasant but generally uninspired artist, was in
his own time more highly esteemed than his father. Eventually, around 1811,

1. By Susumu Suzuki, *Uragami Gyokudō
Gashū* [Collection of Paintings by
Uragami Gyokudō] (Tokyo, 1956), p. 23;
Terukazu Akiyama, *Japanese Painting*
(Geneva, 1961), p. 192; Jon Carter Covell,
Japanese Landscape Painting (New York,
1962), p. 12; and Yukio Yashiro, ed.,
Art Treasures of Japan (Tokyo, 1960), II,
p. 485.

2. See Suzuki, *op. cit.* (n. 1 above),
pp. 3-7, 13-17 (*nempu* or yeartable);
English summary, pp. 21-24.

Gyokudō settled in Kyoto and stayed there until his death in 1820. In Kyoto he
had a number of friends who were Nanga painters, including Chikuden and
Beisanjin. Most of his works, and the best of them, date from his last years,
his sixties and seventies.

The earliest work in the present exhibition, "Building a House in the Mountains" (No. 30), is dated to 1792, two years before Gyokudō left feudal service
and began his wanderings. The poem on it reads:

"I build my house where mountains lean on void;
Here people are at leisure, as in antiquity.
I pass the morning watching mists disperse;
At midnight, rain falls on the chilly pond."

The painting is unusual among Gyokudō's works in being painted on silk with
extensive washes of color; later he usually worked on paper, in ink monochrome
or with only touches of color. Starting from a fairly stable and conventional
foreground, the composition moves rapidly upward through tall, leafy trees to
a crowded cluster of mountaintops. Gyokudō's fully developed style is antici-
pated in a few points—the rows of horizontal strokes along the edges of rocks,
the fondness for arching and rounded forms, the constant movement of line
that denies stability. But the deliberate repetitions of shapes and brushstrokes
that unify the later works are not to be seen here; instead, a diversity of foliage
patterns in the trees, so marked as to make up a major theme in the picture,
seems aimed at an effect of disarray. This textural variety and the varied washes
of color produce a pleasantly disordered richness—an achievement still far
short, however, of the power of his mature style.

That style seems to have come into being in the first decade of the nineteenth
century. One point to be made about it immediately—and we must add that
it does not take us very far toward accounting for Gyokudō's greatness—is that
Gyokudō seems to have been the first Japanese painter to understand and make
use of one basic feature of Chinese literati painting style. It is a feature that can be
observed only in good original paintings, and Gyokudō's awareness of it may
have been a consequence of the importation to Japan, by his time, of more and
better Chinese paintings than Taiga and the other early masters had been able
to see. This stylistic feature is the manner of building up a rich pictorial texture
by overlaying and interweaving brushstrokes of different kinds: dry and wet,
broad and fine, deep-toned and pale. As the Yüan dynasty masters of China had
discovered in the fourteenth century, the fabric of brushwork achieved in this
way can constitute the very substance of the forms, which are brought into being
not by the traditional means of delineating and then shading or coloring, but
by defining their surfaces and their bulk through a gradual amassing of brushstrokes, as one might weave a textured fabric. An area of painting treated in this
way can have the remarkable capacity of seeming to draw the eye in and out,
providing a sense of depth at the same time that it sets up a visually exciting
surface agitation in these traces of the actual motion of the brush.

These are the means that Gyokudō uses superbly, and in an extremely personal
manner, in the works of his middle period, his sixties. An ideal painting to introduce this group is the "Green Pines and Russet Valleys" ("*Seishō tangaku*,"
No. 31) which he painted in 1807 as a gift for the sixty-third birthday of the
mother of a man named Hirota. The colors are only in the title; the painting,
like most of Gyokudō's later works, is in ink monochrome. The composition is
fairly simple: a V-shaped valley, at its base a small hut with a man inside reading
a book, and hills beyond. On the slopes of this terrain grow pine trees, drawn

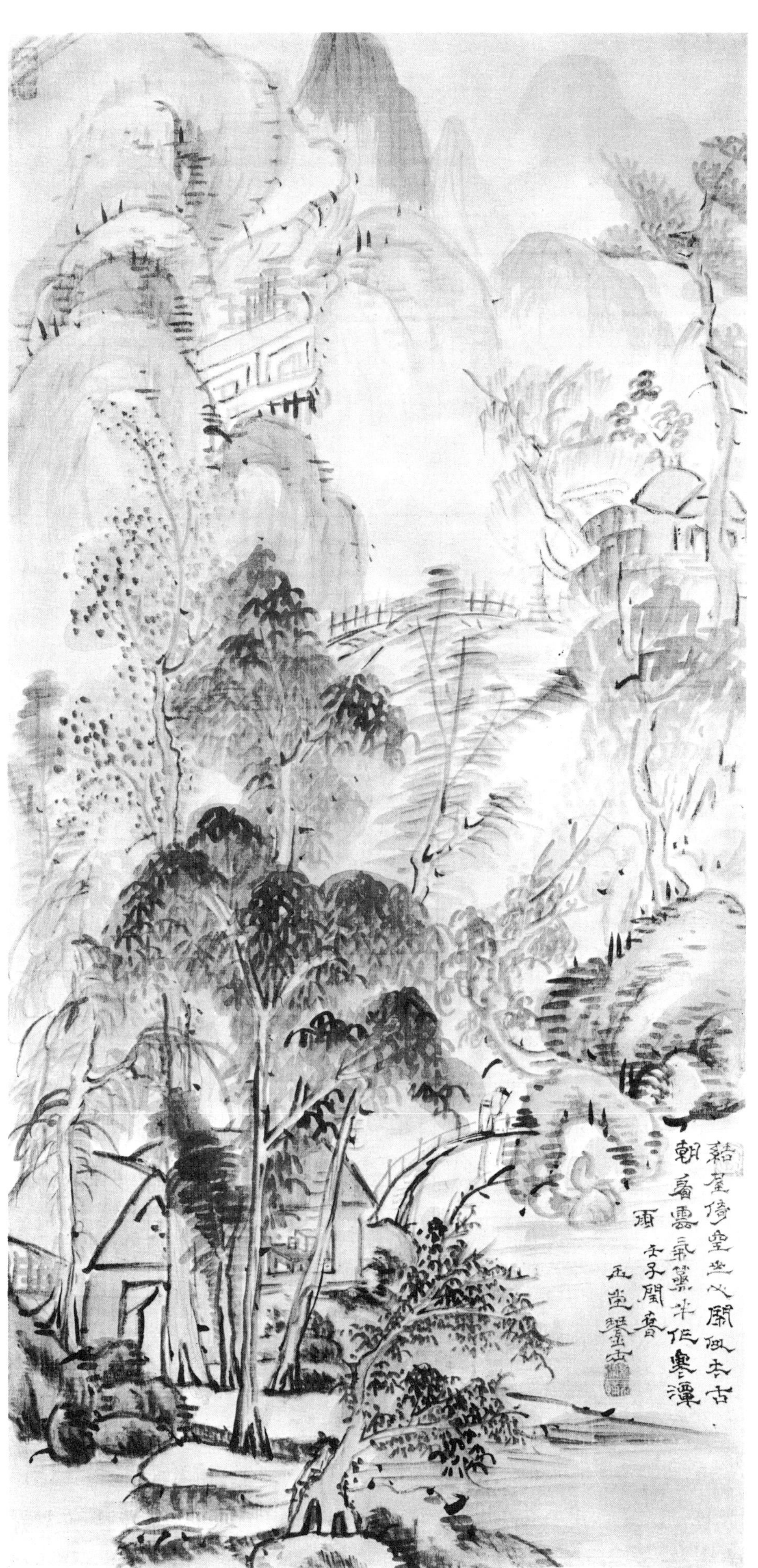

30 Uragami Gyokudō Building a House in the Mountains *(Sanchū Ketsuro)*, 1792. Hanging scroll, ink and light colors on silk. H. 26 in. (66 cm.)

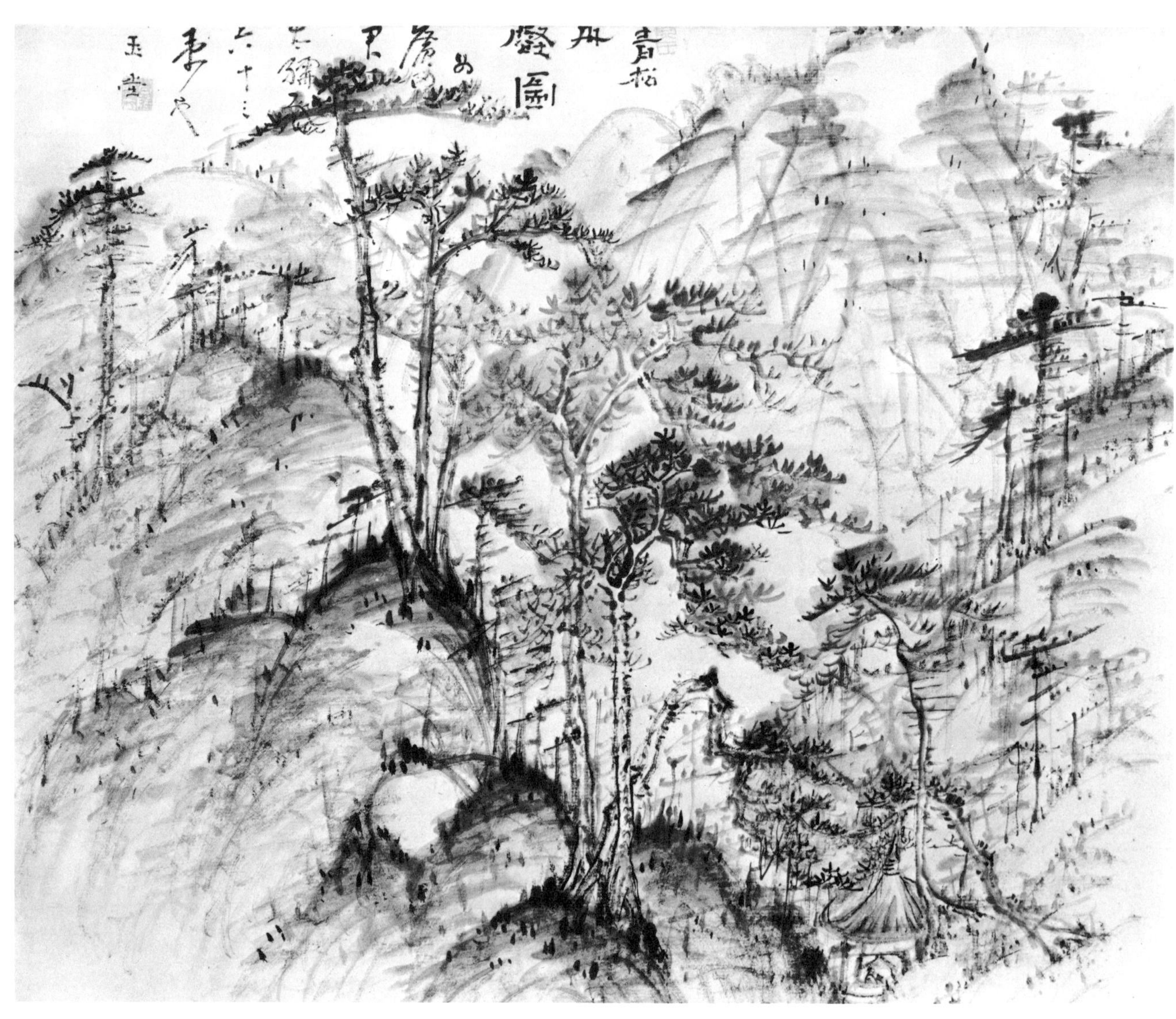

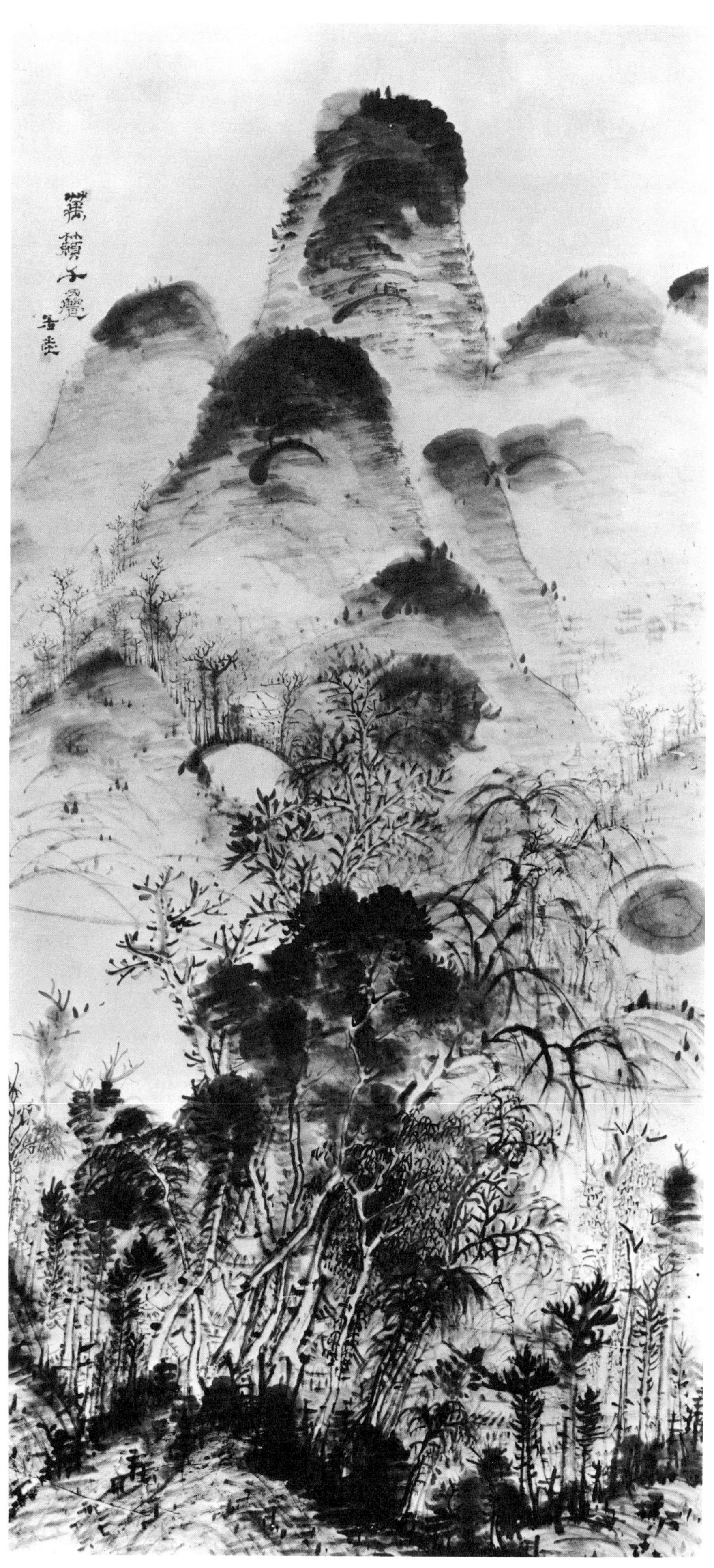

32 Uragami Gyokudō A Myriad Sounds and Thousand-layered Peaks *(Banrai Senjō)*. Hanging scroll, ink and light colors on paper. H. 53⅛ in. (135 cm.)

large so as to give us the feeling of being in the forest instead of only gazing at it from a distance. What pulls the picture into powerful unity is the rhythmic repetition of certain forms: the rounded hillocks, proceeding upward to the left, echoed in lighter tone by the hills in the distance; the pines, varying in size, shape, and tone, marking out depth; and, most of all, insistently repeated horizontal strokes in pale ink, all slanting slightly leftward, representing nothing in particular but imparting to the composition the soft vibrance of a world alive with wind and air. Variety is sacrificed to a typically Japanese kind of surface unity, the same kind that we noted in some works of Taiga and Buson: a few simple pictorial elements—here, pine trees and sketchily drawn hills— comprise nearly the entire matter of the picture and are spread out over its surface so as to fill most of it, as a closely integrated fabric. The painting is thus read first as a kind of all-over design, but certain parts of it gradually draw our attention: the hut at the bottom, the darkest parts of the trees, or the round, white shape on one of the near hillocks, a motif we will encounter later in more radical and conspicuous form.

Gyokudō is one of the few Nanga masters who can move from a small size to a large with no loss of either structure or sensitivity. His larger compositions generally offer a much greater variety of forms and types of brushwork, but have the same depths and subtleties as the smaller ones. Most of his hanging scroll landscapes follow, with variations, a single compositional type. Two that can serve to introduce the type, both undated but probably belonging to the decade of his sixties, are "A Myriad Sounds and Thousand-layered Peaks" (No. 32— the translation is approximate, his titles being hard to render) and "Idle in the Mountains" (No. 33). In each, a grove of tall trees grows on a knoll in the fore- ground; a river cuts across the middle ground, and round-topped hills rise beyond to fill the upper part of the picture. A few houses and pavilions are half hidden among the trees. In both pictures, oval shapes much lighter or darker than their surroundings are repeated on the mountainsides, representing, if anything at all, flat tops of truncated hillocks, sharply tilted to face the viewer.

In other respects the two pictures represent divergent directions. "Idle in the Mountains" is more static, with the shapes of the severely vertical exposed trunks of trees repeated in a waterfall behind, and all the forms squarely im- planted on level bases. Heavy applications of staccato horizontal strokes in black ink and large, slightly blurred dots render the foliage of the trees and suggest vegetation on the distant mountains. This technique, and other features of Gyokudō's style as well as the motif of the white oval shapes on the hillsides, suggest that he may have known the landscapes of the Chinese individualist painter Kung Hsien (d. 1789) whose works had reached Japan by the early nine- teenth century. Gyokudō is a far less systematic painter than Kung Hsien, however, and attempts no such naturalistic effects of sunlight and shadow; instead, constant alternations of light and dark occur throughout the com- position.

The painting "Myriad Sounds" is executed in a less patient, more nervous manner; slashing, upward-arched strokes appear everywhere. Somber weight is given to the trees and mountains by heavy washes of dark ink. The center of the composition is alive with a dense mass of tree branches and leaf patterns, forming in some areas spidery linear designs of a peculiarly agitated, somehow incoherent character. The different networks of brushstrokes—dry and wet, heavy and light—seem to occupy different levels of depth, probably because the combining of fine line and broad, blurred strokes somehow reproduces the

33 Uragami Gyokudō Idle in the Mountains *(Sanchū Buji).* Hanging scroll, ink on paper. H. 69³/₈ in. (176.1 cm.)

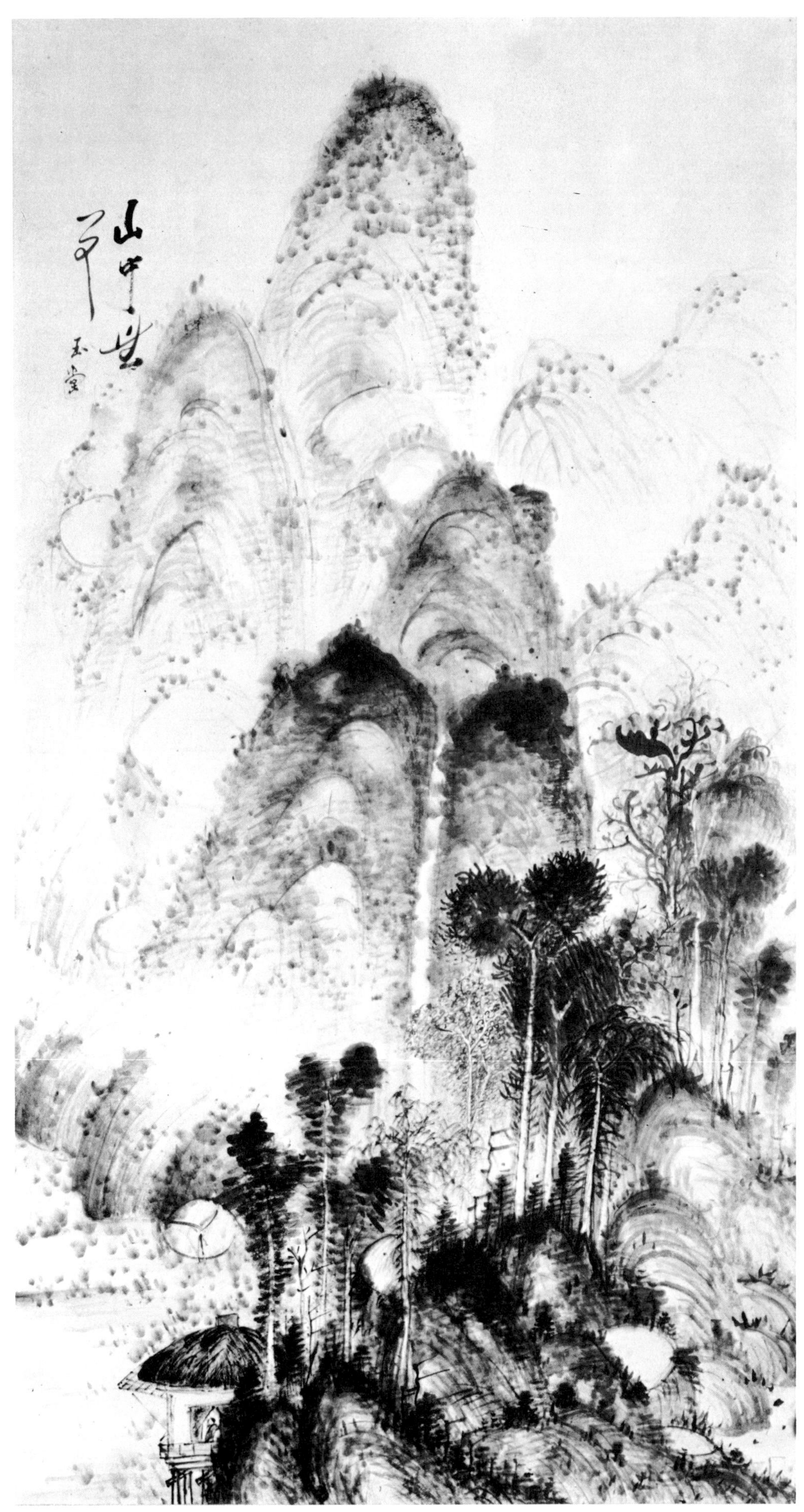

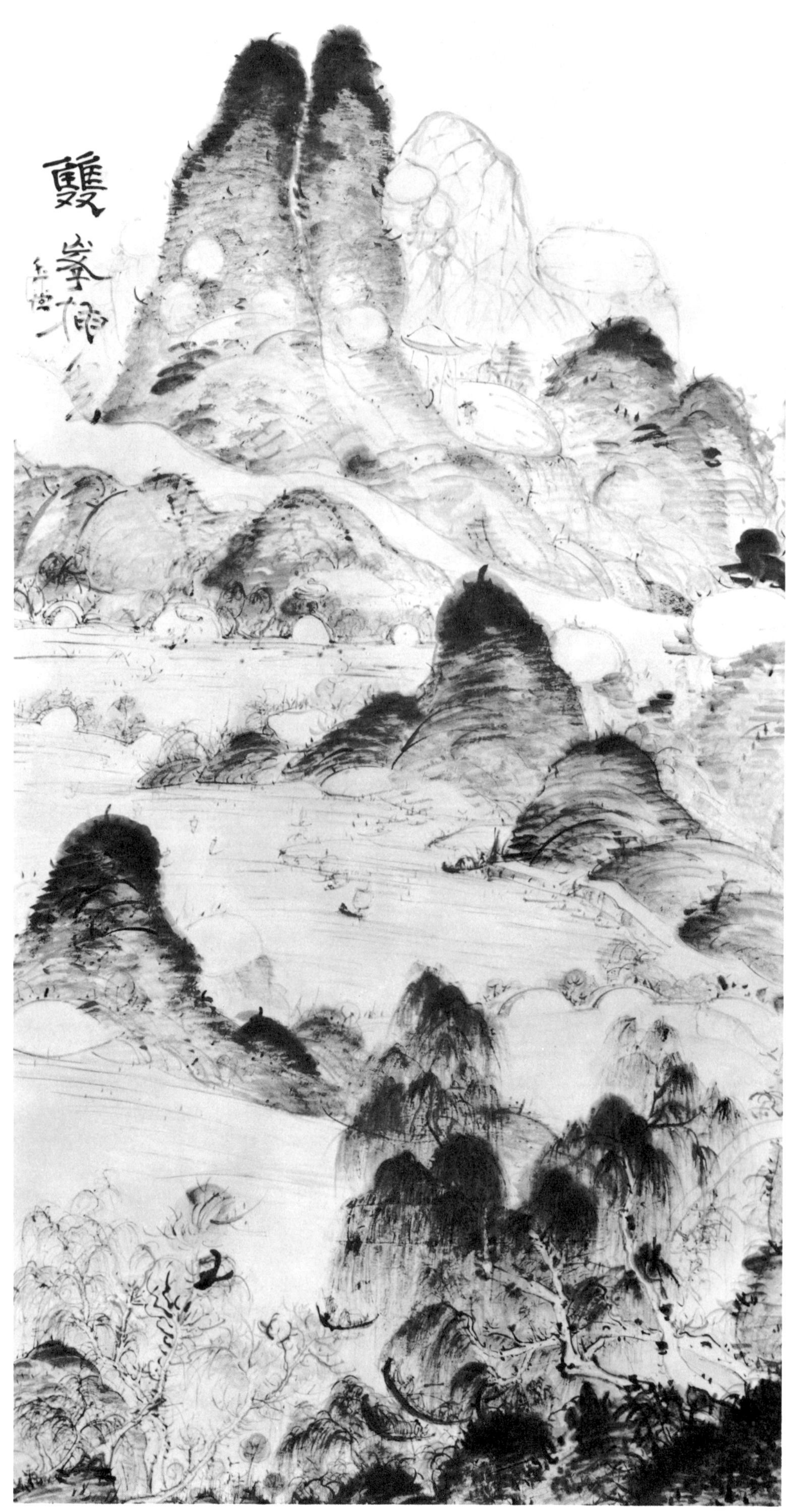

雙
峯
挿雲

effect of sharp-focus and diffuse, as one sees objects at different distances in actual vision. However it is accomplished, it is an extraordinary visual experience, perhaps not paralleled by anything in Western art, and by very little in that of the Far East.

It would appear from the titles that Gyokudō wrote on his paintings and from his poems, as well as from the paintings themselves, that he saw nature in a state of continual change, with its forms interacting dynamically with their surroundings. One of his best-known paintings is titled "Two Peaks Embracing Clouds" ("Sōhō Sōun," No. 34). The nature of the painting warns us, however, against assuming too quickly that Gyokudō "painted nature as he saw it"; the extreme, almost perverse manipulations of space and form make this seem rather a world of the artist's mind. The impulses that impelled the brush on its sometimes erratic course were evidently unrestrained by any urgent necessity to describe nature as it is perceived, or to make the landscape plausible; the urgent need was rather to objectify an emotional state. The expression of that state, whatever it may have been, seems to have required the compulsive reiteration of certain semi-circular and rotary movements, which produce arched and ovoid forms everywhere in the composition. All the tree branches and clusters of willow tendrils conform to this movement, the boats are bent by it into half-moon shapes, and semi-circular bridges traverse the lake, inspired perhaps by some memory of the famous embankments on the West Lake near Hangchow in China, which Gyokudō must have seen in pictures. (A painting of the West Lake by Taiga is close enough to this in composition to suggest that Gyokudō may have been inspired by it.[3]) The "clouds" of the title are represented only by a serpentine band of white that lies sluggishly along the foothills below the split peak. A figure approaching a pavilion on one of the plateaus in the far distance is as large as the figures in the foreground, and considerably larger than sailing boats in middle ground. There are traces of incompleted ideas and changes of plan throughout the composition. The title is written large and with an unusual degree of calligraphic abandon. Gyokudō does not add in this case, as he does in some others, "painted while drunk," but the picture makes one wonder. It is nonetheless an exciting work, particularly in the near-ecstatic painting of the foreground.

One of the recognized masterpieces of Gyokudō is the album titled "Enka-jō," or "Album of Mists and Clouds" (No. 35). Colophons attached to it by the artist's son Shunkin and the painter Tanomura Chikuden, dated 1811, indicate that the album was painted shortly before that year. Most of the leaves are rendered in Gyokudō's excited, running-line manner, and are perhaps the finest examples of that style. The leaf most often reproduced however, is a relatively quiet one, the eighth, the superb "Green Mountains and Red-leafed Grove" (No. 35H). This is an autumn scene, to which red-brown color (taisha) has been applied in scattered suffusions that scarcely seem to adhere to any particular forms. Here again, the finer patterns of branches set against amorphous patches of ink and color create a sense of depth that is independent of any ordinary compositional means, even those of Gyokudō's own earlier landscapes. The eye is drawn in and out, entering hollows of space that contain buildings and sketchily drawn figures, pulled back by the twisting trees. There is no point of rest, and yet the whole exists as an integrated and stable entity.

A few of the leaves seem only shorthand renderings of compositional formulae to be seen in Gyokudō's larger works. The sixth (No. 35F), for instance, presents the familiar scene of a man crossing a bridge that spans the gap between two

3. Susumu Suzuki et al., Ikeno Taiga Sakuhin-shū [Collection of Works by Ikeno Taiga] (Tokyo, 1960), pl. 599.

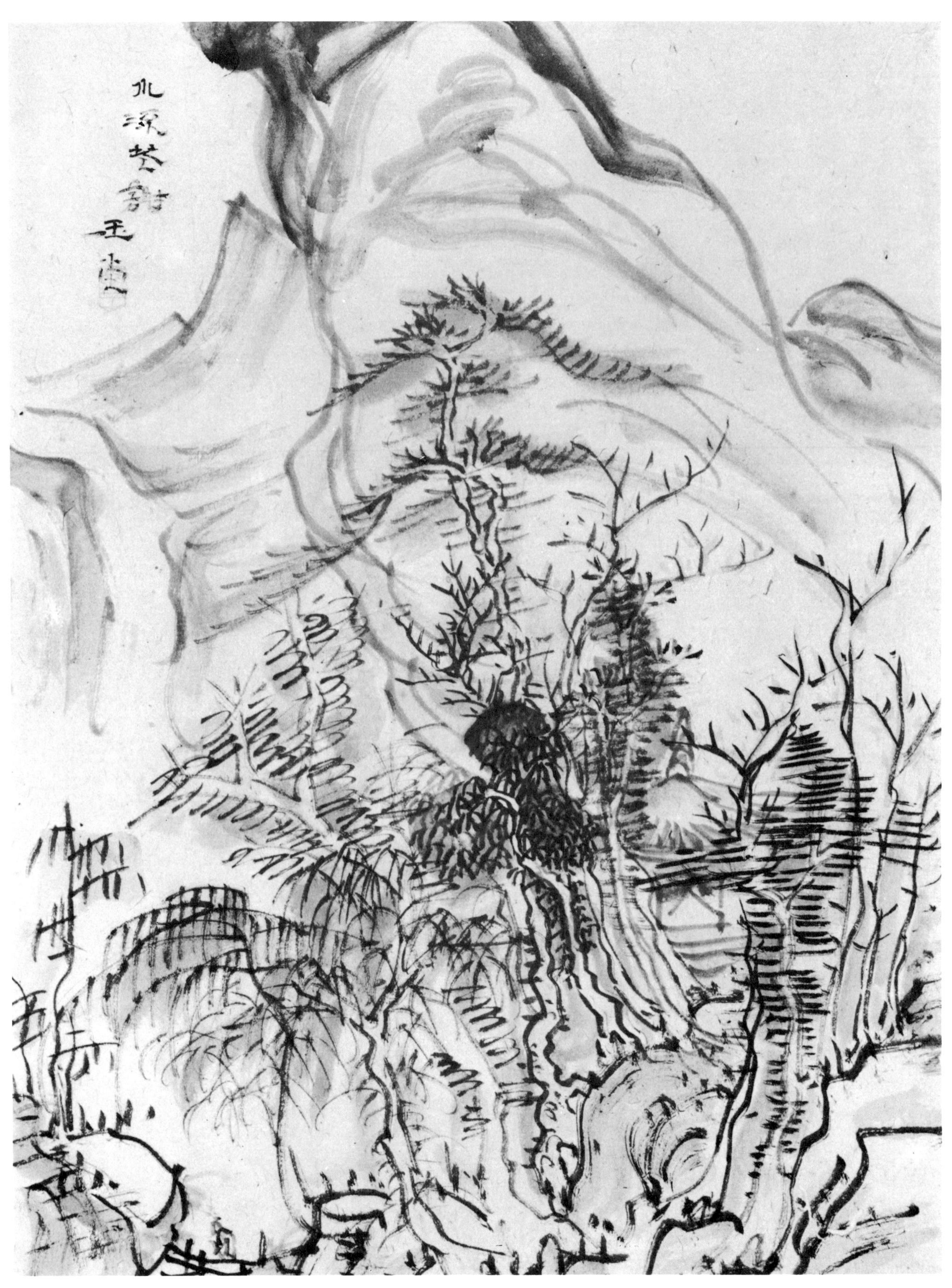
九溪苓社
玉山

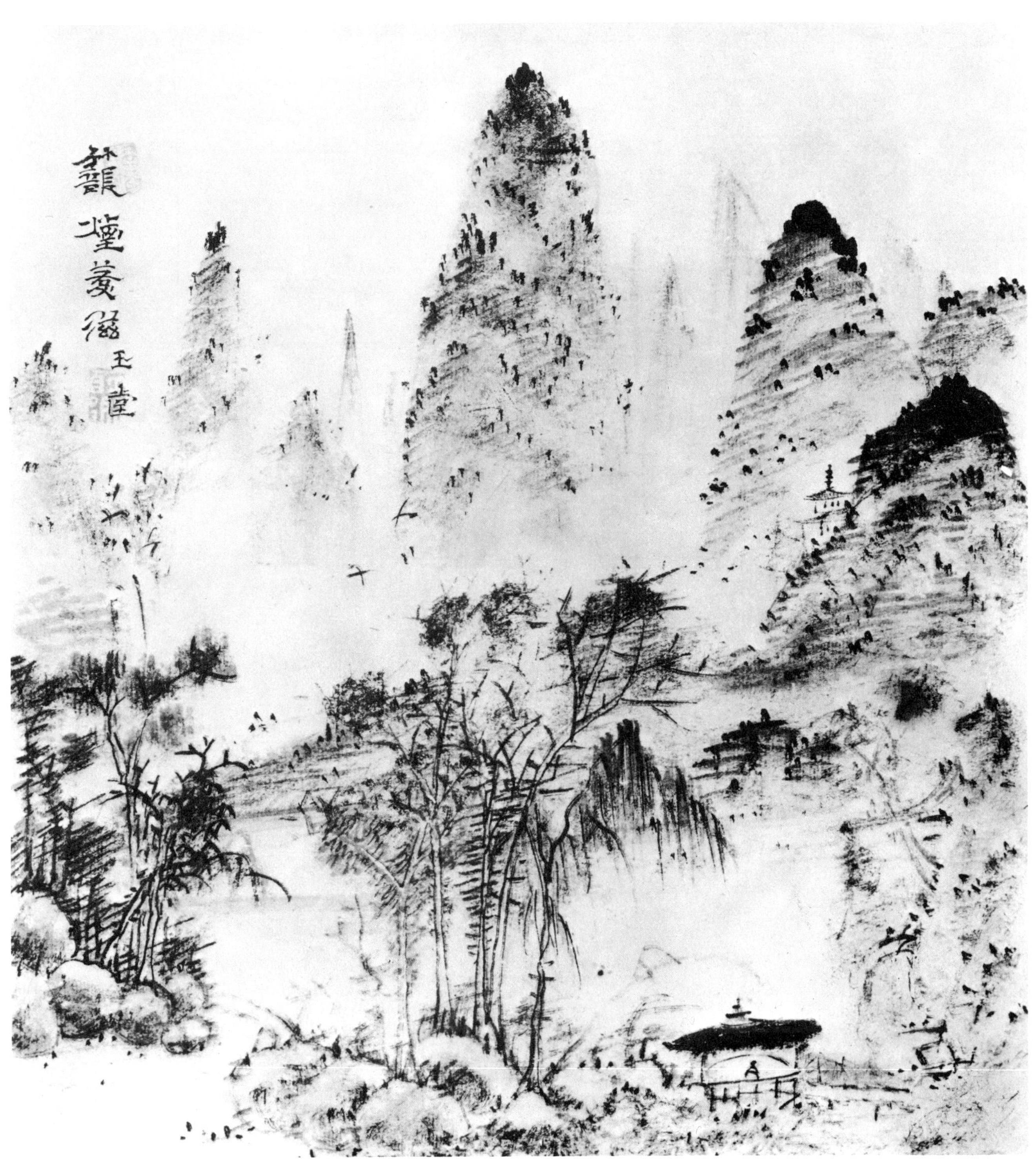

35 Uragami Gyokudō Album of
Mists and Clouds *(Enka-jō),* 1811.
Leaf G from an album of twelve
leaves, ink and light colors on
paper. Each leaf, H. 11-7/16 in.
(29 cm.)

36 Uragami Gyokudō Enveloping
Mists Arouse and Nourish *(Rōen
Jakuji).* Hanging scroll, ink on
paper. H. 10-5/16 in. (26.2 cm.)

37 Uragami Gyokudō Many
Houses Seen from On High *(Kōka
Sūka).* Hanging scroll, ink on
paper. H. 11-13/16 in. (30 cm.)

38 Uragami Gyokudō Streams
and Rocks in a Deep, Damp
Valley *(Yūkan Senseki),* 1816.
Hanging scroll, ink and light
colors on paper. H. 43-9/16 in.
(110.6 cm.)

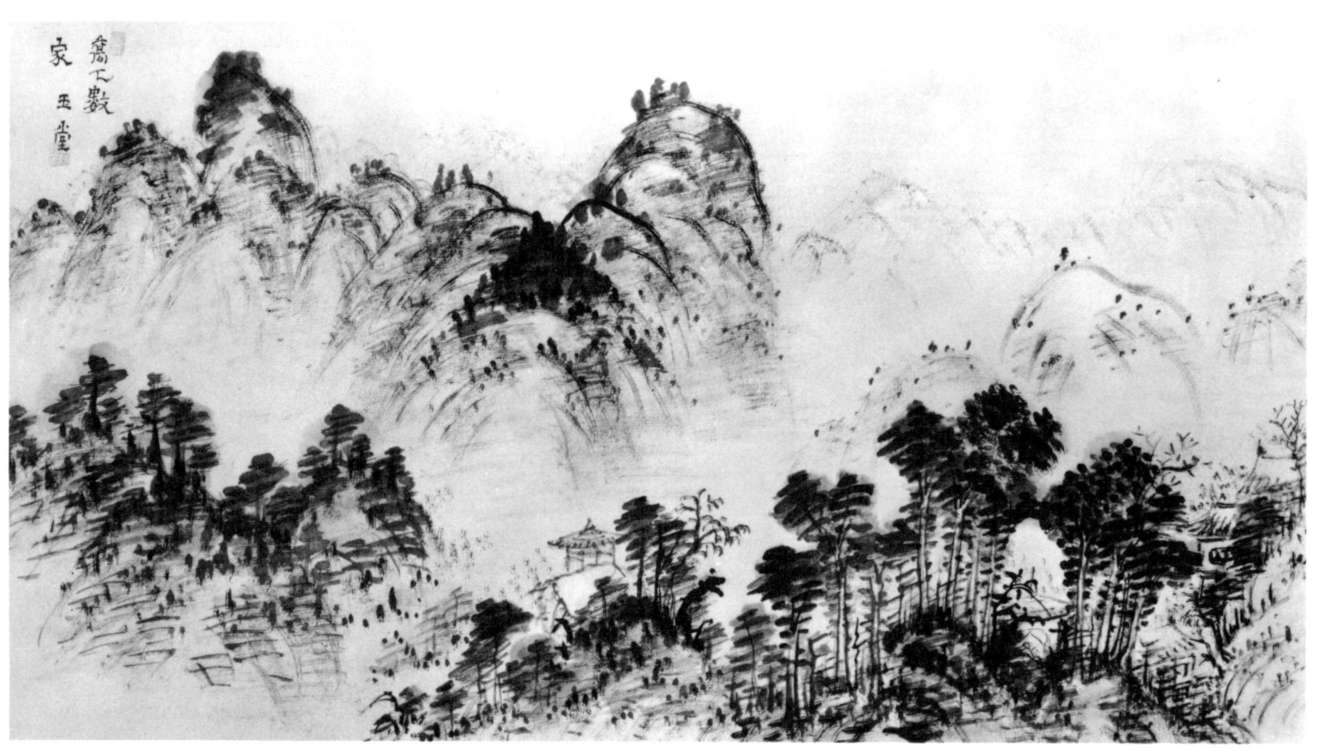

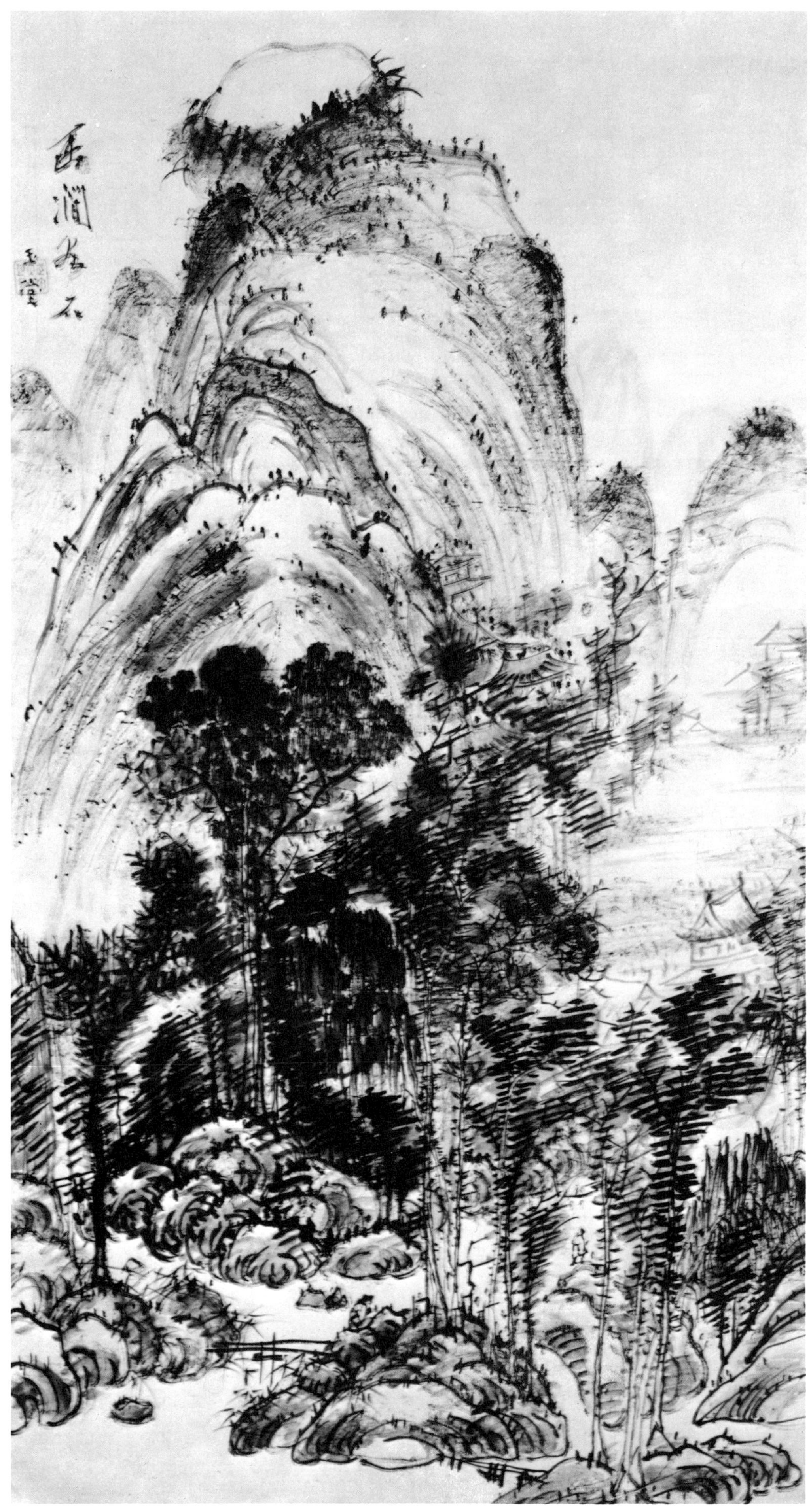

banks in the foreground; the banks are surmounted by trees, as always, and hills
rise conventionally to the upper corner. But the near-frenzied manner in which
the picture is painted makes it difficult to read as a scene at all, except by
remembered references to more restrained treatments of the same motifs.
It is not so much truth to nature as the extreme tension between the artistic
image and some image in nature left far behind that gives the painting its force.
As in some of Taiga's pictures, the title is written large and plays a role in the
design scarcely different from some of the pictorial elements, which seem
almost equally "ideographic."

The following leaf, the seventh, is titled "Water Flows, Flowers Fade" (No.
35G) but the meditative mood is in the title only. The restriction of the washes
to a few light touches in limited areas, and the total elimination of the systematic
texturing of his other style, gives the picture a quality of transparence and
weightlessness; this is a world of pure energy, seemingly devoid of substance.
The slender, wavering trunks of trees, drawn in fluid line, begin a rushing ascent
culminating in the mountain peak that twists out the top of the picture like an
explosion. Here, too, the forms are read as movement, the products of dancing
motions of the painter's brush, and this in turn as a revelation of the painter's
state of consciousness. That the picture can also be seen as a powerful expression
of the impermanence suggested in the title, of the world as composed of
transient phenomena rather than immutable forms, is beyond question; but
more than anything else, it affects us as a transfiguration of reality into a vision
charged with the intensity of some moment of exhilaration, or intoxication, in
the artist's life.

In his late years Gyokudō subsides, in most of his works, into a gentler mood.
His concerns are again with light and space, and arrangements of solid forms
with tactile surfaces. These surfaces are built up either with the familiar accumulations of horizontal or slanting touches, or with a dry-brush application of ink.
The latter technique is seen at its best in *"Rōen Jakuji"* or "Enveloping Mists
Arouse and Nourish" (No. 36), a small picture that probably was painted around
Gyokudō's seventieth year. The artist's brush, slower-moving and more con-
trolled, has sketched soft, earthy hills that seem partially dissolved in haze. The
very dryness of the style here precludes any bravura brushwork; the rubbed ink
textures on the hills look as though they might have been applied with a piece
of charcoal. A similar fragility pervades the rest of the drawing, notably in the
trees. The effect of this sensitivity of execution is an impression of light and
space surrounding the forms. Black dots scattered over the hills serve here to
stabilize, where elsewhere, apart from the masses, they set up vibrations. The
parts of the composition have been arranged carefully within the nearly square
shape, and the feeling is of clarity and calm.

A horizontal painting titled "Many Houses Seen from On High" (No. 37,
"Kōka Sūka," a somewhat enigmatic title perhaps taken from a poem) is a work
of his seventies. It is related compositionally to the "Green Pines and Russet
Valleys" (No. 31) in the way two diagonal recessions, forming a V-shape, draw
attention to a pavilion in the foreground, located at their point of intersection.
But unlike the "Green Pines," in which the elements of the picture fill the space
fairly evenly, this composition is sharply divided into four distinct units, two
each in foreground and background. The contrasts of heavy and light ink, wet
and dry brushwork, are also more pronounced. There are none of the geologi-
cally perverse forms of some of his earlier pictures; all in all, this is one of his
more conservative works.

Also conservative, but more impressive, is "Streams and Rocks in a Deep, Damp Valley" (No. 38, *"Yūkan Senseki"*), painted in 1816. It is one of Gyokudō's rare essays into the monumental landscape type, with massive forms and deep space. The movements into depth and the spatial ordering are far more complex than in his typical paintings. A diverging stream leads leftward into a dense mass of trees, from which the ridge rises steeply to the plateau-topped peak, and rightward to the screened entrance of a receding valley. The piling up of diagonal and vertical strokes in the foreground is more than usually insistent, setting up vibrations and counter-vibrations that relieve the rotundity of the rocks and hills. Again, there are no anomalies in the terrain; in these late works, Gyokudō seems to have arrived at a state of harmony between his inner and outer worlds, although at the expense of some drama and intensity.

It is one of the tragedies of Nanga that the magnificent achievements of Gyokudō were not followed up by any other artist, unless it be, in a limited way, Okada Hankō, or much later Tomioka Tessai, who in his late and finest landscapes can sometimes create a similar kind of fervor and excitement. Gyokudō's son Shunkin, as we have already noted, was one of the tamest of painters. The emphasis on individualism that was one of the strengths of the Nanga School proved to be a weakness as well, depriving it of cohesiveness and continuity. Its greatest masters remain in the end isolated figures, with little significant following.

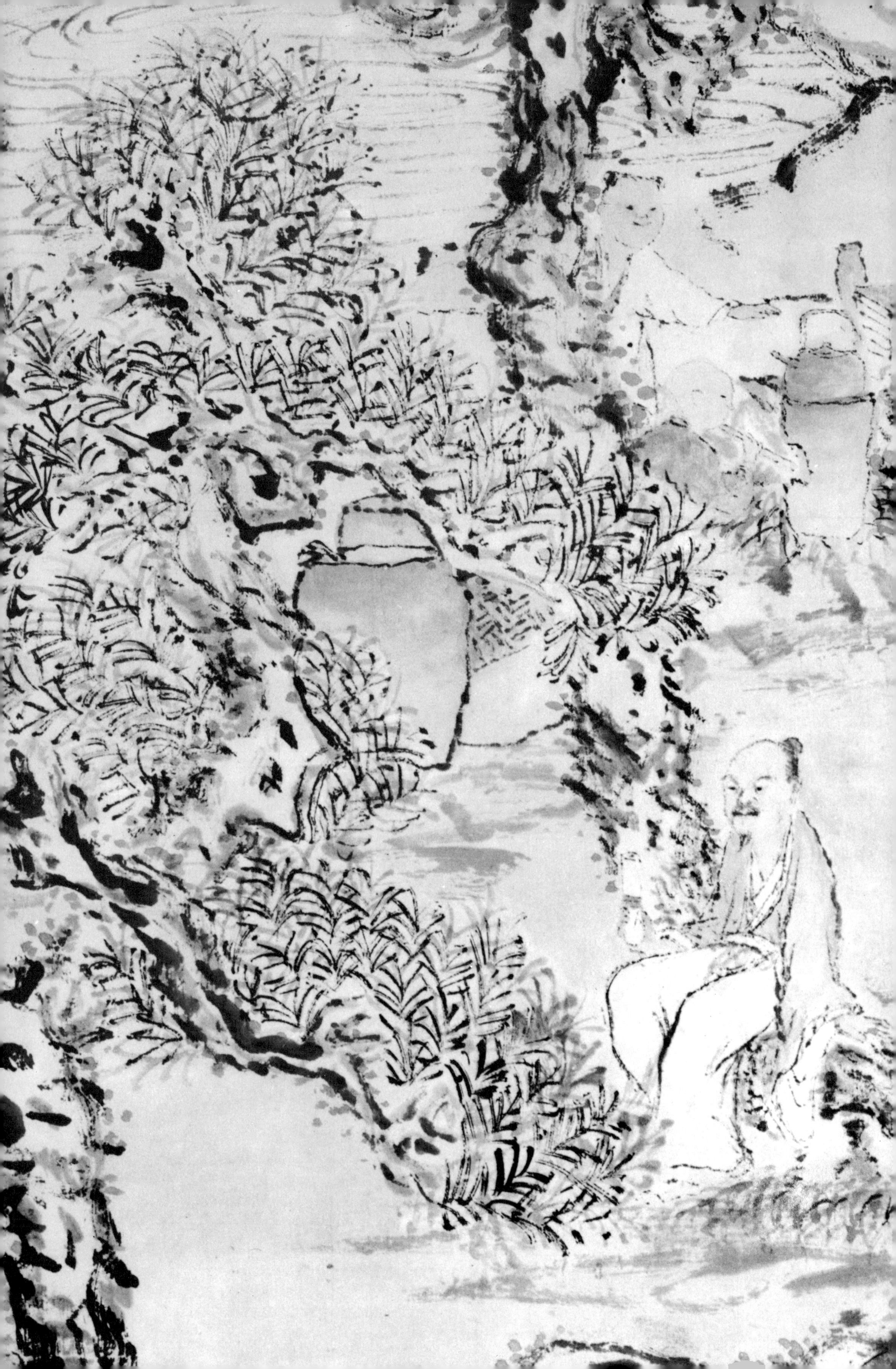

Chapter VI: Mokubei and Chikuden

By the late eighteenth and early nineteenth centuries, Nanga was solidly estab-
lished in the Kyoto-Osaka area as a thriving school of painting and as a lively
alternative for artists and patrons who found the older and more conservative
schools no longer interesting. Scholars, poets, calligraphers, and painters came
from many parts of Japan to participate in this new intellectual and artistic
scene. Their interests and talents varied widely, but they shared an admiration
for Chinese literature, art, and learning, and tended to be men who had somehow withdrawn from, or been ejected from, the highly stratified and static
structure of the feudal society. Some of them, such as Gyokudō, Chikuden, and
Rai Sanyō, began as clan officials but renounced their clan and family ties to
lead more independent lives than those had allowed. They lived by their learning and their art; their patrons were *sake* makers, merchants, and other rich
men of the Kyoto-Osaka area and the region to the west, located in such
places as Itami, Fushimi, and Tango. These men entertained the scholar-artists in
their homes and bought their works, through a conventionalized system of
exchange in which the painting was ostensibly given as a gift but the recipient
was expected to reciprocate with a gift of a more negotiable kind.

Living in Osaka was the scholar-merchant Kimura Kenkadō (1736-1802) who
had a store that provided the literati with such necessities as brushes and ink.
Nearly all the scholars and painters who came to Osaka visited him. He was a
collector of books and objects of art, and a minor painter himself, who had
studied under Taiga in his youth. In the following generation, the leader of
Kyoto's scholarly-literary circle was Rai Sanyō (1780-1832), a Confucianist who
had fled from his official post with the Hiroshima clan and opened a private
school in Kyoto. He too was a minor painter, but was better known as a poet
and calligrapher. Among his friends were educated men of many sorts—
Buddhists priests, doctors, writers, artists, including Gyokudō's son Shunkin
and two more important artists, Aoki Mokubei and Tanomura Chikuden.

Aoki Mokubei (1767-1833) was the son of a restaurateur and brothel keeper
in the Nawate district of Kyoto. As a young man he studied the connoisseurship
of antiquities under Kō Fuyō, a painter, seal-carver, and connoisseur who had
been a close friend of Taiga. A turning point in Mokubei's life evidently came
when, around 1796, he saw and read at the home of Kenkadō a Chinese
book on ceramics called the *T'ao-shuo* (Japanese, *Tōsetsu*) and decided to
become a potter. He made wares for use in *sencha,* a kind of tea ceremony,

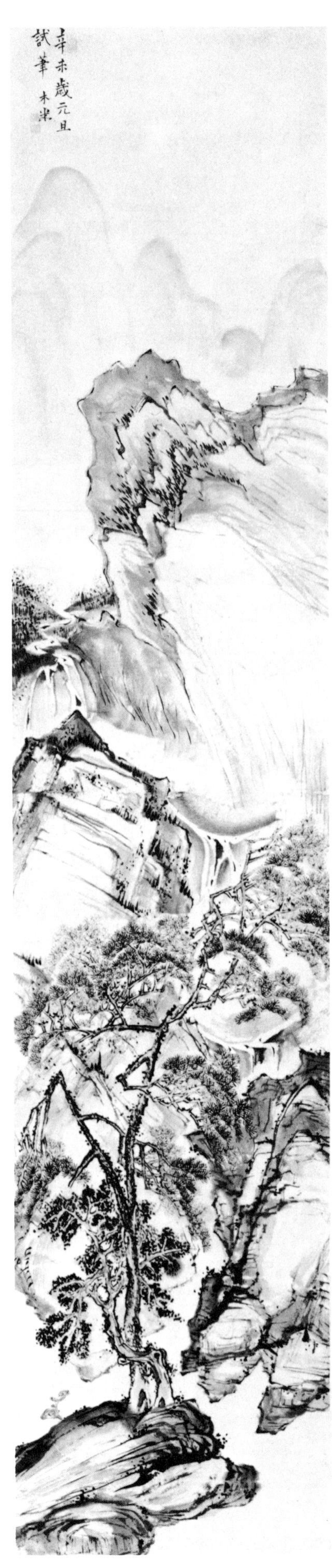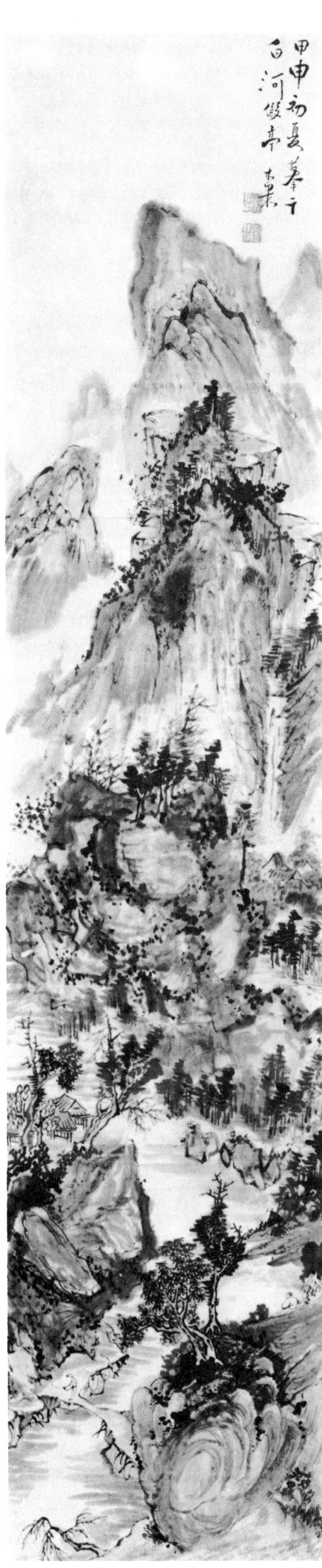

39 Aoki Mokubei Mount P'eng-lai *Hōrai-zan)*, 1811. Hanging scroll, ink and colors on paper. H. 53-1/16 in. (134.8 cm.)

40 Aoki Mokubei Autumn Landscape, 1824. Hanging scroll, ink and light colors on paper. H. 53³/₈ in. (135.6 cm.)

favored by the Sinophile scholars, which was less formal than the *cha-no-yu.*
He was best known in his time as a ceramist, but his fame today rests primarily
on his paintings, most of which he did in his late years and purely as an amateur,
giving them to friends. Chikuden tells us that Mokubei's painting style was
based on the painted designs used to decorate pottery, and that this is why he
works in bold, black strokes, using little wash, "with a strange flavor and
unusual ideas." This judgement has been much repeated; but, with all respect
to Chikuden, it sounds like one of those forced efforts to relate the different
creative activities of a single man. In fact, very few of Mokubei's paintings reveal
anything that could possibly derive from ceramic decoration, and most of
them use a great deal of wash, very effectively. He seems to have been self-
taught, and painted little; his works are relatively scarce today.

The landscape titled "Mount P'eng-lai" ("Hōrai-zan," No. 39) is considered
to be an early work, although Mokubei was forty-four when he painted it in
1811. For it he uses the tall, narrow shape that he was to favor throughout his
life, and fills it with active forms that seem to strain the boundaries of the
picture. A bank in the foreground thrusts abruptly and diagonally inward from
the lower left corner; two roughly rectangular masses of rock, above at the
right and further up at the left, take up this movement, slanting less sharply in
the same direction; the peak at the top counters this directional emphasis by
pushing powerfully to the left. Relieving the starkness of the plan are the tall
pine tree that occupies the middle area and a series of cascades dropping
between the rocks. The drawing is in heavy ink-line, the colors fairly strong.

The changes that take place in Mokubei's style as he moves into his mature
period are apparent if we compare this work of 1811 with his "Autumn Landscape" of 1824 (No. 40). The subject is similar, a mountain gorge with steep cliffs,
but the scene is now enlivened, as it is in virtually all his later pictures, with
buildings and figures. These follow standard Nanga practice in being for the
most part conventional: Buddhist temples, pagodas, bridges with scholars
crossing or pausing on them, fishermen in boats, woodcutters. The shape of the
1824 picture is the same as that of the earlier one, tall and narrow, and it is still
crowded with leaning masses. The composition is more spacious—a recession
along a river from foreground to middle ground precedes the precipitous ascent
—and somewhat more stable, although Mokubei still avoids, except for the
waterfall, any prominent vertical or horizontal elements that might offset the
dynamism of the slanting forms. The principal difference is in the rendering
of the rocks and peaks, which is in the new manner he was to favor from this
time on. Heavy shading gives bulk and dramatic light-dark contrasts. The coloring, blending a red ocher and indigo (*taisha* and *ai*) with the ink, is subtler, so
much so that in some passages the effect is only of slightly warmer or cooler ink.
Mokubei now avoids continuous, firm contour drawing, preferring dry and
broken strokes in deep black ink (the Chinese *chiao-mo,* Japanese *shōboku*),
so that his forms seem soft-edged and crumbly. This softer manner, in which
trees and rocks are blurred so as to merge with each other and with the surrounding space, has the effect of a slightly atmospheric rendering. The resulting
erosion of clarity may seem excessive in the middle ground, making it look
muddled, but this passage provides a relief from the strong convexities above
and below. Mokubei's strength was not in composition; his pictures sometimes
look as though they had been pieced together of lumpy parts. This is one of
his better organized works, and the brilliance of the brushwork and the ink and
colors compensate for whatever structural weaknesses there are.

Mokubei's most famous composition, one that he himself was so pleased with
that he repeated it several times, is the "Morning Sun at Uji" (No. 41). The
version we include was painted in 1824, only about four months after the
"Autumn Landscape." It presents a bird's-eye view of the Uji River, which flows
through this famous tea growing region near Kyoto. The Byōdōin, the temple
best known for its great Phoenix Hall built in 1053, is seen through pine trees in
the lower right corner. The roofs of the town appear on the further shore.
Even this quiet scene Mokubei manages to dramatize, turning the low hills that
surround Uji into lunging peaks, which slant inward from each side. They draw
the eye to the point at which the river enters, to curve steeply downward to
the left, marked by a broad stroke of blue wash. Mokubei's characteristic
blending of reddish-brown and blue colors with grey washes of ink is especially
beautiful here, giving a generalized effect of cool sunlight and shade. The composition is a departure from Mokubei's favorite type; the horizontal shape
allows him to surround the features of his terrain with more space, and so to
create a more expansive feeling in the landscape.

The temptation for painters whose natural tendency was toward compositional fragmentation—and Mokubei was certainly one—was to seize upon some
simple unifying device and exploit it for all it was worth. It was probably the
viewing of some Chinese landscape painting in which the entire composition
was threaded on a single, winding movement into distance along a rising ridge,
an extreme form of the "dragon-vein" device of later Chinese painting which
was especially common in the seventeenth century, that offered Mokubei such a
temptation. Whatever the source, Mokubei succumbed to the idea, as can be
seen in his "New Verdure Wet with Rain" of 1826 (No. 42). The movement
of the picture begins beyond a stretch of open water, on a river bank where
houses are seen among trees. From this the rounded ridge curves upward and
back, inexorably and a little monotonously, to a summit crowned by a pagoda.
A marked disparity in ground level between the areas at the two sides of the
ridge—higher and flat at left, dropping steeply to an undefined floor at right—
increases the unsettling effect. The picture must have been particularly striking
in its time, as no such composition had been known earlier in Japan.

Part of Mokubei's amateurism as a painter, and part of his interest, lie in his
refusal to settle into a really consistent style and to continue its practice until a
point of comfortable mastery had been reached. He preferred to experiment
and take chances; and we can agree that an artist with this attitude, unless he is
purely capricious, deserves to be forgiven occasional falterings and failures—
provided that we do not treat them as if they were successes. Some of Mokubei's
paintings that survive, and no doubt a great many more that he threw away,
testify to unsuccessful experiments with unorthodox compositions and techniques. But others are brilliantly successful, and indeed bring to Nanga, as
Chikuden says, "a strange flavor and unusual ideas." As noted above, however,
some of these ideas may not have been entirely new; like others of his generation he learned a great deal from recently imported Chinese paintings. His
"*Tempō Kyūjo*" (No. 43, "Heaven Protects the Nine Similitudes," meaning all
creation, a reference to one of the poems in the ancient Chinese *Book of Odes*),
painted in 1830, suggests that he may have seen some painting, perhaps a copy
or forgery, in the style of the fourteenth century Chinese master Fang Ts'ung-i.
The trees in the foreground are in the distinctive style associated with Fang,
as are the lunging mountain masses, the extensive concealing mists, and the
consciously achieved instability of the whole. For most of the picture he dis-

41 Aoki Mokubei Morning Sun
at Uji, 1824. Hanging scroll, ink
and light colors on paper.
H. 19^{1}/$_{8}$ in. (48.5 cm.)

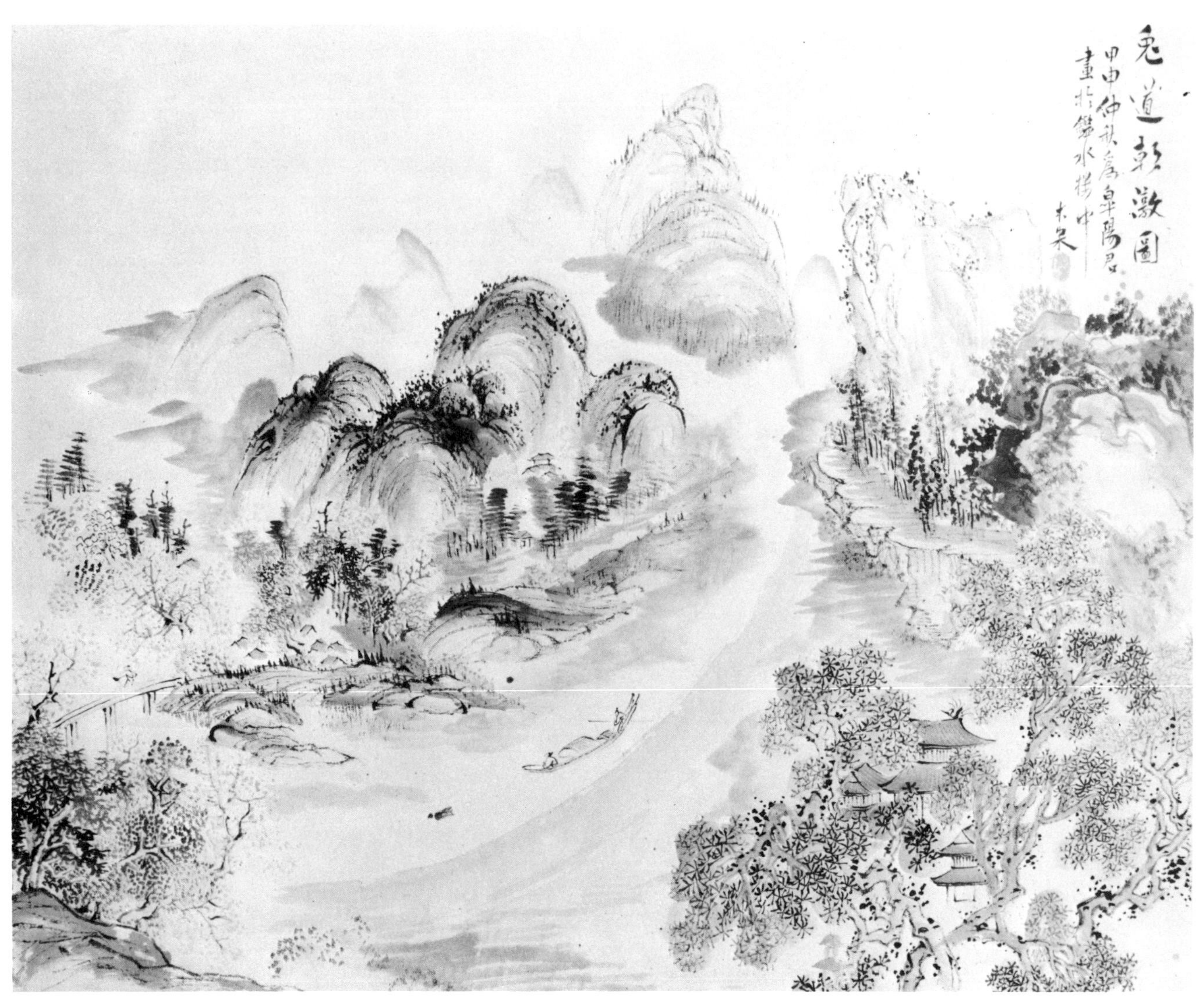

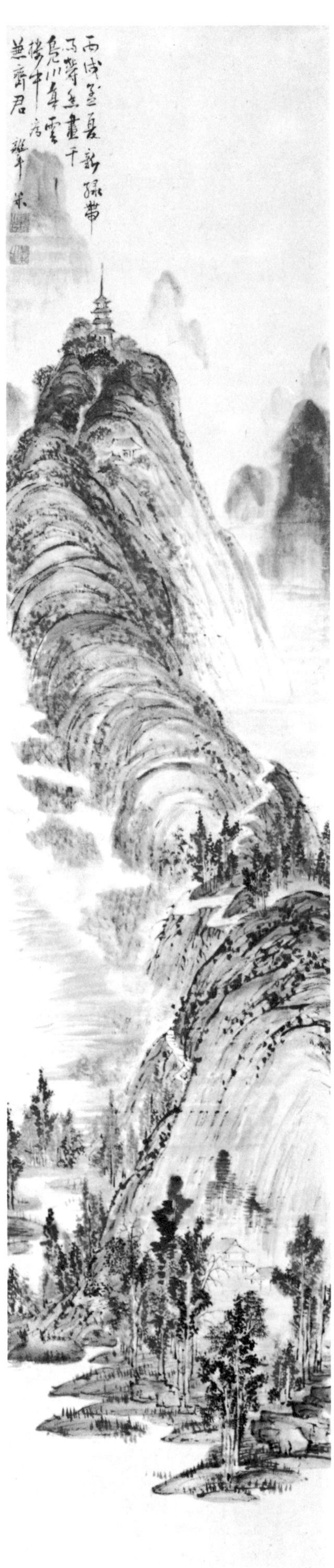

42 Aoki Mokubei New Verdure Wet with Rain, 1826. Hanging scroll, ink and light colors on paper. H. 52½ in. (133.4 cm.)

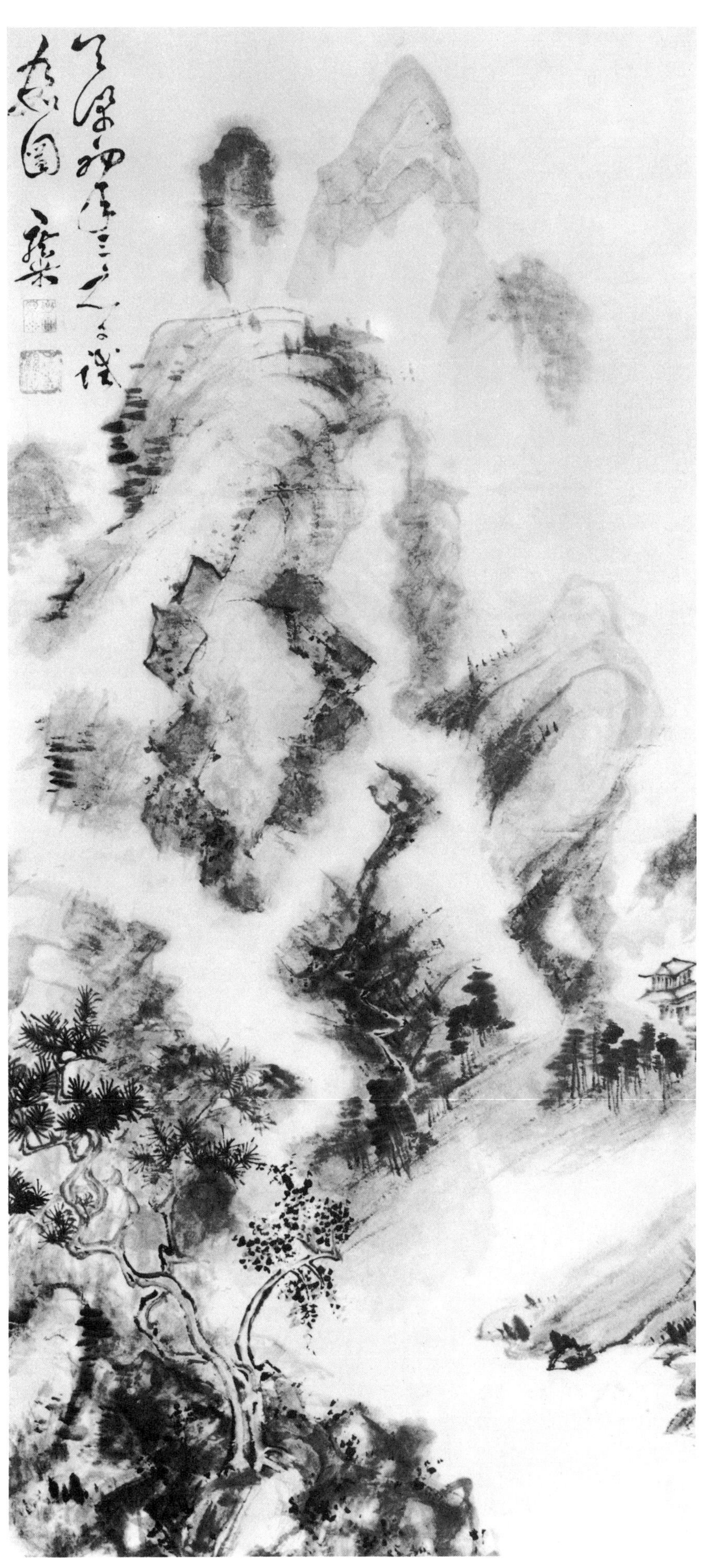

43 Aoki Mokubei Heaven Protects the Nine Similitudes *(Tempō Kyūjo),* 1830. Hanging scroll, ink and light colors on paper. H. 41³/₈ in. (105 cm.)

penses with outlines almost entirely, working only in rough patches of wash and dark accents, with a few dry, ragged strokes to mark the edges of his boulders and cliffs. The slanting of the water surface is a device also used by Taiga; but here the diagonal movement is carried through the whole composition, as if all nature were in a state of turbulence or taking part in some wild dance.

At the other extreme is a small picture titled "Clouds Around the Base of a Mountain" ("*Unshutsu Sanyō*," No. 44), one of Mokubei's gentler works and one of the loveliest. It is undated, but surely belongs to his late period. For whatever reason—perhaps as a guide to the mounter—he has drawn a rectangular frame for the picture with ruled lines and painted within this frame. The use of suffusing ink washes with touches of *taisha* is extremely sensitive here, as is the contour drawing in *shōboku*, literally "roasted ink," a technique in which dry, black ink is used for the final drawing, tracing over earlier, paler strokes. This is an important feature of Mokubei's style, giving a special crispness to his drawing and attractive tonal contrast to his pictures. The combination of these fluid washes and crisp lines imparts a feeling of flow to the earth forms, bringing them into harmony with the serpentine band of mist that twists from lower left into upper right, countering the main movement of the land masses. This main movement is marked and clarified by a path that enters in the lower right corner, crosses a bridge, and climbs the peak to a small temple near the top.

Mokubei's more famous friend Tanomura Chikuden (1777-1835) shares with him some features of style, such as the use of color with ink washes and the dry-wet contrasts in brushwork. But the scenery he paints, and the manner in which he paints it, are generally at an opposite pole from Mokubei's landscapes. Where Mokubei is often wild, Chikuden seldom relaxes his tight control over his brush; where Mokubei was inclined to experiment, Chikuden usually stays safely within his technical limits.

What we know of his life would not indicate any such cautiousness. It follows the typical pattern of the intellectual dropout from the feudal system. Chikuden's family served as clan physicians to the Oka clan of Bungo, near modern Oita in northern Kyūshū. Chikuden received the standard Confucian training, and around 1810 became the head of his family, and of the clan school. In 1811, a farmer's insurrection in the area spurred him to submit a memorial proposing reforms in the clan administration. His suggestions were not adopted. The insurrection was put down, but broke out again the following year, and again Chikuden submitted his memorial. Again it was rejected. Chikuden thereupon turned over the leadership of the family to his son and resigned his position. For the rest of his life he earned his livelihood as a scholar, poet, and painter. He had studied painting with a local artist in his home village, and also, by correspondence, with Tani Bunchō, whom he met on a trip to Edo in 1801. After resigning from his post he went to Osaka and Kyoto, where he learned more about the styles and techniques of Nanga from artists such as Okada Beisanjin, a painter whom we shall consider in the next chapter. In Kyoto he became a good friend and protégé of Rai Sanyō. The remainder of his life he divided between the Kyoto-Osaka region and his home in Kyūshū, traveling back and forth frequently. His health was poor, a fact sometimes cited by Japanese writers to account for a certain frailty and unassertiveness in many of his paintings. The most scholarly Nanga artist of his generation, he wrote numerous books on poetry and painting; his *Chikuden Shiyū Garoku (Record of the Painting of Master Chikuden and His Friends)* gives valuable information on the period.

In the inscription on his "Autumn Landscape" of 1827 (No. 45) Chikuden

44 Aoki Mokubei Clouds around
the Base of a Mountain
(Unshutsu Sanyō). Hanging scroll,
ink and light colors on paper.
H. 12-1/16 in. (30.6 cm.)

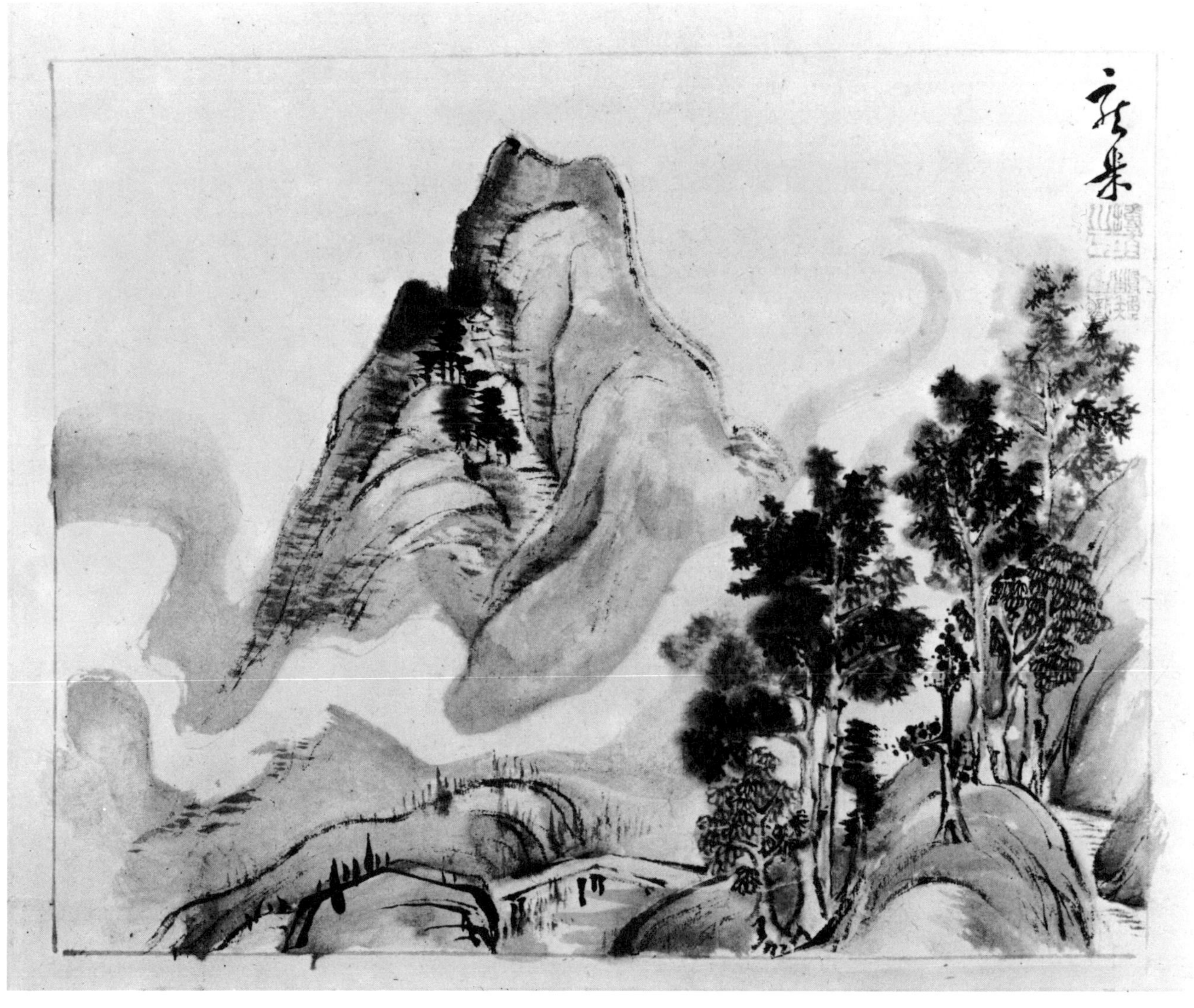

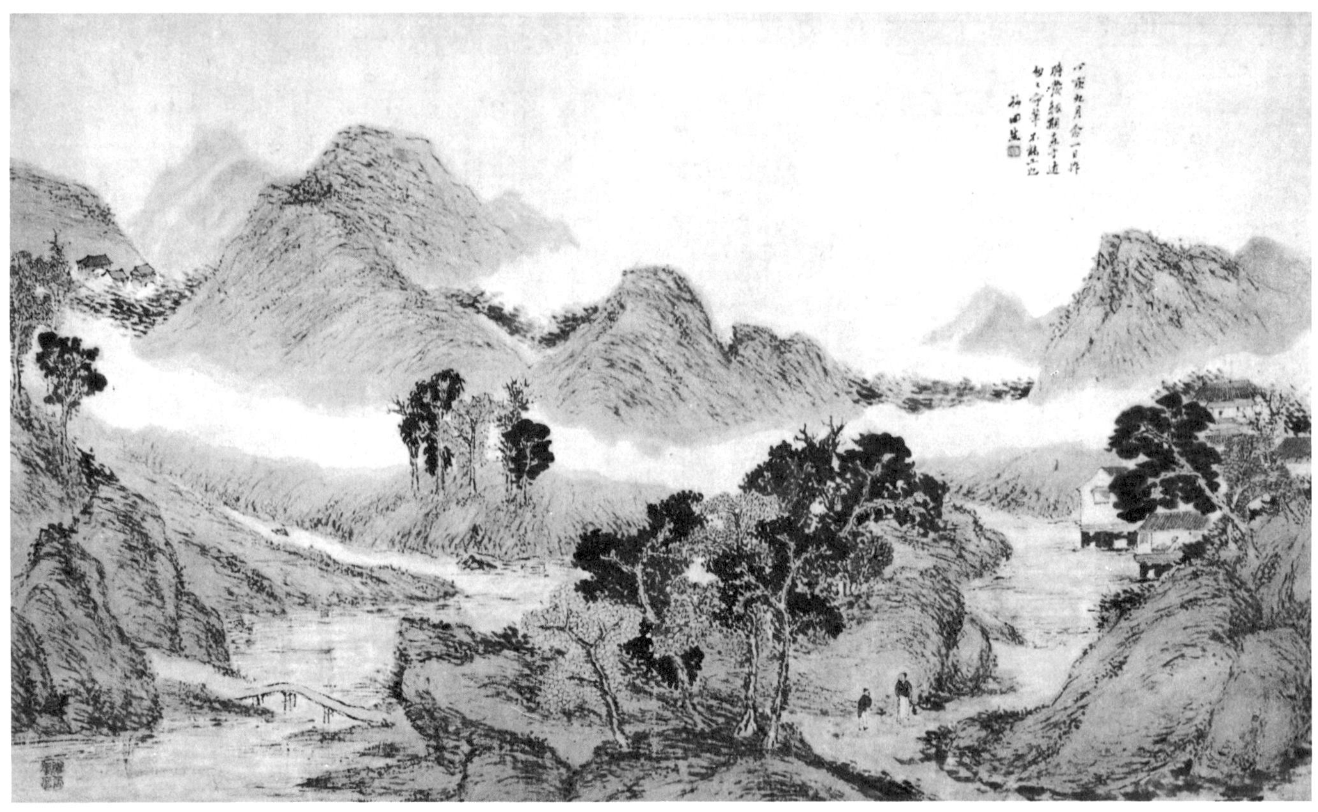

45 **Tanomura Chikuden** Autumn
Landscape, 1827. Hanging scroll,
ink and light colors on paper.
H. 20⁷/₈ in. (53 cm.)

writes apologetically that the man to whom it is dedicated asked him for a painting when he was unable to give enough time to it, so that he "couldn't do it skillfully." The painting is in fact, however, a carefully planned, tightly structured composition. A man and his servant stand at the juncture of two paths, about to turn off to visit a friend who is seen through the window of a house at the right. The hills enclose a large space in the center, its corners marked with four groups of trees. His treatment of the crests and slopes of the hills shows a mastery of the Chinese technique of combining texture strokes *(ts'un)* and dots *(tien)* to give them a convincing tactile reality that is beyond anything possible in earlier Nanga; again we have unmistable evidence of a new and deeper understanding of Chinese styles. The brushwork is restrained, concerned with defining form and building textures rather than with calligraphic brilliance.

In the winter of 1829 Chikuden painted what is perhaps the most beautiful of his larger compositions, *"Inagawa Shūyū"* or "Boat Trip on the Inagawa" (No. 46). This river flows near the town of Itami, where Chikuden, Rai Sanyō, and others had been staying with a patron, a rich sake maker named Sakagami Tōin. When Chikuden was ready to leave by boat, some of them came to the river to see him off. It may be the artist himself who appears in a small boat at the bottom of the picture, with a friend in an adjoining boat; they are fishing and drinking from wine pots beside them. The river, its shores densely lined with bushes and trees, winds upward into distance, fading back into the twilight. As in some compositions of Taiga and Buson, soft masses of leafage fill much of the picture area, with darkly drawn trees set at intervals within these. The extraordinarily subtle play of many hues and values of blue and green, interspersed with some touches of red, is new to Nanga; its similarity to the coloring used by some Chinese artists of the Yangchow School in the later eighteenth and early nineteenth centuries, particularly Ch'ien Tu (1763-1844), suggests that Chikuden may have seen some work of theirs; but he could also have developed this new manner of coloring independently, inspired only by the Japanese love for decorative color and the infinite variegation to be seen in nature. In place of the strong color contrasts generally preferred in other schools of Japanese painting, however, he juxtaposes hues closely related in value, or slight variants of a single color, in keeping with the mild and subtle character of his work.

A river scene of a very different kind, sparse and thin where *"Inagawa Shūyū"* is rich in textures; done in ink on silk where the other is in colors on paper, is the undated "Returning by Boat on a Cold River" (No. 47). The couplet written on it by the artist reads:

"A cold river; the sky darkens to dusk.

With shortened oar, he rows home into the wind."

The composition is simple but original. Hills slope down to the shore, extending finger-like spits into the river, so that land and water seem to interpenetrate. This bland and uncomplicated plan is broken only by three repeated motifs: rows of bare trees on the two nearest spits, rocks in the shallows, and dark patches of vegetation widely spaced on the slopes. The tops of the trees all lean rightward, blown by the wind. Through this device and also by slanting the ground and water plane so that the boat seems to move uphill, Chikuden suggests the effort with which the boatman is poling into the wind toward shore, where his destination, a group of houses, may be seen.

Chikuden's love of Chinese learning comes out in the subjects of some of his paintings, such as "Feeding Cranes Beneath Pine Trees," a work of 1830 (No. 48). The crane represents longevity or immortality in China, since it was believed

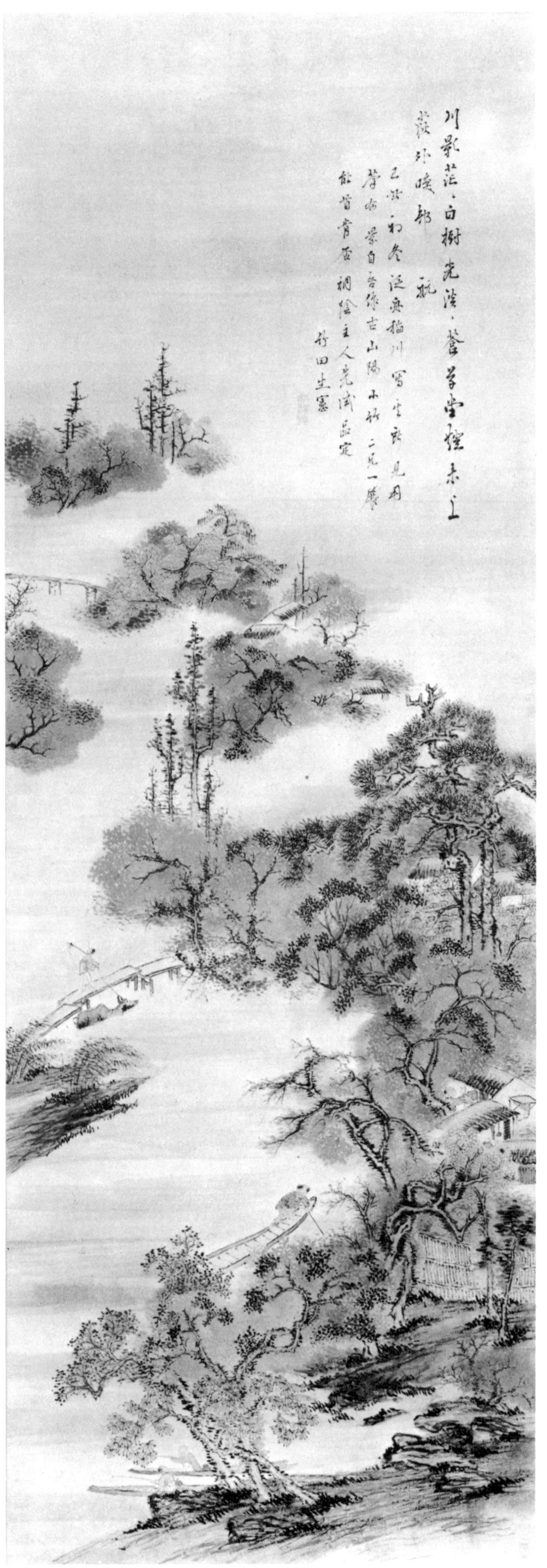

46 Tanomura Chikuden A Boat Trip on the Inagawa, 1829. Hanging scroll, ink and light colors on paper. H. 52³/₈ in. (133 cm.)

47 Tanomura Chikuden Returning by Boat on a Cold River. Hanging scroll, ink on silk. H. 48-9/16 in. (123.4 cm.)

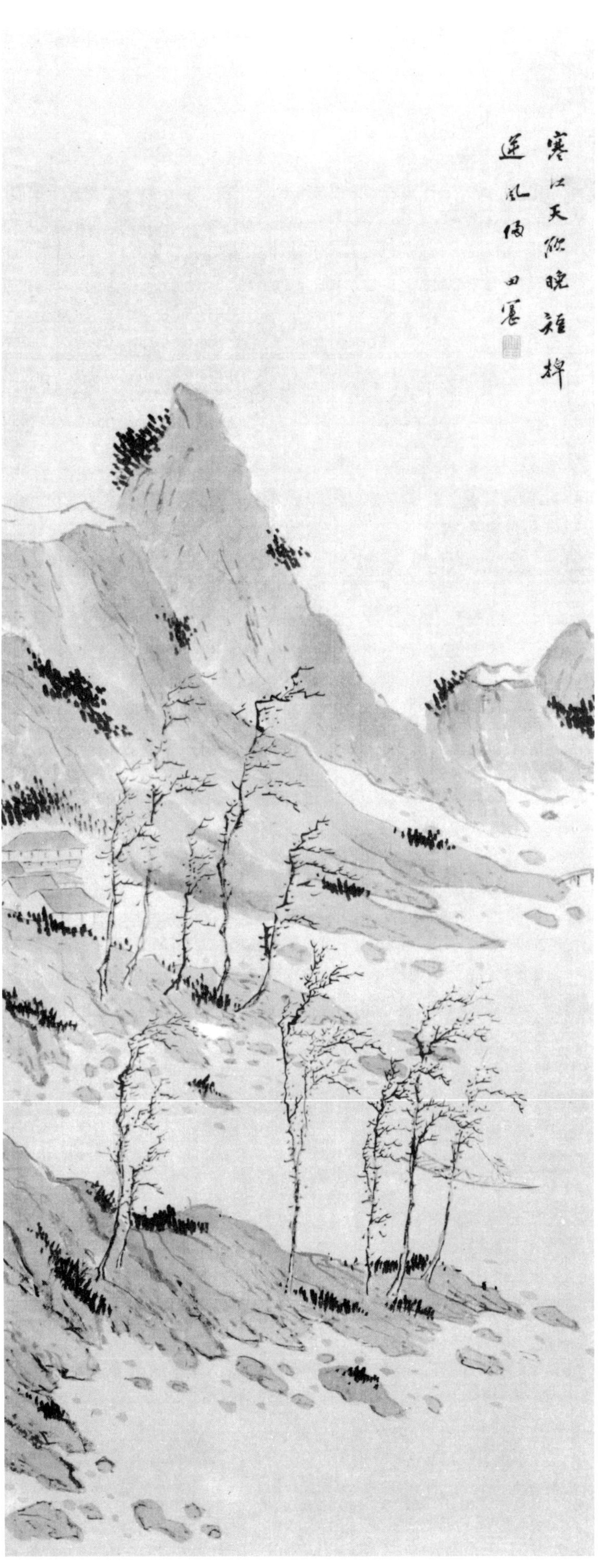

to live more than a thousand years, and since Taoist immortals were said to fly to
P'eng-lai, the Isle of Immortals, on its back. The pine tree also symbolizes
longevity, because of its own slow-changing nature and tenacious hold on life.
The presentation of a painting of these subjects thus carried the meaning of
wishing long life to the receiver. The birds in Chikuden's painting are being fed
by a servant boy, while the master watches, seated on a horizontal pine trunk.
The spacing of three pine trees from foreground to middle ground defines the
space within which this action takes place. The peak, composed of oddly
bulging forms, reveals Chikuden to have been as fascinated as his friend
Mokubei with the new means of achieving rotundity in landscape masses.

Also like Mokubei, he chose the tall and narrow shape for most of his hanging
scrolls. But instead of building his picture principally out of massive forms, as
Mokubei does, Chikuden typically organizes his composition around the
repeated patterns of such motifs as bare trees, bushes, or flowering plum trees,
or repeated areas of texture such as foliage or masses of pine needles. These are
frequently set along an evenly receding or rising ground plane, over which one
moves backward from one side of the picture to the other by a series of diagonal
movements. One painting that follows this formula generally but is unusual in
the variety of the vegetation—leafy trees of different kinds, bamboo, banana
palms—is *"Kōban-zu"* (No. 49). The title is loosely translatable as "Living in
Seclusion," since the word *kōban* (Chinese *k'ao-p'an*), literally "to build a hut,"
occurs first in the *Book of Odes* with that meaning, which it retains in Chinese
literature. The group of gentlemen in Chikuden's painting who are enjoying
the pleasures of the secluded life are placed in the middle ground on the bank
of a stream, and are seen beyond a passage of trees and rocks, suggesting by this
removal from the viewer their remoteness from human society, apart from their
own. They sit in relaxed postures, one dangling his foot in the water, others
engaged in conversation with bundles of books and scrolls beside them. A
servant behind a tree prepares wine for them to drink. On the opposite shore
is a gaming board, and further back a small kiosk with seats, from which they can
admire the scenery. All these are references to ideal leisurely pastimes. The
very lushness of the landscape, with its profusion of plants among soft, furry
rocks, has the same implication of an easy and pleasurable existence.

From all these we can define the special qualities of Chikuden's style: poetic
and delicate rather than bold; building up forms fastidiously with patient
accumulations of soft strokes and fine, dry line; tending to pale and cool colors.
It is a style suited to the depiction of mild, undramatic themes, and to the expression of subtle feelings by embodying them in pictures of moments and
situations with which those feelings are associated.

The finest expression of such themes in Chikuden's works is not in his large
hanging scroll paintings, but in two albums dating from his late years. One is the
Senso Shogi, or "Scenes Viewed from a Boat Window," a pictorial record of a
trip that he made in 1829, with his son Josen and his disciple Takahashi Sōhei,
through the Inland Sea. The other, painted in 1831-32, is the justly famous
Mata-mata Ichiraku-jō, or "Yet Again One More Pleasure" album (No. 50). It
contains thirteen paintings: seven landscapes, three figure pictures, and three of
flowers. The paintings all bear inscriptions by the artist, some written in his
spidery, precise script, others in broader and more cursive manners. They set
forth in words the themes of the paintings, which deal with especially satisfying
moments in a life that is basically in repose, the pleasures of a refined sensibility:
playing the flute in a boat by moonlight, being visited by a friend in one's

48 Tanomura Chikuden Feeding
Cranes Beneath Pine Trees, 1830.
Hanging scroll, ink and light
colors on paper. H. 49½ in.
(125.8 cm.)

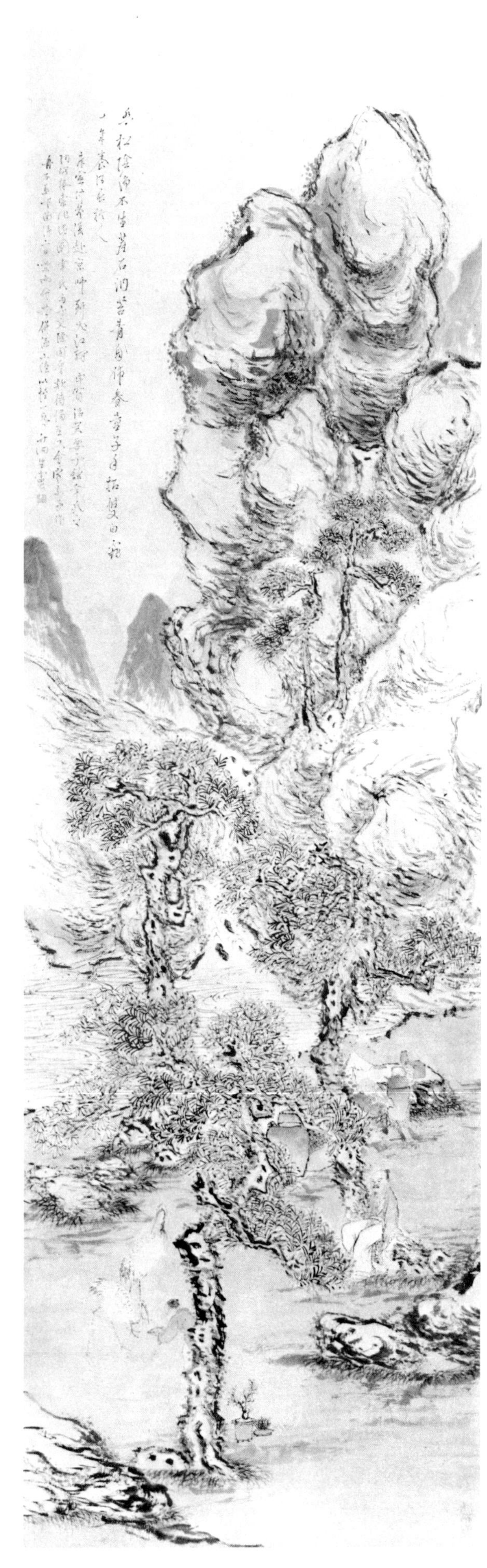

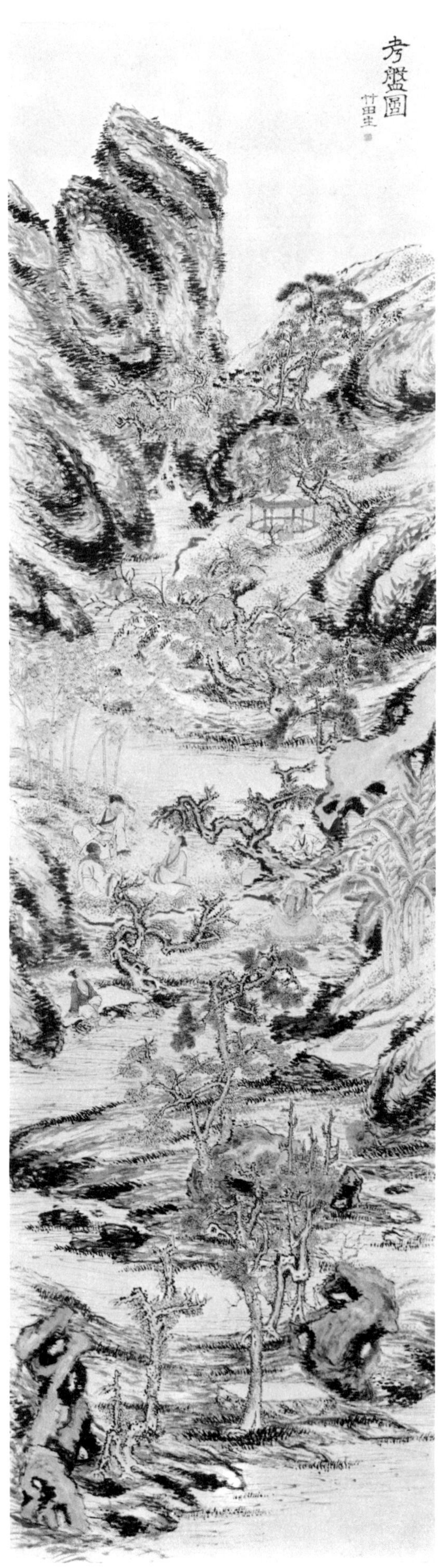

49 Tanomura Chikuden Living in Seclusion *(Kōban-zu)*, 1832. Hanging scroll, ink and light colors on paper. H. 69³/₈ in. (176.1 cm.)

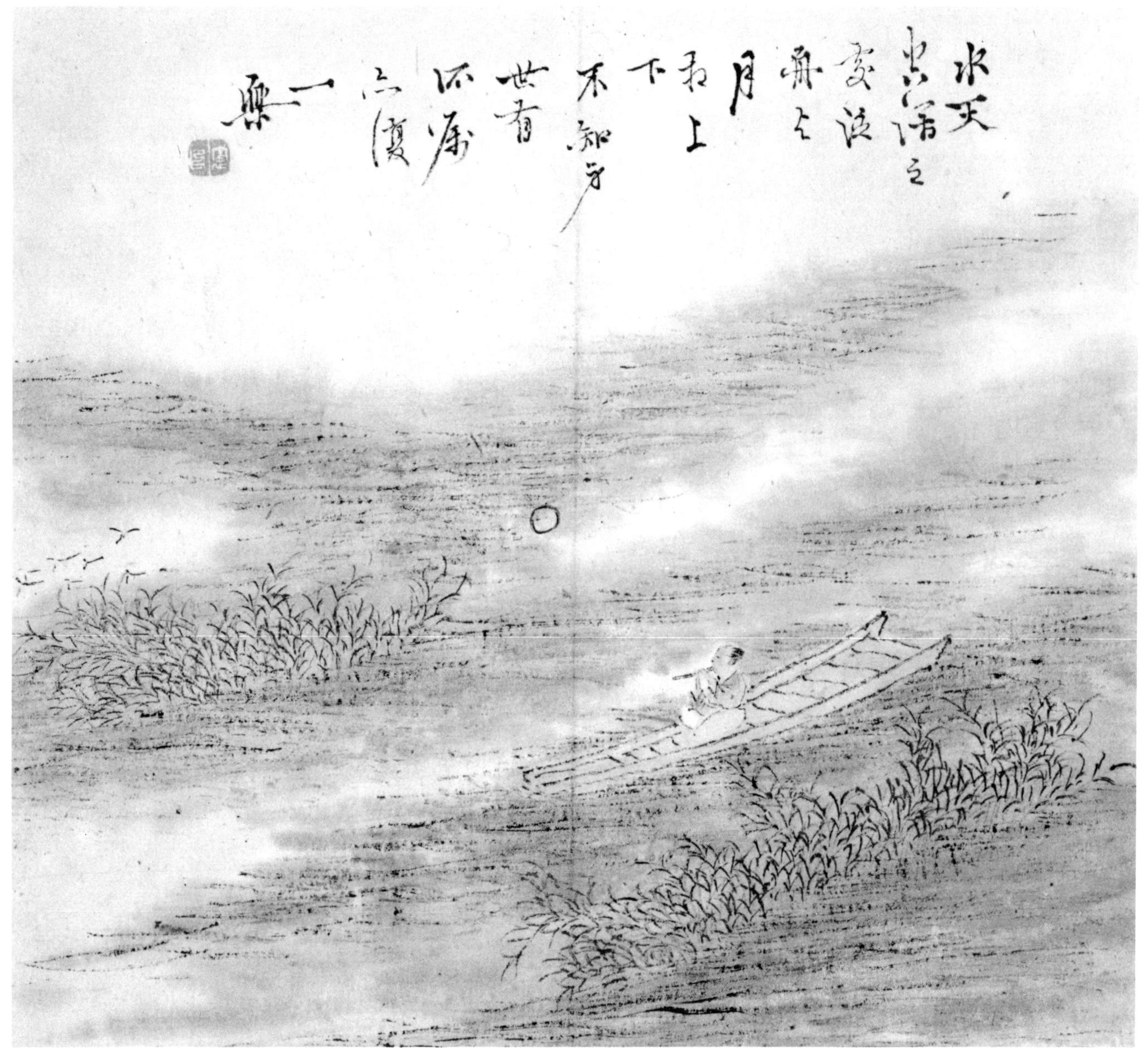

103

mountain retreat, discussing and judging paintings and calligraphy, staying indoors and drinking warm wine with companions on a stormy night. Each inscription ends: "This is yet again one more pleasure."

The entertaining story of the circumstances under which the album took its present form tells us something about the relationship of Nanga artist and patron. The album, originally of ten leaves only, was intended for an Osaka doctor and collector, Matsushita Suiko. After painting these leaves in 1831, Chikuden asked Rai Sanyō to add a colophon to the album. What happened next is related by Sanyō himself in a postscript to the laudatory lines he wrote:

"Kun-i (Chikuden) brought me this album, asking for a colophon. I put it in my desk, taking it out from time to time to leaf through, and came to realize how lovable it is. In the end I have decided to take it by force and make it mine. This is yet again one more pleasure!"

Chikuden, caught by this extension of his own idea but also moved by the friendship and gratitude he felt toward Sanyō, acquiesced and gave the album to him. In the following year he added three more paintings, the flower pictures, and wrote another long inscription on six more leaves, which now precede the paintings, giving his own account of the whole affair. Matsushita Suiko was eventually presented with a different album.

The seven landscapes are in every way a delight. The conceptions are fresh, the compositions original and strong; the colors have the cool harmony that is part of Chikuden's special flavor; the execution gives to each picture a richness and consistency of surface that few Nanga painters could achieve. Working on unsized or lightly sized paper, Chikuden can exploit the contrasts of wet (suffused) and dry brushwork for effects of rough-textured or slightly blurred forms. Dry strokes are overlaid on washes or traced over paler drawing in a technique that Chikuden learned from Chinese styles but had made his own. His distinctive line drawing must be seen close up and in the originals to be appreciated. He draws with the very tip of the brush, which is sufficiently loaded with ink to leave a small blot wherever it pauses. In the lyrical picture of a lonely figure in a boat playing a flute to a few wild geese and the reflection of the moon (50B), the slowness and slight hesitancy implied in this drawing adds another element of calm to an already placid scene.

The three figure paintings are charming, ingenuous, perhaps a touch too open in their appeal. The flowers were done with special care, since they were for Rai Sanyō. Among them the peony, painted large and in full bloom, its petals done in pure pink color without outlines, is (for some very Japanese reason that may elude foreigners) the most often reproduced of all Chikuden's works.

Chikuden's principal disciple Takahashi Sōhei (1802-1833) was born into a merchant family in Kizuki, Bungo (modern Oita Prefecture) in Kyushu. He learned painting while quite young, and at the age of nineteen was discovered by Chikuden, who took him as a student. Chikuden looked upon the young man as his future successor, but unhappily Sōhei died early, before his master, leaving Chikuden to lament that he had never fully developed his talent. Sōhei imitates Chikuden closely in both landscapes and flower paintings, without notable originality in either. The pair of paintings representing "Peonies and Hydrangeas" and "Birds in a Flowering Tree" (No. 51a, b) were done in 1832, the year before his death. The branches are bent into decorative curves, the groups of leaves flattened into two-dimensional patterns. Such paintings may have been popular with the merchants for whom the Nanga masters painted much of the time, but do not add significantly to the glory of the school.

51a, b Takahashi Sōhei a. Peonies and Hydrangeas; b. Birds in a Flowering Tree, 1832. Pair of hanging scrolls, colors on silk. Each, H. 48⅛ in. (122.1 cm.)

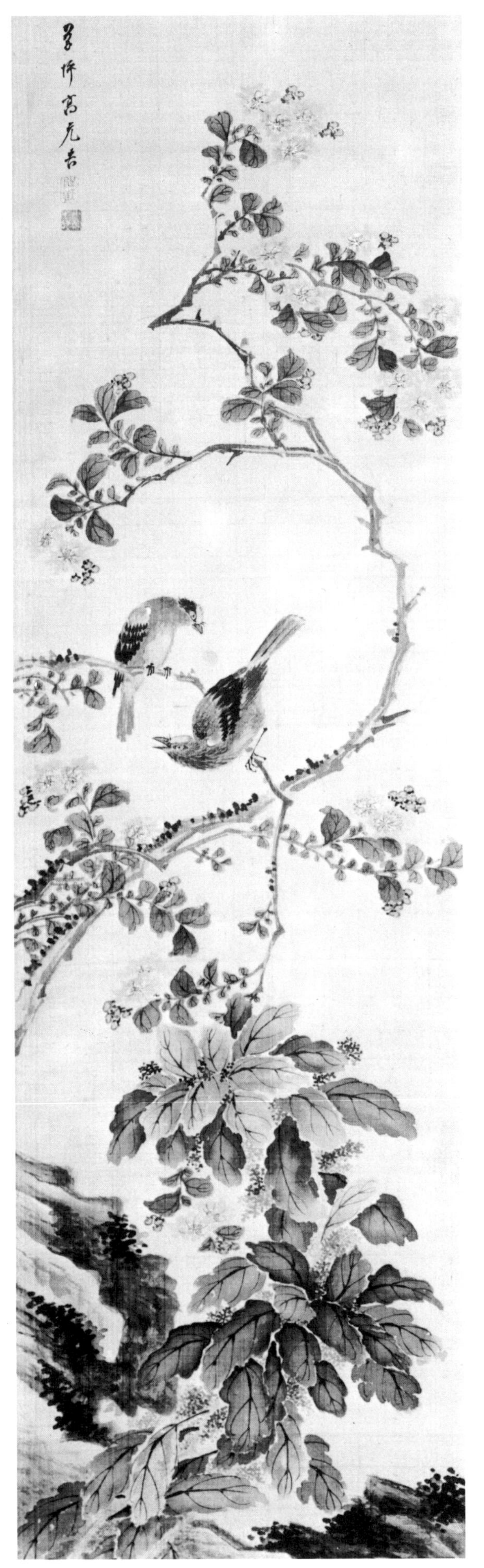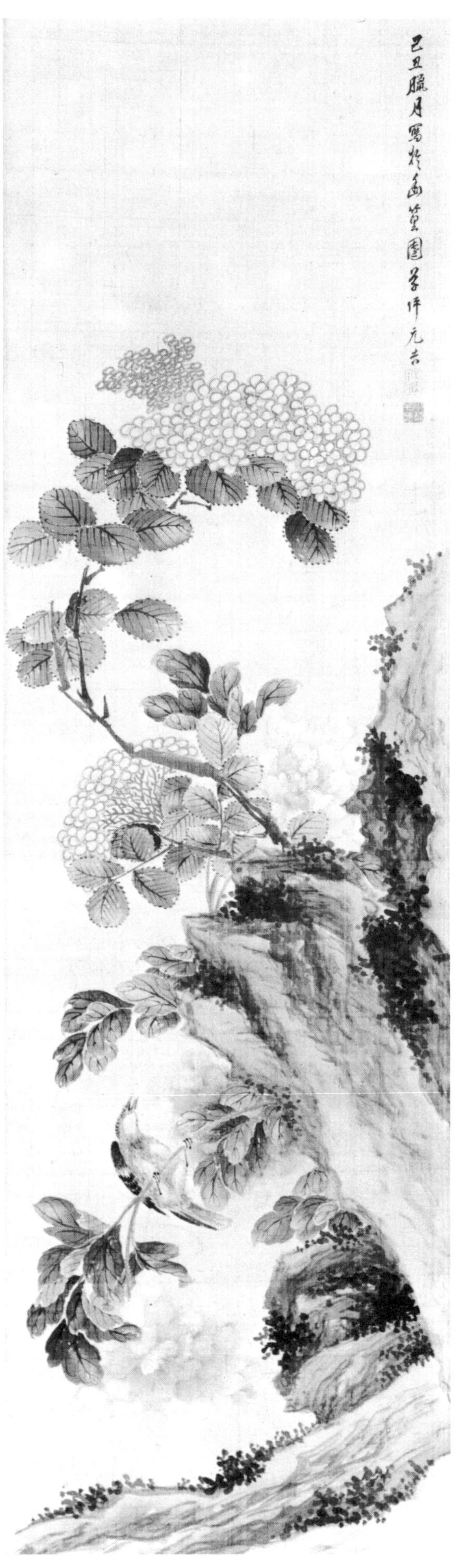

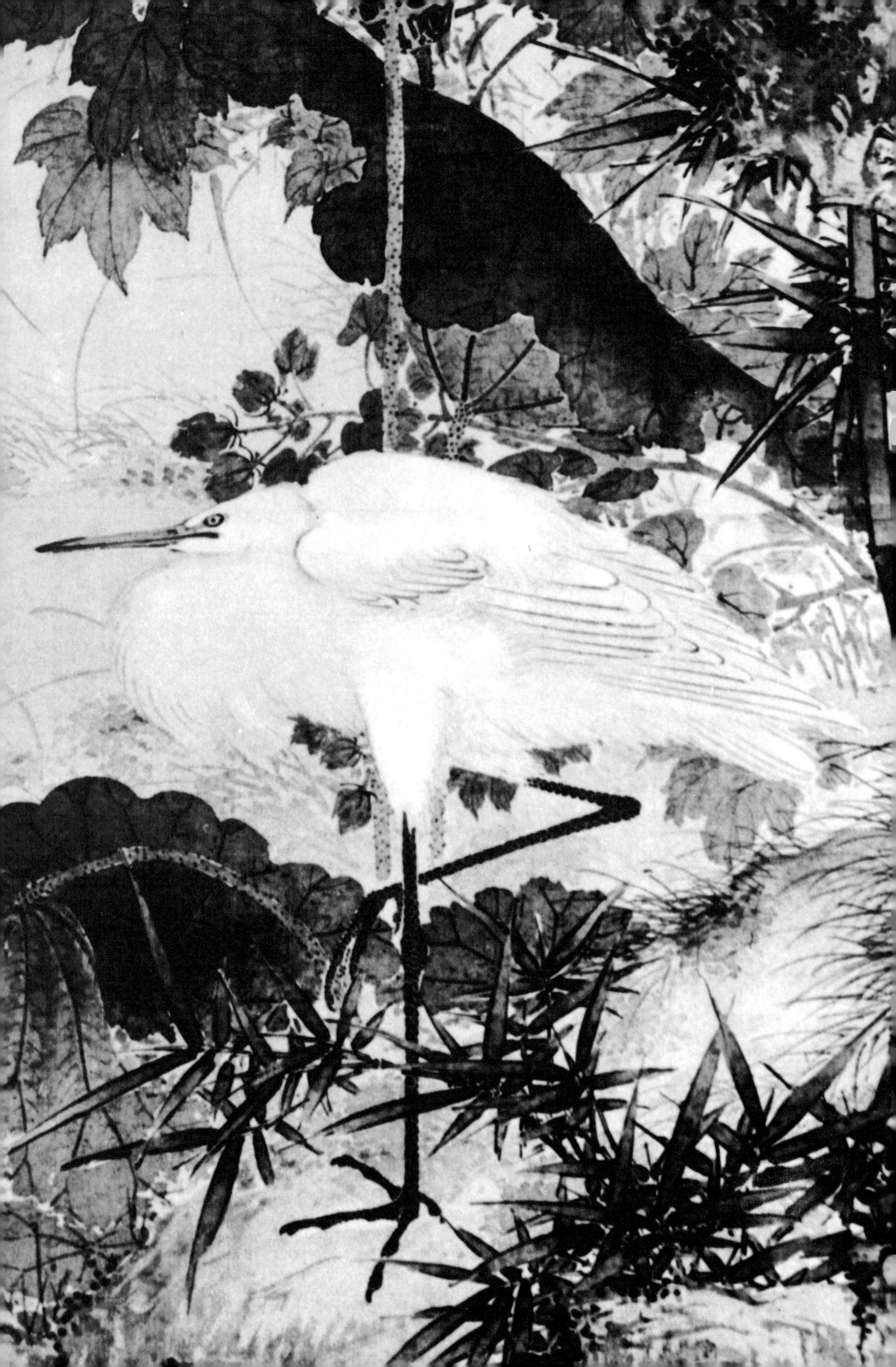

Chapter VII: The Spread of Nanga

By the later part of the eighteenth century, Nanga, which in its earlier stages
had been chiefly a Kyoto phenomenon, had gained adherents among painters
in a number of other artistic centers. Its diffusion was linked with the Chinese-
oriented literati culture, as its origin had been. Coteries of scholars, similar to
that surrounding Rai Sanyō in Kyoto, came together in other cities; visits were
exchanged, as these men tended to travel widely and frequently. Freedom and
fluidity of movement, a degree of independence difficult to achieve in the
late Tokugawa society, were part of the ideal they adopted from their Chinese
counterparts; it was an ideal that sometimes brought them into conflict with
authority, and was not wholly realizable, as in fact it had seldom been in China.
This did not make it less appealing. The situation was similar to the early
twentieth century Japanese fascination with an idealized vision of the free
and uninhibited life as lived by artists in Paris: the truthfulness of the vision,
and its applicability to the situation of Japanese artists, had nothing to do with
the attraction it exerted. So the ideal of the Chinese literatus spread through the
intellectual world in Japan, and with it Nanga.

The literati of Osaka were in such constant contact with Kyoto that they can
scarcely be considered a separate branch of the school. Kimura Kenkadō was
mentioned in the previous chapter; his home was a gathering place for scholars
and artists of this persuasion. Gyokudō visited him a number of times. Another
important figure in the Osaka circle was Okada Beisanjin (1744-1820). His birth-
place is unknown. He is said to have studied by reading books while working
in the rice fields as a youth. For a time he served the lord of Tōdō at Ise. Around
1772 he moved to Osaka and set himself up as a rice merchant, while continuing
to be active in scholarship. The *Bei* of his adopted name means "rice," but is also
the family name of the Chinese landscapist Mi Fu, whose landscape style,
featuring the short horizontal strokes called "Mi dots," Beisanjin sometimes
imitated. Beisanjin no doubt had both meanings in mind when he took the
name. He seems to have been self-taught as a painter. He painted figures, in a
half-comical style that suggests he did not take figure painting very seriously, and
landscapes in the highly formalized manner for which he is best known. Round-
topped hills of symmetrical shape nearly always occupy most of the space of
his pictures, their slopes covered with long, stringy, parallel strokes which have
no discernible representational meaning; they represent only an extreme
schematization of the "hemp-fiber texture-strokes" convention of Chinese

landscape. Once more, we are probably dealing with a re-translation into brush painting of a woodblock rendering of that convention. With the hills he combines trees that similarly follow Chinese type-forms, rocks of uniform size and shape that are often curiously striped, and standard *staffage:* strolling scholars, servant boys carrying zithers for the scholars to strum, fishermen, and the rest. His repertory of forms is limited, both within any single picture and in his works as a whole. This need not in itself be a fault—the same could be said of the paintings of his friend Gyokudō; but Beisanjin's works seem, in motivation and method, more intellectually calculated, less impassioned and less pictorial. His "Landscape with Pine Groves" of 1807 (No.52) is one of his most pleasing works, not so severely schematic as others and better supplied with depth and space. This is particularly true of the lower part, where the artist has convincingly created a cool hollow among the pines in which to locate his figures.

Beisanjin's son Okada Hankō (1782-1846) was a more serious, more versatile, altogether better painter: at times he may have been undervalued in the past through being thought of as Beisanjin's son rather than as a self-sufficient artist. Like his father he served the lord of Tōdō for a time, but resigned in 1822 and came to Osaka, where he made his living as a painter. His friends included Chikuden, who stayed with him on trips to Osaka, and others of that group. Hankō first learned painting from his father, but expanded the range of his styles greatly by studying Chinese paintings that were coming to Japan around this time. The Chinese artists he studied and imitated, as we know from his inscriptions on paintings, included Mi Fu of the Sung period, Wu Chen and Huang Kung-wang of the Yüan, Tung Ch'i-ch'ang of the late Ming, and Wang Hui of the early Ch'ing—all highly respectable models for a literatus-painter, although the last-named might be said to carry the germs of the orthodoxy that afflicted Kaiseki.

Hankō's *"Shunai Kia"* or "Crows Taking Flight Through Spring Haze" (No. 53), painted in 1841, is loosely based, according to his inscription, on a painting of a similar subject by Tung Ch'i-ch'ang (1555-1636). Whether any genuine work of that master had reached Japan by Hankō's time is open to question, but the authenticity of the painting Hankō saw is not crucial to his own work, which is in a style very different from Tung's. Evident in it is a new mastery of the representation of landscape forms in light and atmosphere, and of their convincing interrelationship in space. The mists are not schematically treated at all, but drift naturally through the scene, obscuring or softening trees and hillsides. Color is used expertly to suggest a cool, somewhat dimmed sunlight. The viewer can move back smoothly, in imaginary exploration of the landscape, from the fishing boats in the foreground across the river, past a villa and a riverside pavilion, over a bridge to a Buddhist temple set among the trees, and upward past a waterfall to the highest peak, with no dislocation or forced transition at any point. Among other Nanga artists perhaps only Yamamoto Baiitsu, of whom we will speak later, was capable of an achievement of this kind, which seems to have been technically beyond the capacities of both earlier and later masters. This is not to suggest that either Hankō or Baiitsu was ultimately of the artistic stature of Gyokudō, Buson, or Taiga; but only that they had gained, largely through study of Chinese paintings, new representational means—special skills in drawing, composition, and spatial rendering—that raised Nanga, in their period, to a new height of technical mastery, from which it was to decline shortly after.

Nanga did not take root in Edo, or modern Tokyo, until the late eighteenth

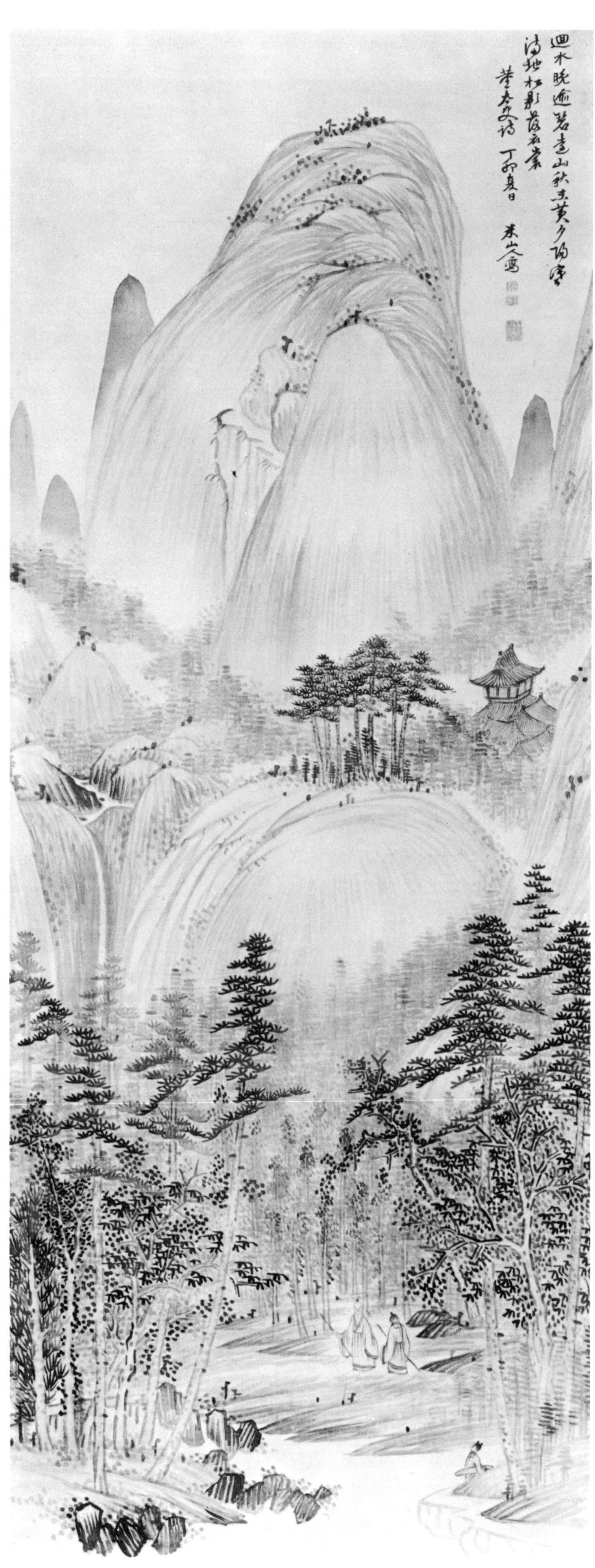

52 **Okada Beisanjin** Landscape with Pine Groves, 1807. Hanging scroll, ink and light colors on silk. H. 51-7/16 in. (130.6 cm.)

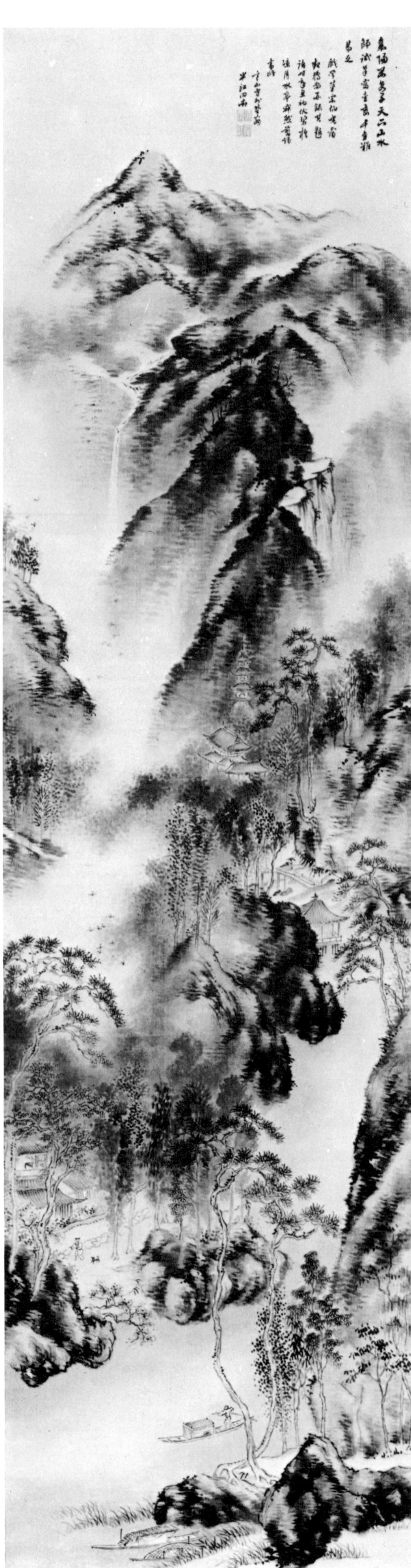

53 Okada Hankō Crows Taking Flight through Spring Haze *(Shunai Kia)*, 1841. Hanging scroll, ink and colors on silk. H. 51-11/16 in. (131.4 cm.)

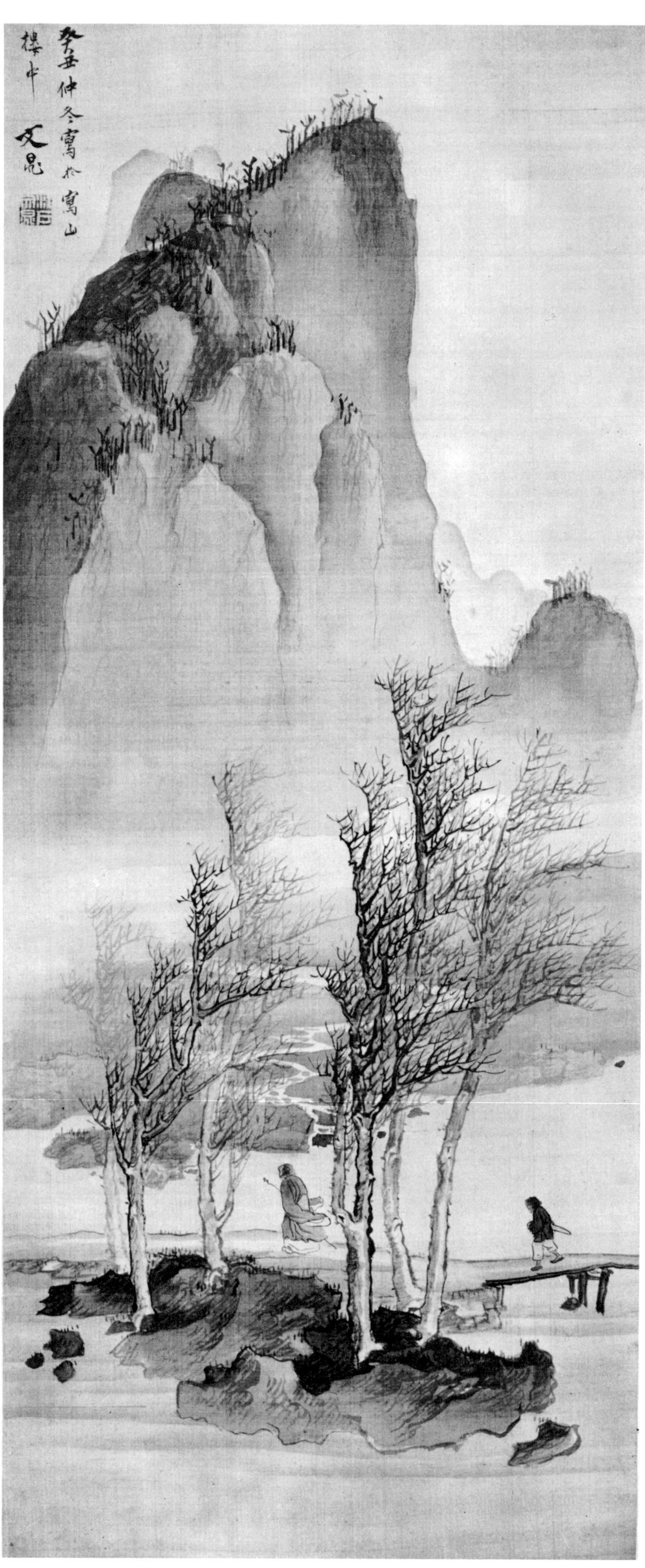

54 Tani Bunchō Landscape with Figures, 1793. Hanging scroll, ink and colors on silk. H. 27 in. (66.5 cm.)

century, and after that was always a somewhat hybrid plant. The artist credited
with introducing it to Edo is the famous Tani Bunchō (1763-1840). He was born
in Edo, the son of a poet, and began painting at an early age. He studied the
styles of various schools under a number of masters—Kanō, Nagasaki, Nanga,
Western-style painting, and later the Maruyama-Shijō styles as well as others.
He also saw, and learned from, a great many Chinese paintings, some of which
he copied carefully. He did illustrations for books, and paintings of a wide range
of subjects: birds, flowers, animals, and figures of all kinds. But he was at his
best as a landscapist. He was the most famous of Edo artists in his generation,
and his only contemporary there who could be considered to rival him in versatility and technical proficiency was Katsushika Hokusai (1760-1849). Also like
Hokusai, Buncho was extremely prolific; the profusion of second-rate works he
painted, especially in his later years, has recently led to a downward re-evalua-
tion of his position in Japanese painting. The Japanese maintain that he produced
his finest works in the Kansei era (1789-1801).

The two paintings we include date from that period. The "Landscape with
Figures" in the Tokyo National Museum (No. 54) was painted in 1793, when
Bunchō was only thirty years old. The composition is simple but unhackneyed,
and must have seemed fresh and original within the context of Edo painting.
A gentleman in a red robe with a staff hurries along a path behind a row of bare
trees, followed by his boy servant carrying the usual *ch'in*. The man's sleeves
are blown back by the wind, as are the branches of the trees. Behind the figures,
a winding river and a zone of fog indicate the deep space that separates them
from the mountain beyond. Cool grey-green washes suggest that the time is late
afternoon or evening. The composition is worked out, and the painting executed, with a logic and formal control that relate it more to Sung dynasty painting
than to the scholar-painters' tradition in China; the combination of sharp, clear
drawing and graded washes, as well as the evocative relationship of the figures
and their setting and the overall spaciousness and moodiness of the scene,
belong to a landscape mode that began with the masters of the Southern Sung
Academy in China and was carried on by Ming artists such as T'ang Yin (1470-
1523). Bunchō must have been familiar with some works of his, or of his
numerous followers. This mode was not properly Southern School at all; but
as we have seen, the range of styles in Nanga was far wider than any stylistic
definition based only on the artist's choice of Chinese models could possibly
encompass. The Edo branch of Nanga, in particular, tended to make use of styles
that were outside the scholar-painters' world.

Some time around 1800 Bunchō traveled to Kōnodai, the present Ichikawa
City in Chiba Prefecture, and painted a series of travel sketches, originally in the
form of an album but now mounted as a handscroll (No. 55). The sketches were
surely not considered to be finished works by the artist, who would normally
have reworked them as formal compositions. He has jotted notes freely on some
of them, and in places roughed in his intention in a summary way. The pictures
seem all the more fresh and firsthand for their extemporaneous character; in the
context of Far Eastern painting, where carefully and artificially composed scenes
were the rule, they may strike us as quite unarranged and naturalistic, an
impression that would last only until one put them beside certain European
sketches from nature, or photographs, and could see what a relative matter this
is. Bunchō's technical skill is apparent everywhere in the ease with which he
lays out each scene in convincing scale and perspective. The pictures are of
historic monuments and other notable sights in the city and its environs, or

simply portray the scenery that the artist encountered. Included also in the scroll are what appear to be simplified copies of paintings he saw on the trip.

Of Bunchō's many followers, the most famous is Watanabe Kazan (1793-1841), one of the fascinating and tragic figures of Japanese art. He was a retainer to the Tahara clan in Mikawa, modern Aichi Prefecture, but was born and raised in Edo. The Tahara clan was poor and Kazan lived in poverty during his early years; he began painting as a means of augmenting his income. From 1809 he became a pupil of Bunchō, after studying painting earlier under several other masters. Eventually he succeeded to the position of patriarch of the family and was put in charge of coastal defenses for the clan, besides having other responsibilities in the clan administration. His broad learning extended to *Rangaku,* a term meaning literally "Dutch studies" but also used more generally for European studies; Kazan was particularly interested in the politics and economics of European countries. Useful as such knowledge must have been to him in his official functions, in the end it was his undoing. In 1839 the Tokugawa government launched a rigorous suppression of Rangaku among the common people. Kazan was arrested, and only escaped execution through the intervention of his teachers and friends. He was ordered to return to the clan seat and remain there under house arrest. He lived nearly two years in confinement, doing some painting and writing. In 1841 he killed himself.

Like Bunchō, Kazan as a painter was extremely eclectic, and his range of styles is difficult to circumscribe. He too learned the realistic Nagasaki bird-and-flower painting, the new Western-influenced realistic styles, and the Nanga styles of landscape, in this last imitating Chinese artists such as Lan Ying and Yün Shou-p'ing (the former not a "Southern School" painter at all, in Chinese terms). He was a pioneer of realistic portraiture in Japan and a master of lively genre figure subjects. Behind all of these one senses a fundamentally intellectual approach to painting; Kazan does not seem really to think in images. With an object before him to be depicted faithfully, or an existing realistic style such as the Nagasaki School or European pictures to follow, he can do penetrating studies that seem to be trying to cut through barriers of style and to grasp visual reality almost in its raw state. His pictures composed in the usual manner out of conventional images, on the other hand, can be quite dry and thin, with little appeal to the eye.

Several works that are believed to have been painted by Kazan during his last years, his period of incarceration, are inscribed by him with earlier dates. The reason is that although he desperately needed money and had to paint to raise it, he could not do so openly, as he had been forbidden to sell his paintings. He was forced to write false dates on them and smuggle them out to friends who sold them as productions of his earlier years. His painting of "Playing Fish" (No. 56), for instance, bears a date corresponding to 1834, but was probably done in 1840, since it agrees with a description that Kazan wrote late in that year, in a letter to his follower Tsubaki Chinzan (1801-1854), of a painting he had just completed. He wrote that he had done a picture of fish deep in the ocean, a subject that the old masters had never treated. He adds, however, that he had painted the waves in a traditional style. The painting reveals just such a contrast. The fish are portrayed realistically, both as individual forms, in the shading of their bodies and absence of conventions in the brushwork, and in their grouping, with unstudied overlappings and the creation of depth through diminution and tonal dimming of the further fish. The rendering of the waves in a manner that recalls Kōrin does indeed, in this context, seem anomalous.

55 Tani Buncho Travel Sketches of Konodai. Handscroll (section illus.), ink and light colors on paper. H. 6-7/16 in. (16.3 cm.)

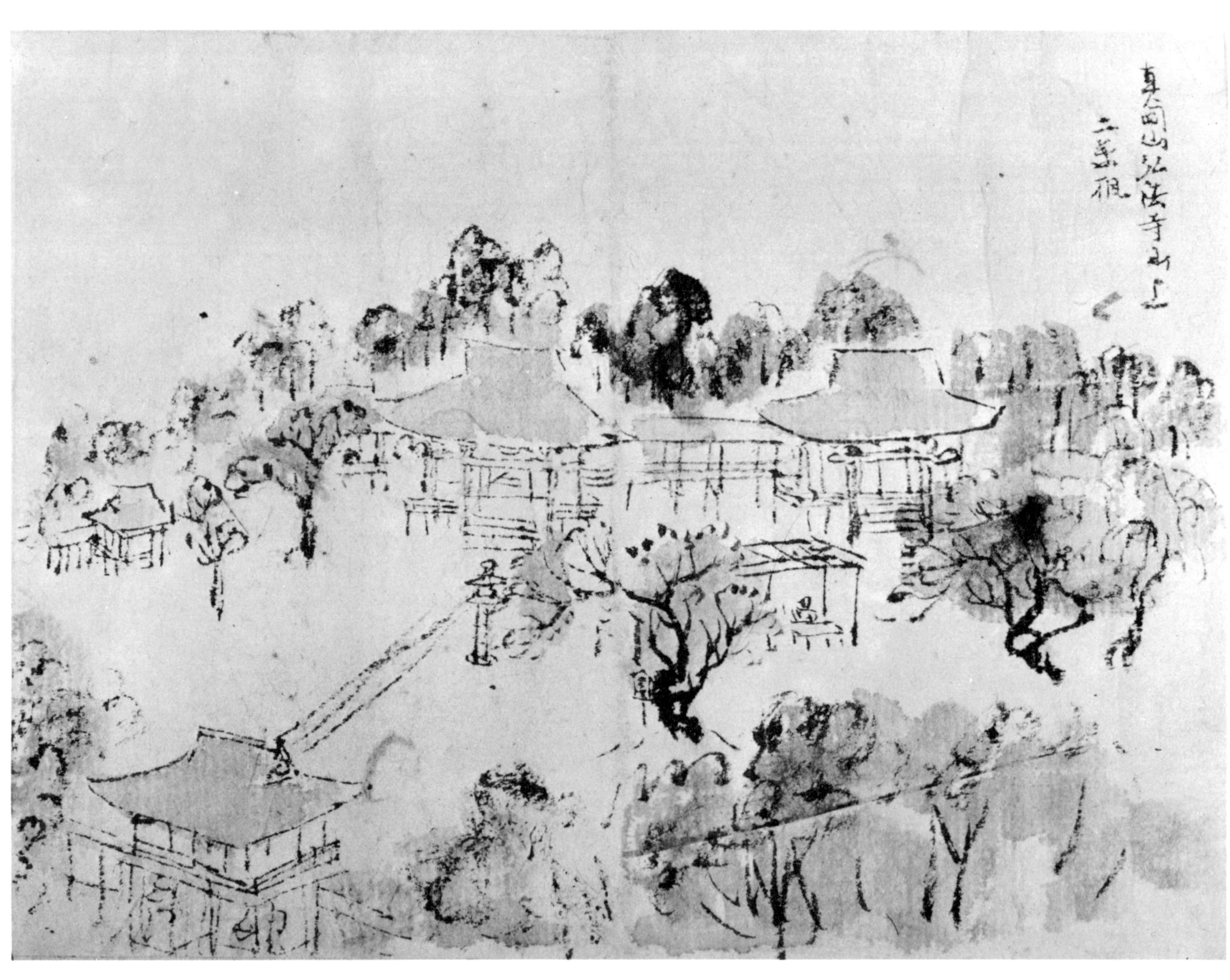

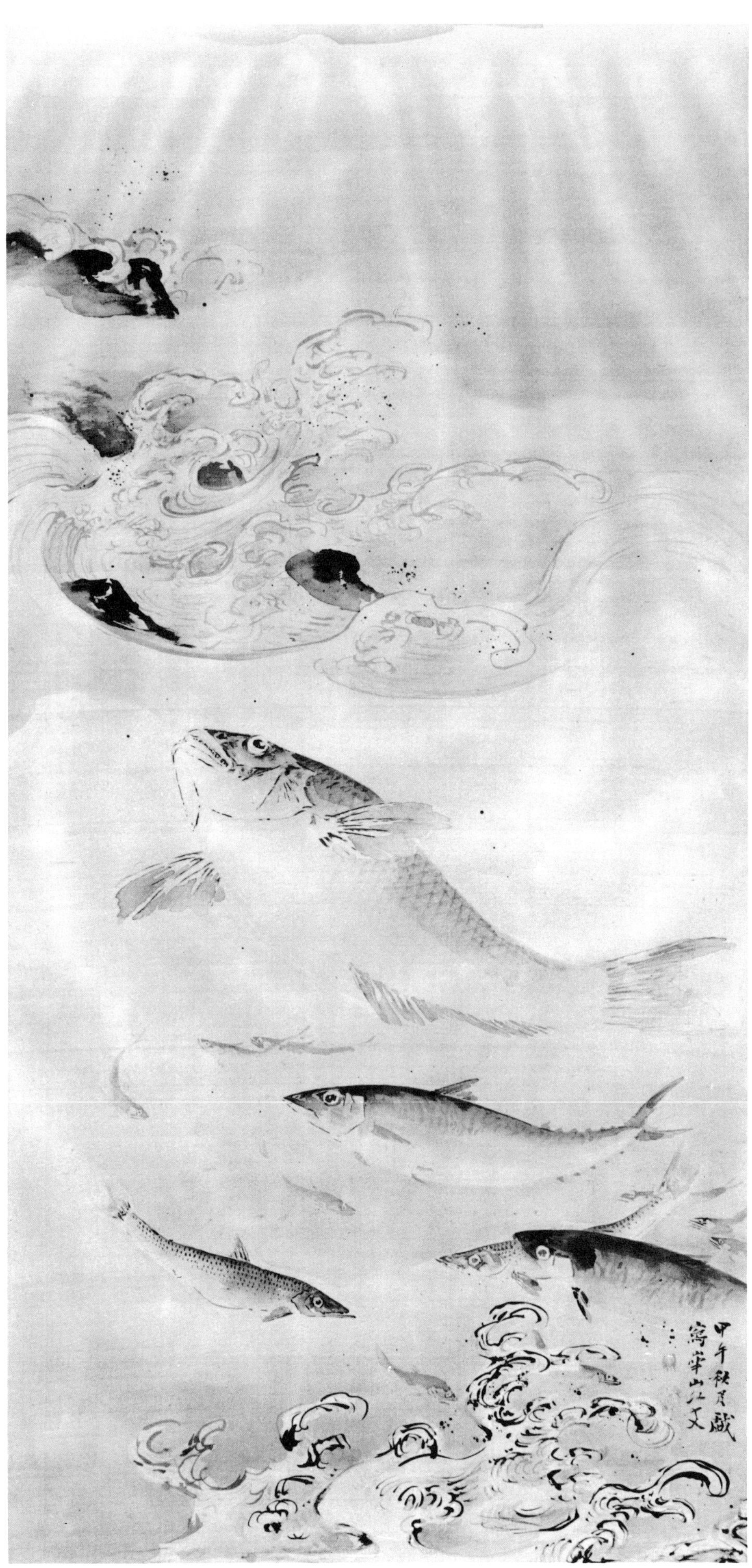

56 Watanabe Kazan Playing Fish, dated 1834 but probably painted in 1840. Hanging scroll, ink and colors on silk. H. 44³/₈ in. (112.7 cm.)

A more ambitious and altogether more interesting work is "Weaving by Moonlight" (No. 57), which is also believed to date from Kazan's period of house arrest, although the date he has written on it is 1829. Here the realism is even more marked, and even more obviously dependent on his acquaintance with European pictures, giving the painting the appearance of a scene analytically observed and accurately rendered. In fact, it is an imaginary scene of life in the Yangtze River region of China, as envisioned by Kazan. The subject carries Confucian overtones of the belief that agriculture and industry are the foundations of the state, a belief encouraged by the Tokugawa government, so that pictures of such subjects are fairly common in the Edo Period. Kazan's is unusual, however, in its air of specificity. Within the buildings in the foreground, which are open on the side facing the viewer, women are seen spinning thread and weaving by lamplight. Behind these buildings is a pond with ducks, and on its shores rows of houses, drawn in a detailed, matter-of-fact way, with no obvious dependence on old models. A horizontal zone of thick fog at the base of the hill is a concession to traditional landscape, but the hill itself and the night sky with clouds return us to the realistic mode. Here, as in his portraits, Kazan attempts the objective and quasi-scientific approach to painting that he learned through his fatal fascination with the West. When one considers this aspect of the painting, and realizes that part of the motivation for its impressively meticulous execution was Kazan's desire to sell it for badly needed money, it acquires a quality of poignancy which, however irrelevant to the quality of the picture proper, must affect one's experience of it.

Sakurama Seigai (1786-1851) was a close friend of Kazan who began his artistic career as a figure painter but later, like Kazan, fell under the influence of Bunchō, and still later of Kazan himself. Seigai's best works are those of his fifties, and his best known painting, the landscape now in the Tokyo National Museum (No. 58), probably dates from that period. Seigai did not sign it, but impressed his seal in the lower right corner. Once more we must see the painting, and the ways it differs from earlier Nanga works, in the light of new Sinicization of Nanga styles brought about by closer acquaintance with Chinese originals. Here, more than with any other work we have considered, the possibility exists of mistaking it for a Chinese painting, and in any case it would be difficult to define any Japanese qualities in it. To say so is not to judge its success as a landscape, but only its originality; the composition is strong, the brushwork varied and sure, and the ceaselessly undulating contours and the texture strokes give an interesting restlessness to the forms. However, it demonstrates that along with the gain of new technical means went a loss of some qualities that had been the particular strengths of Nanga, particularly those that had made it compatible with the native Japanese traditions of painting. The freshness of approach of Taiga and Buson, their simple, strong designs and decorative patterns, have largely disappeared with the development of this new, further Sinicized sophistication.

A minor branch of the Nanga School was located in the city of Nagoya, and included two of the best of the later Nanga painters, who were close friends: Nakabayashi Chikutō (1776-1853) and Yamamoto Baiitsu (1783-1856). Chikutō was the son of a doctor, but at the age of fifteen became the protégé of a rich Nagoya businessman and collector named Kamiya Tenyū. At Tenyū's house he saw and studied Chinese paintings and met artists, including Baiitsu who was similarly sponsored by Tenyū. As the story goes, Tenyū once invited the two young painters to a temple where they saw two Chinese paintings of bamboo

57 **Watanabe Kazan** Weaving by
Moonlight, dated 1829 but
probably painted ca. 1840.
Hanging scroll, ink and colors on
silk. H. 49-15/16 in. (126.9 cm.)

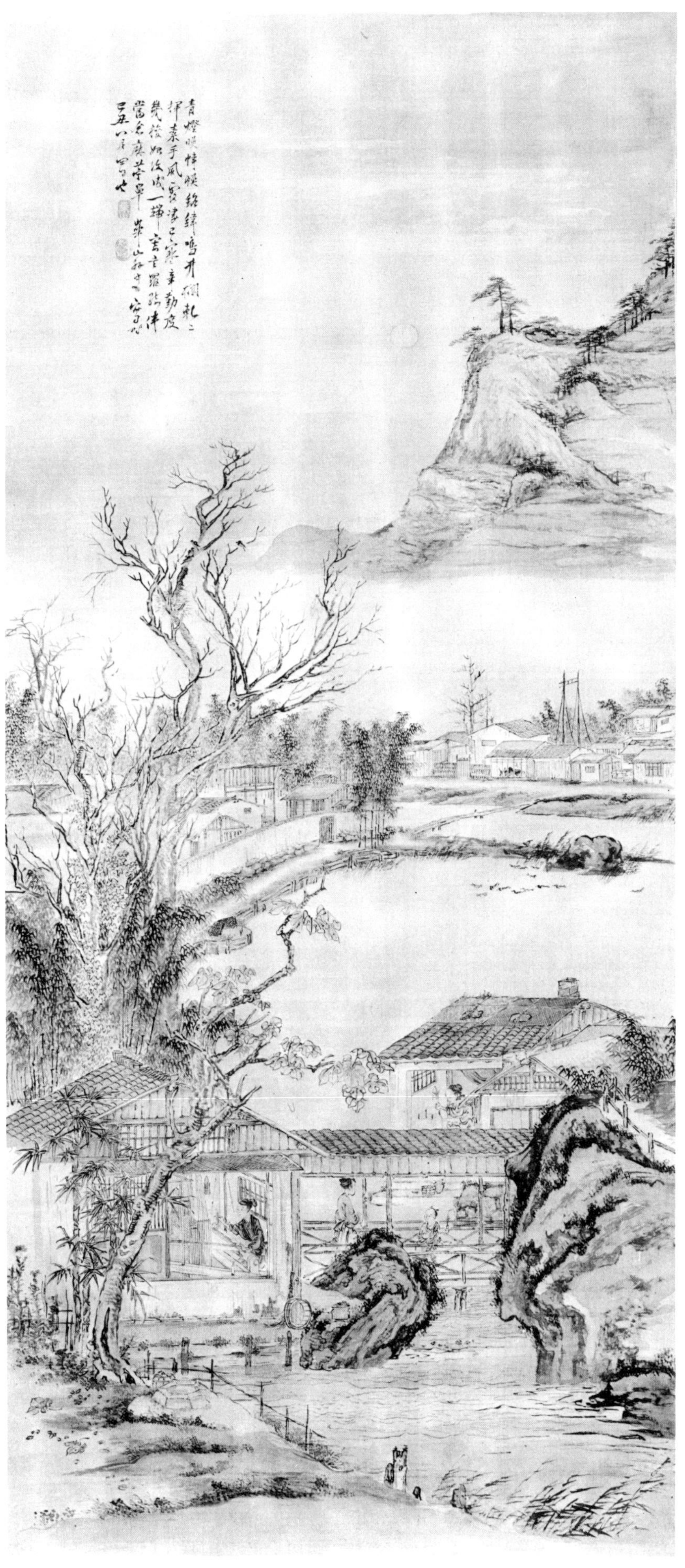

58 Sakurama Seigai Landscape.
Hanging scroll, ink and light
colors on paper. H. 51-3/16 in.
(130 cm.)

60 Yamamoto Baiitsu Bamboo
Groves and Waterfalls. Hanging
scroll, ink on silk. H. 51³/₈ in.
(130.5 cm.)

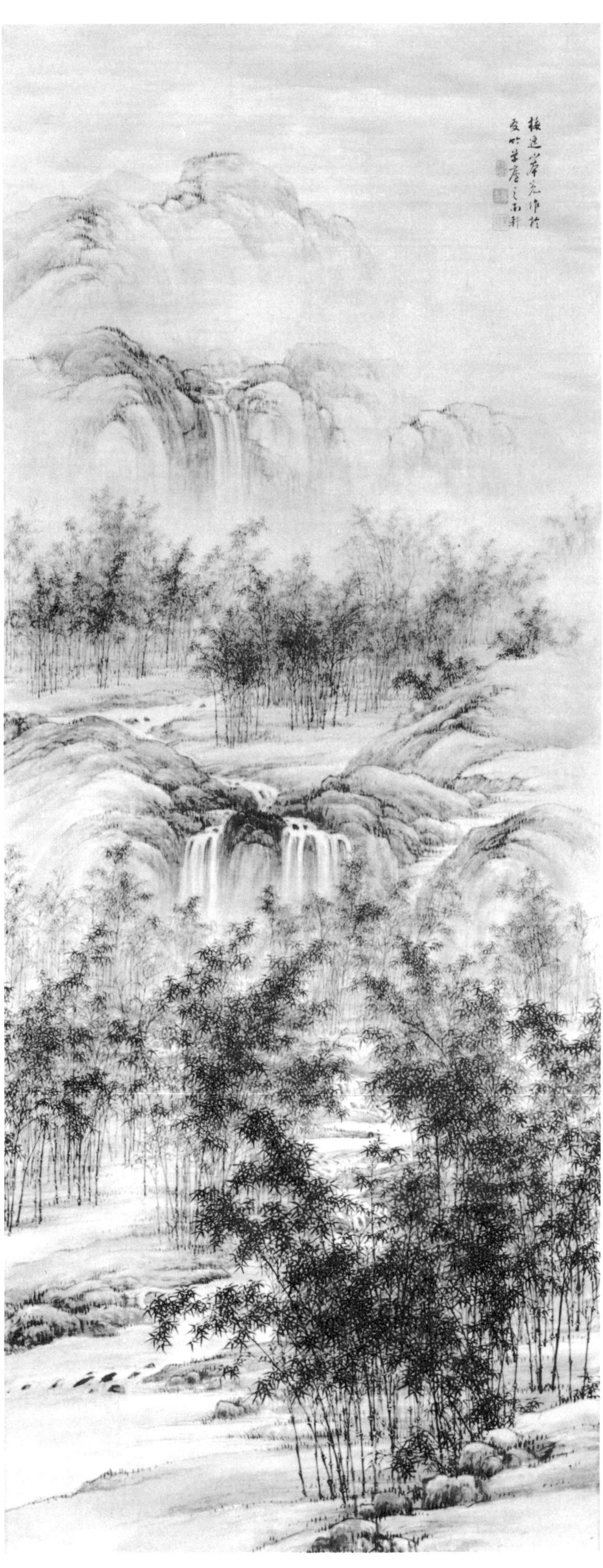

and blossoming plum; inspired by these, he bestowed on them their artists' names: Chikutō ("Bamboo Grotto") and Baiitsu ("Plum Leisure"). In 1802, both painters went to Kyoto, but soon returned to Nagoya. Chikutō moved to Kyoto permanently in 1815, and joined the circle of Rai Sanyō. He also became a friend of the Zen priest Yōzan, who was abbot of the Zakke-in, the temple where the landscape we include, "Summer Mountains Washed By Rain" (No. 59), is still preserved. It probably dates from the artist's sixties.

For all his experimenting with a variety of Chinese traditions and manners, Chikutō stays within a fairly narrow stylistic range in his paintings. He was the author of many volumes on art theory and guidebooks for painters, setting forth the most correct and orthodox Southern School doctrines and styles, and the same didactic attitude comes out in his own works, which tend to be rather static and conventional in composition. They acquire their interest and attractiveness chiefly through the decorative value of the brushstroke patterns and small forms which Chikutō will repeat tirelessly throughout a picture. (He himself would probably have been offended by this judgement, since the whole direction of Nanga theory is against decorative styles.) In the case of "Summer Mountains," it is the "Mi dots" of the Mi Fu manner, previously encountered several times in the works of earlier Nanga masters, which are repeated systematically to give substance to hills and trees. The picture that Chikutō produces with these means is pleasant, serene, uneventful.

Yamamoto Baiitsu is an artist of another kind altogether—versatile, inventive, concerned with pictorial values rather than doctrinary ones. He was the son of a sculptor in Nagoya and, after returning from his short stay in Kyoto with Chikutō, became a painter for the Tokugawa clan. He was one of the most accomplished of later Japanese artists, and perhaps can be said to have attained a better technical command of the Chinese-derived styles than any other Nanga master. Nevertheless, his reputation in Japan is not high, partly because, like Bunchō, he painted many rather superficial pictures. At his best, however, he can be dazzlingly good. He handles brush and ink with a finesse that few others in Japan could match; he is another of the few whose works could be mistaken, at times, for Chinese paintings. This is in itself no recommendation, of course; the same could be said of the most slavish imitations, if they were faithful enough. But Baiitsu is by no means a simple imitator of Chinese styles; he is a painter of originality and feeling. He is represented in the United States by a number of fine works, among which a superb pair of screens in the Freer Gallery of Art is outstanding.[1] His best known landscape in Japan is "Bamboo Groves and Waterfalls" (No. 60), painted in ink monochrome on silk. The device of atmospheric perspective, by which more distant objects are drawn in lighter tone, had seldom been so beautifully handled in Japanese painting. It gives the picture a sense of air and sunshine as well as depth. The definition of planes of height and depth is also masterly. The stream flows downward from one level to the next, issuing finally from the bottom of the composition, binding the whole together. Particularly admirable is the lower part, in which this stream is seen winding through the tall bamboo. The entire scene is thoroughly convincing spatially, truly "a picture one can walk around in."

Baiitsu's fame as a painter of bird-and-flower compositions in color has somewhat obscured his stature as a landscapist and has led to his being regarded sometimes as a facile and decorative artist. The style of his bird-and-flower pictures is also based ultimately on Chinese styles, particularly that of a late Ming master of such subjects named Chou Chih-mien (active ca. 1580-1610), whose

1. See Junkichi Mayuyama, ed., *Japanese Art in the West* (Tokyo, 1966), pl. 290.

59 Nakabayashi Chikutō Summer
Mountains Washed by Rain.
Hanging scroll, ink on silk.
H. 48-15/16 in. (124.3 cm.)

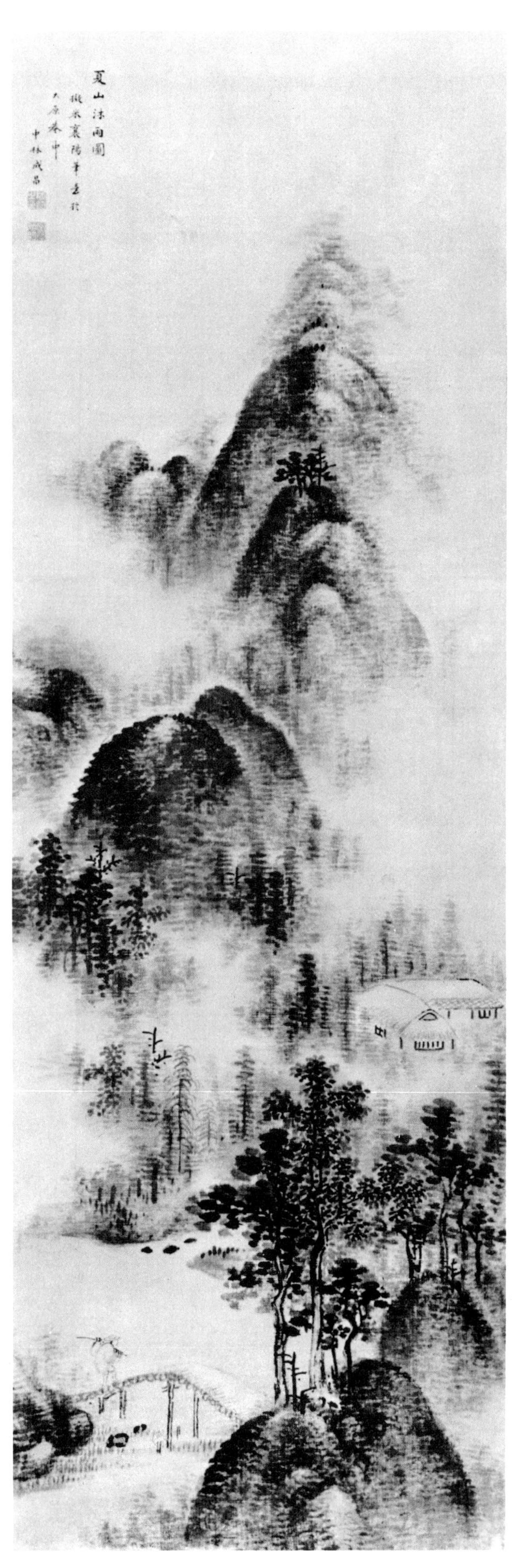

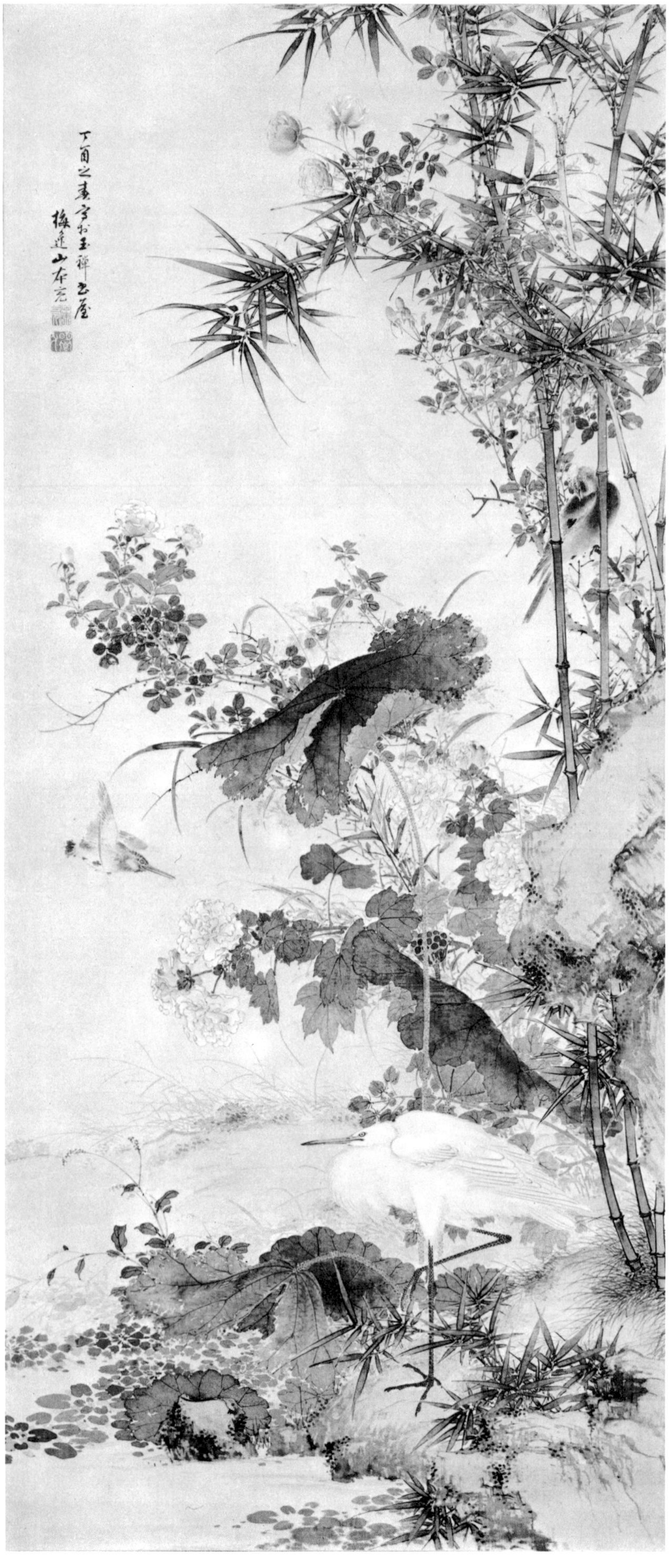

61 **Yamamoto Baiitsu** Birds and Flowers, 1837. Hanging scroll, ink and colors on silk. H. 64³/₈ in. (163.5 cm.)

62 **Tomioka Tessai** Fishermen on the Great River, 1916. Hanging scroll, ink and colors on paper. H. 58⁷/₈ in. (149.5 cm.)

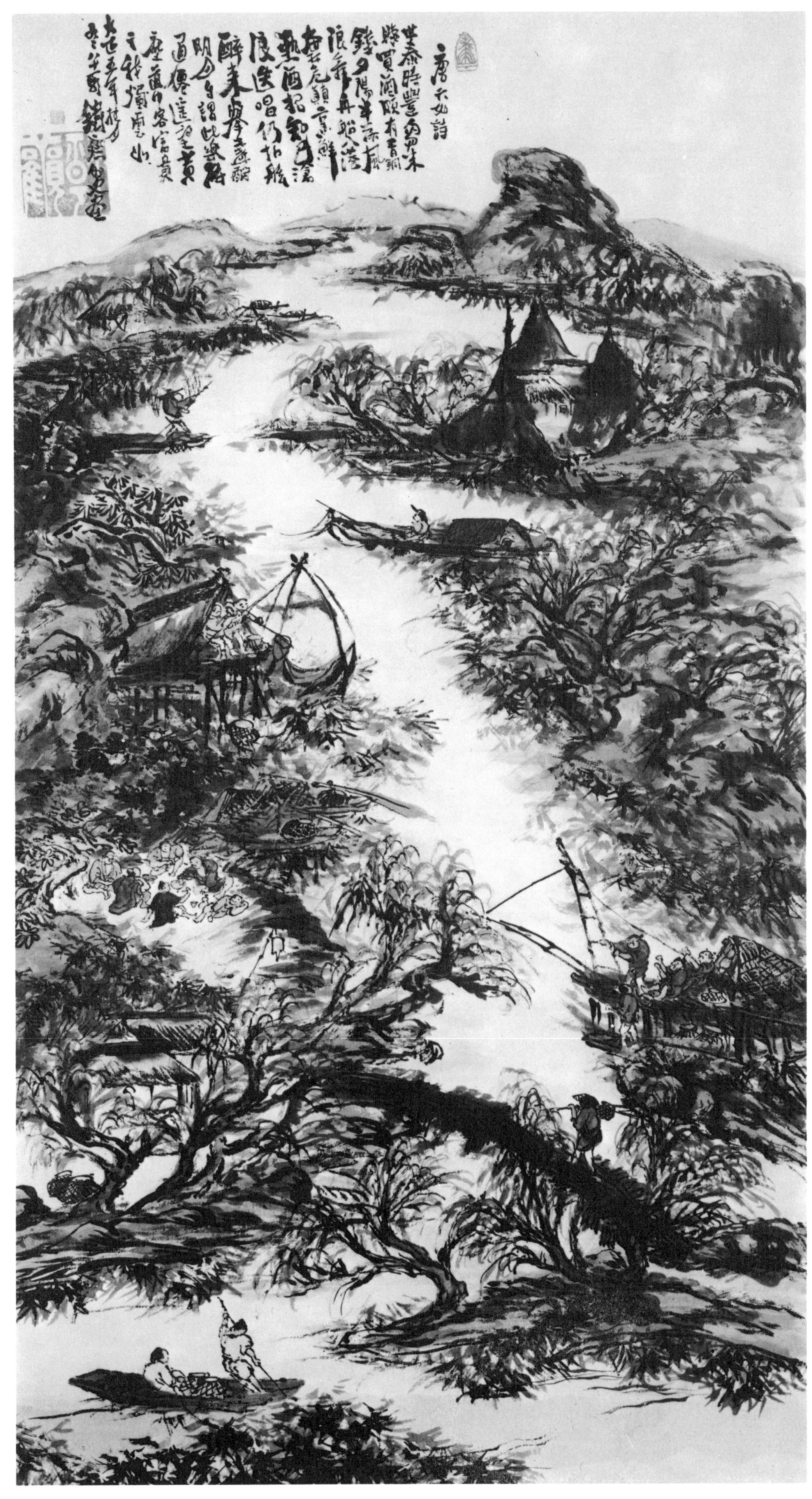

works were to be seen in Japan by then. Baiitsu works in washes of color, mixed sometimes with ink, in a variety of the so-called "boneless" manner which largely or completely dispensed with outline drawing in ink. A good example is his large bird-and-flower painting of 1837 (No. 61). The birds and plants are distributed in the composition in a purely decorative, artificial arrangement, as they had been in Kanō School pictures of this type and in Ming dynasty academic pictures before that. Baiitsu's work differs from those of the Kanō tradition in his far more sensitive and realistic rendering of the individual elements. Baiitsu understood how plants grow and how bamboo stalks bend, the weight of flowers and the structure of leaves, and describes them in sharp crisp drawing. The colors, although richly varied, are mostly muted with ink—he often, for the leaves, adds light washes of color to a graded ink-wash base—and the general effect is one of coolness and precision.

Nanga artists working after the middle of the nineteenth century had little that was new to offer. In 1868 the Meiji Restoration ended Japan's long isolation and opened it to the modern world. It ended also the conditions under which Nanga had grown and flourished, and the school can scarcely be said to have continued into the Meiji era and beyond as a living force in Japanese art.

An exception to these statements, and to most others one might make about twentieth century Japanese painting, was Tomioka Tessai (1837-1924), in whose works, especially those of his late period, Nanga has a brief, last flowering. Tessai has been seen in the United States in two traveling exhibitions, and so is familiar to most people interested at all in Japanese art; it should not be necessary to repeat the facts of his life or discuss his style at length.[2] We conclude this exhibition with two of his works. "Fishermen on the Great River" (No. 62) was painted in 1916, and is based loosely on a work by T'ang Yin (1470-1523), whose poem Tessai has copied at the top.[3] This is still another Japanese artist's vision of an idealized China, where fishermen live easy lives on the luxuriant banks of the river, picnicking in the interludes between their pleasant labors. The execution matches the subject in its seemingly effortless, loosely disciplined drawing. The composition obviously belongs to a type used earlier in Nanga, particularly by Chikuden (cf. No. 49), which is axially organized around a single winding recession moving up the center, with points of interest located to one side and the other along the way. Tessai imitates Chikuden closely in some of his early works, especially his early figure paintings, and was obviously influenced by other Nanga masters as well—Mokubei in his use of ink and color, Gyokudō in the freedom and fervor of his style.

Tessai's most brilliant productions are those of his very last years; he painted prolifically until his death at the age of eighty-nine. In these late works he uses ink lavishly, in a way analogous to recent Western expressionist painters' impasto use of oils, for powerful compositions that typically build vertically within the picture space with no real attempt to establish any depth beyond occasional hollows and narrow openings. In the painting of "Hakuin Visiting the Hermit Hakuyūshi" (No. 63), painted in 1920, the remoteness of Hakuyūshi's cave in the mountains is suggested by the old device of placing it at the end of a path, supposedly far back in the picture. In fact, since the path reads as nearly vertical, the cave seems nearly as close to the viewer as the trees in the foreground; it is typical of Tessai's late works in giving more or less equal value to the parts of the picture, while providing at the same time a focal area through compositional direction and the concentration of brighter colors there. The dramatic massing of black ink, and the occasional areas of depth achieved by

2. For a good account of his life and artistic development, see Tarō Odakane, *Tessai: Master of the Literati Style*, trans. and adapted by Money Hickman (Tokyo and Rutland, Vt., 1965). See also James Cahill, "The Painting of Tessai," in *The Works of Tomioka Tessai* (Berkeley, 1969).

3. It is impossible to say what painting, or copy of a painting, by T'ang Yin was the source of Tessai's composition; it must have been compositionally similar to the "Farmers' Dwellings in Chiang-nan" now in the Palace Museum, Taipei. See Peking Palace Museum, *Ku-kung shu-hua chi* (Peking, 1932), XXIII.

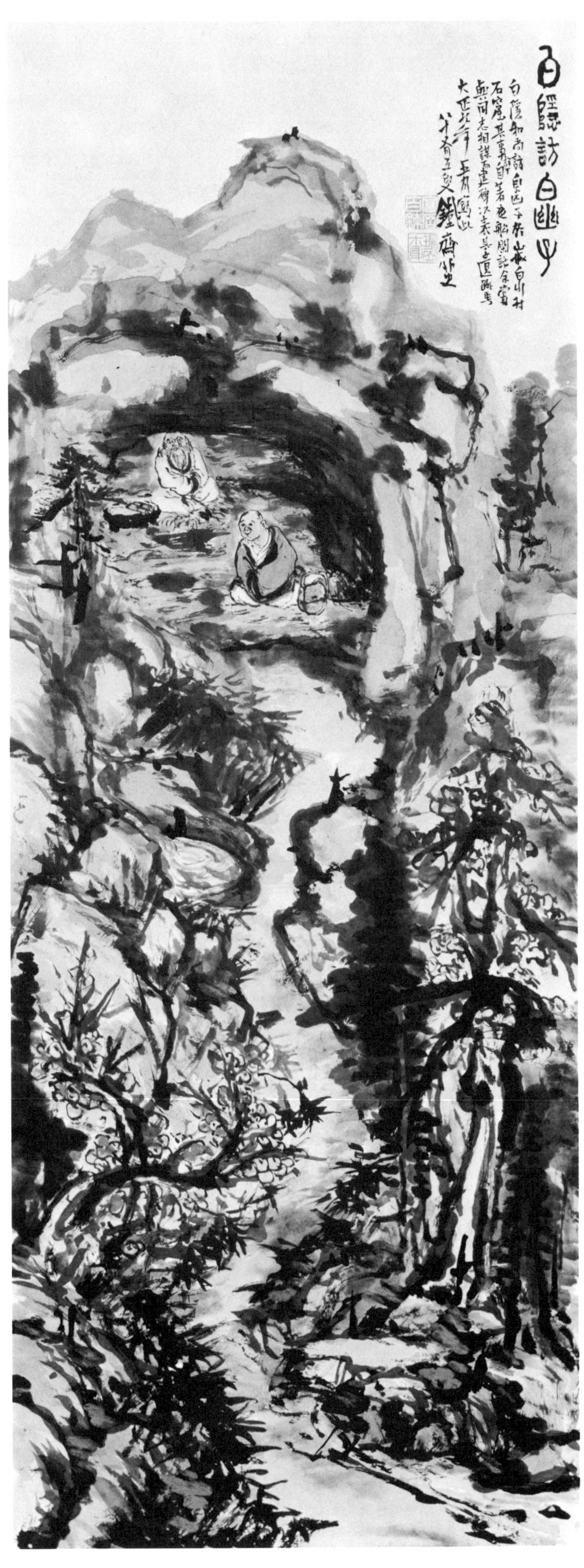

63 Tomioka Tessai Hakuin
Visiting the Hermit Hakuyūshi,
1920. Hanging scroll, ink and
light colors on paper. H. 52¼ in.
(132.6 cm.)

moving through a wide range of tonal values within a small area of the picture, again recall Gyokudō, whose work Tessai knew and admired.

It was only through the extraordinary longevity and productivity of Tessai that Nanga survived into the twentieth century, which clearly offers no climate congenial to the growth of such an art form. Even Kyoto, for two centuries the home of Nanga, retains little of the classical Chinese-oriented culture that nourished it. The kind of education and background that the Nanga artists and their friends received, their bookishness and attachment to the past, seem little suited to our time, and in any case virtually unattainable in it. Lacking that background, we may admire the paintings for reasons that the artists themselves might not always have considered to be the right ones, or at least the most important ones. But the capacity of works of art to evoke different responses in people with different sets of values is the very basis of their survival, and so it is with Nanga paintings: their multi-level meanings and their failure to conform consistently to any particular value system, whether Chinese or Japanese, is in the end the source of their strength, allowing them to hold their fascination and attraction long after the original "proper" context for their appreciation has ceased to exist.

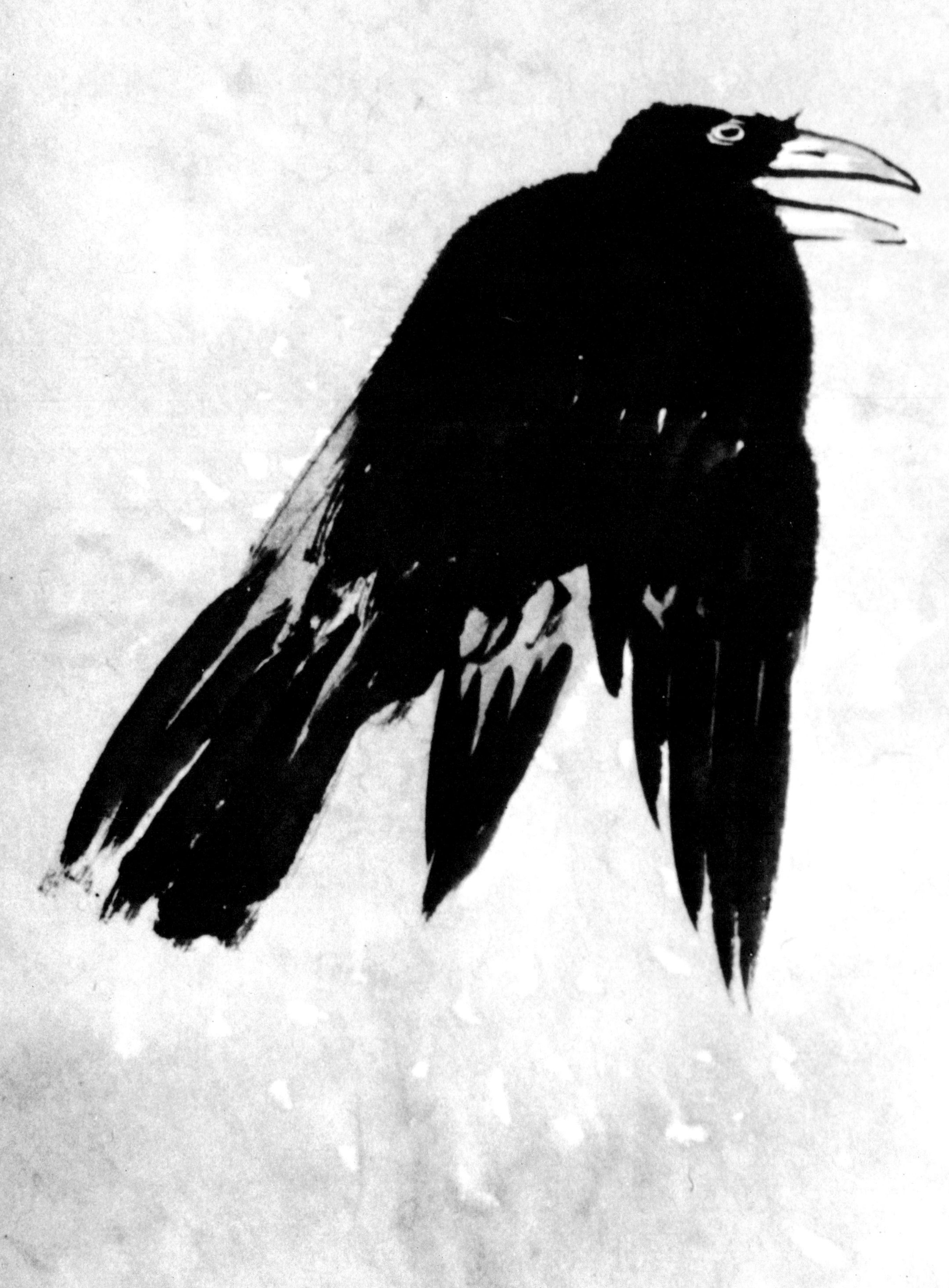

Catalogue

21 **Yosa Buson** A Crow in a
Wintry Sky (detail)

1 **Gion Nankai (1676-1751)** Landscape
Hanging scroll, ink and light colors on
paper
H. 47^1/$_2$ in. (120.6 cm.), W. 10-13/16 in.
(27.5 cm.)
Published: Bibl. 17, pl. 1
Tokyo National Museum

2 **Gion Nankai** A Branch of Blossoming
Plum
Hanging scroll, ink on paper
H. 38^3/$_8$ in. (97.6 cm.), W. 21 in. (53.3 cm.)
Published: Bibl. 14, pl. 93; Bibl. 15, pl. 8;
Bibl. 17, pl. 2
Mr. Kinsuke Wanaka, Wakayama

3a, b, c **Yanagisawa Kien (1704-1758)**
Flowers of the First, Fifth, and Ninth
Months
Three hanging scrolls, colors on silk
Each, H. 38^7/$_8$ in. (98.8 cm.), W. 16^1/$_8$ in.
(40.9 cm.)
Published: Bibl. 17, pl. 3
Japanese Imperial Household Collection

4a, b **Yanagisawa Kien** Landscape of the
West Lake at Hangchow
Pair of hanging scrolls, ink and light colors
on paper
Each, H. 53^3/$_4$ in. (136.6 cm.), W. 22^3/$_4$ in.
(57.8 cm.)
Published: Bibl. 14, pls. 95, 96
Tokyo University of Fine Arts

5 **Sakaki Hyakusen (1697-1752)** River
Landscape with Willows, 1745
Hanging scroll, ink and light colors on
paper
H. 52 in. (132.2 cm.), W. 21^3/$_8$ in. (54.4 cm.)
Mr. Kōzō Yabumoto, Hyogo

6 **Sakaki Hyakusen** Li Po Gazing at a
Waterfall
Hanging scroll, ink and light colors on
paper
H. 53^1/$_2$ in. (135.9 cm.), W. 21^5/$_8$ in. (55 cm.)
Mr. Kōzō Yabumoto, Hyogo

7 **Nakayama Kōyō (1717-1780)** Landscape
of Matsushima, probably painted in 1772
Hanging scroll, ink and light colors on
paper
H. 38^1/$_4$ in. (97.1 cm.), W. 10-5/16 in.
(26.2 cm.)
Published: Bibl. 16, pl. 67
Homma Art Museum, Yamagata

8 **Ikeno Taiga (1723-1776)** Essay on
Enjoying One's Will (*Rakushi-ron* or
Lo-chih lun), 1750
Handscroll, ink and light colors on paper
H. 11^1/$_8$ in. (28.3 cm.), L. 53-5/16 in.
(135.4 cm.)
Published: Bibl. 10, pl. 19; Bibl. 11, pl. 46;
Bibl. 14, pl. 9; Bibl. 16, pl. 5; Bibl. 18,
pl. 124
Umezawa Memorial Hall, Tokyo

9a, b **Ikeno Taiga** The Daibutsu-kaku and
Tōfukuji, from Six Sights in Kyoto
Two hanging scrolls from a series of six.
Daibutsu-kaku: ink on paper. Tōfukuji:
ink and light colors on paper
a. Daibutsu-kaku: H. 51^1/$_2$ in. (130.9 cm.),
W. 20^3/$_4$ in. (52.7 cm.)
b. Tōfukuji: H. 50^1/$_2$ in. (128.2 cm.),
W. 20^5/$_8$ in. (52.4 cm.)
Published: Bibl. 10, pls. 216-222; Bibl. 14,
pl. 16 (Daibutsu-kaku); Bibl. 18, pl. 96
Mr. Gihei Hamaguchi, Chiba

10 **Ikeno Taiga** The Poetical Gathering at
the Orchid Pavilion (*Lan-t'ing*)
Six-fold screen, ink and colors on paper
H. 64^1/$_8$ in. (162.8 cm.), W. 141^1/$_8$ in.
(359.1 cm.)
Published: Bibl. 2, pl. 3 (detail); Bibl. 10,
pl. 241
Mr. and Mrs. Jackson Burke, New York

11 **Ikeno Taiga** Landscapes in the Blue,
Green, and Gold Style, 1763
Album of ten leaves, ink, colors, and gold
on silk

Each leaf, H. 8⁵/₈ in. (22 cm.), W. 11⁵/₈ in.
(29.5 cm.)
Published: Bibl. 10, pl. 446; *The Kokka,*
No. 710 (May 1951), pls. 1-10
Suntory Art Gallery, Tokyo

12 Ikeno Taiga White Clouds and Red Trees
Hanging scroll, ink and colors on silk
H. 47⁷/₈ in. (121.5 cm.), W. 15³/₄ in.
(40.1 cm.)
Published: Bibl. 10, pl. 506; Bibl. 11, pl. 34;
Bibl. 18, pl. 101
Mr. Yoshio Sekizumi, Tokyo
Important Cultural Property

13a, b Ikeno Taiga The Six Distances, 1766
Two hanging scrolls from a set of six,
ink on paper
Each, H. 53¹/₂ in. (136 cm.), W. 23¹/₄ in.
(59 cm.)
Published: Bibl. 10, pl. 459; Bibl. 11, pl. 37;
Bibl. 16, pl. 4; Bibl. 18, pl. 38
Tokyo National Museum

14 Ikeno Taiga A Real View of Kojima Bay
Hanging scroll, ink and colors on silk
H. 39¹/₄ in. (99.6 cm.), W. 14³/₄ in. (37.4
cm.)
Published: Bibl. 10, pl. 557; Bibl. 14, pl. 13;
Bibl. 15, pl. 1 (detail) and fig. 25
Mr. Ryō Hosomi, Osaka

15 Ikeno Taiga The Nachi Waterfall
Hanging scroll, ink and light colors on
paper
H. 49¹/₂ in. (125.7 cm.), W. 22³/₈ in.
(56.9 cm.)
Published: Bibl. 10, pl. 616; Bibl. 11, pl. 42;
Bibl. 18, pl. 116
Tokyo National Museum

16 Ikeno Taiga Eight Views of the Hsiao-
Hsiang Region
Album of eight fan-shaped paintings, ink
on paper, accompanied by eight fan-
shaped leaves of calligraphy
Each, H. 7⁷/₈ in. (20 cm.), W. 20⁵/₈ in.
(52.5 cm.)
Published: Bibl. 10, pl. 772; Bibl. 11, pl. 49;
Bibl. 14, pls. 17, 18; Bibl. 15, figs. 2, 28;
Bibl. 16, pl. 10; Bibl. 18, pl. 103
Mr. Shōhei Kumita, Tokyo

17 Aoki Shukuya (died 1789) Autumn
Landscape with Mount Fuji
Hanging scroll, ink and colors on paper
H. 45¹/₄ in. (114.9 cm.), W. 14³/₈ in.
(36.4 cm.)
Mr. Kōzō Yabumoto, Hyogo

18 Kuwayama Gyokushū (1746-1799)
Landscape with Figures, 1798
Hanging scroll, ink and colors on silk
H. 37³/₈ in. (94.9 cm.), W. 13 in. (33.1 cm.)
Mr. Kōzō Yabumoto, Hyogo

19 Noro Kaiseki (1747-1828) Autumn
Landscape, 1811
Hanging scroll, ink and light colors on paper

H. 74¹/₂ in. (189.2 cm.), W. 18¹/₈ in. (46 cm.)
Published: Bibl. 16, pl. 81
Tokyo National Museum

20 Yosa Buson (1716-1783) Landscape,
1758
Hanging scroll, ink and light colors on
paper
H. 50¹/₂ in. (128.2 cm.), W. 21⁷/₈ in.
(55.5 cm.)
Published: Bibl. 18, pl. 145
Tokyo National Museum

21 Yosa Buson A Crow in a Wintry Sky
Hanging scroll, ink on paper
H. 43⁷/₈ in. (111.5 cm.), W. 11³/₄ in.
(29.7 cm.)
Published: Bibl. 6, fig. 53 (detail)
Mr. Kinjirō Kitamura, Kyoto

22a, b Yosa Buson The Narrow Road to the
Deep North *(Oku no Hosomichi),* 1778
Two handscrolls, ink and light colors on
paper
a. H. 11-5/16 in. (29 cm.), L. 375¹/₄ in.
(955 cm.)
b. H. 11-5/16 in. (29 cm.), L. 279⁵/₈ in.
(712 cm.)
Published: Bibl. 6, pl. 51; Bibl. 11, pl. 72;
Bibl. 14, pls. 38, 39; Bibl. 16, pl. 21;
Bibl. 18, pl. 176
Mr. Ryōtarō Hirayama, Tokyo
Important Cultural Property

23a, b Yosa Buson The Elysium of the
Peach Blossom Spring, 1781
Pair of hanging scrolls, ink and colors on
paper
Each, H. 54³/₈ in. (138 cm.), W. 21³/₄ in.
(55.2 cm.)
Published: Bibl. 6, fig. 36; Bibl. 11, pl. 65;
Bibl. 18, pl. 151
Mr. Takaya Shimada, Tokyo

24 Yosa Buson En no Gyōja
Hanging scroll, ink and light colors on
paper
H. 51 in. (129.5 cm.), W. 11¹/₈ in. (28.2 cm.)
Mr. Kinjirō Kitamura, Kyoto

25 Yosa Buson Clearing after Rain in
Spring
Hanging scroll, ink and colors on satin
H. 11¹/₄ in. (28.5 cm.), W. 12⁵/₈ in. (32 cm.)
Published: Bibl. 6, pls. 4 (detail), 28; Bibl.
8, pl. 5; Bibl. 11, pl. 61; Bibl. 14, pl. 34;
Bibl. 15, pl. 19; Bibl. 16, pl. 16; Bibl. 17,
pl. 19; Bibl. 18, pl. 162
Mr. Kōnosuke Matsushita, Hyogo
Important Art Object

26 Yosa Buson Cuckoo in Flight over New
Verdure
Hanging scroll, ink and colors on silk
H. 60-9/16 in. (153.8 cm.), W. 31³/₈ in.
(79.8 cm.)
Published: Bibl. 6, pls. 6 (detail), 20; Bibl.
8, colorplate 2 (detail); Bibl. 11, pl. 66;

Bibl. 14, pl. 31; Bibl. 15, pl. 17; Bibl. 18,
pl. 160
Mr. Shinji Hiraki, Tokyo
Important Cultural Property

27 Yosa Buson Mount Fuji
Hanging scroll, ink and light colors on paper
H. 20¹/₈ in. (51.2 cm.), W. 35¹/₄ in. (89.5 cm.)
Published: Bibl. 6, fig. 43
Mr. Sukekurō Satō, Toyama

28 Yosa Buson Bare Peaks of Mount Gabi
(*O-mei*)
Handscroll, ink and light colors on paper
H. 11³/₈ in. (28.9 cm.), L. 94¹/₂ in. (240.3 cm.)
Published: Bibl. 14, pls. 28, 29; Bibl. 15,
pl. 32; Bibl. 16, pl. 20
Mr. Junkichi Mayuyama, Tokyo

29 Yokoi Kinkoku (1761-1832) The Road
to Shu
Hanging scroll, ink and colors on silk
H. 43-7/16 in. (110.3 cm.), W. 13¹/₄ in.
(33.6 cm.)
Tokyo National Museum

30 Uragami Gyokudō (1745-1820) Building
a House in the Mountains (*Sanchū
Ketsuro*), 1792
Hanging scroll, ink and light colors on silk
H. 26 in. (66 cm.), W. 12-13/16 in. (32.5 cm.)
Published: Bibl. 14, pl. 49; Bibl. 18, pl. 178
Mr. Jūrō Sōrimachi, Tokyo

31 Uragami Gyokudō Green Pines and
Russet Valleys (*Seishō Tangaku*), 1807
Hanging scroll, ink on paper
H. 9³/₈ in. (23.7 cm.), W. 13³/₄ in. (35 cm.)
Published: Bibl. 9, pl. 6; Bibl. 11, pl. 88;
Bibl. 14, pl. 44 (detail); Bibl. 15, pl. 23;
Bibl. 16, pl. 38; Bibl. 18, pl. 179
Mr. Fudō Tomitori, Chiba

32 Uragami Gyokudō A Myriad Sounds
and Thousand-layered Peaks (*Banrai
Senjō*)
Hanging scroll, ink and light colors on paper
H. 53¹/₈ in. (135 cm.), W. 24⁵/₈ in. (62.5 cm.)
Published: Bibl. 11, pl. 83; Bibl. 18, pl. 210
Fuse Art Museum, Shiga

33 Uragami Gyokudō Idle in the
Mountains (*Sanchū Buji*)
Hanging scroll, ink on paper
H. 69³/₈ in. (176.1 cm.), W. 37-5/16 in.
(94.7 cm.)
Published: Bibl. 18, pl. 211
Kyoto National Museum

34 Uragami Gyokudō Two Peaks
Embracing Clouds (*Sōhō Sōun*)
Hanging scroll, ink and light colors on paper
H. 69¹/₄ in. (176 cm.), W. 37 in. (94 cm.)
Published: Bibl. 9, pl. 18 (with three
details); Bibl. 11, pl. 84; Bibl. 16, pl. 34;
Bibl. 17, pl. 38 right; Bibl. 18, pl. 216
Idemitsu Art Museum, Tokyo
Important Cultural Property

35 Uragami Gyokudō Album of Mists and
Clouds (*Enka-jō*), 1811
Album of twelve leaves, ink and light
colors on paper
Each leaf, H. 11-7/16 in. (29 cm.), W.
8-13/16 in. (22.4 cm.)
Published: Bibl. 9, colorplate 1, pls. 28-31;
Bibl. 11, pl. 102; Bibl. 14, pl. 53 and figs.
40-43; Bibl. 15, pl. 26; Bibl. 18, pl. 237
Umezawa Memorial Hall, Tokyo
Important Cultural Property

36 Uragami Gyokudō Enveloping Mists
Arouse and Nourish (*Rōen Jakuji*)
Hanging scroll, ink on paper
H. 10-5/16 in. (26.2 cm.), W. 9¹/₂ in. (24 cm.)
Published Bibl. 9, pl. 66; Bibl. 11, pl. 95;
Bibl. 16, pl. 40; Bibl. 18, pl. 229
Idemitsu Art Museum, Tokyo

37 Uragami Gyokudō Many Houses Seen
From On High (*Kōka Sūka*)
Hanging scroll, ink on paper
H. 11-13/16 in. (30 cm.), W. 21⁵/₈ in.
(55 cm.)
Published: Bibl. 9, pl. 60; Bibl. 11, pl. 89;
Bibl. 16, pl. 29; Bibl. 18, pl. 235
Mr. Kazuo Kurimoto, Kanagawa

38 Uragami Gyokudō Streams and Rocks
in a Deep, Damp Valley (*Yūkan Senseki*),
1816
Hanging scroll, ink and light colors on
paper
H. 43-9/16 in. (110.6 cm.), W. 23-11/16 in.
(60.2 cm.)
Published: Bibl. 9, pl. 44; Bibl. 18, pl. 183
Mr. Jūrō Sōrimachi, Tokyo

39 Aoki Mokubei (1767-1833) Mount
P'eng-lai (*Hōrai-zan*), 1811
Hanging scroll, ink and colors on paper
H. 53-1/16 in. (134.8 cm.), W. 11-3/16 in.
(28.4 cm.)
Published: Bibl. 11, pl. 107; Bibl. 17, pl. 41
right; Bibl. 18, pl. 253
Seikadō, Tokyo
Important Art Object

40 Aoki Mokubei Autumn Landscape,
1824
Hanging scroll, ink and light colors on
paper
H. 53³/₈ in. (135.6 cm.), W. 11-5/16 in.
(29 cm.)
Published: Bibl. 11, pl. 108; Bibl. 16, pl. 47;
Bibl. 17, pl. 44 right; Bibl. 18, pl. 245
Mr. Jōji Kanzaki, Kanagawa

41 Aoki Mokubei Morning Sun at Uji, 1824
Hanging scroll, ink and light colors on
paper
H. 19¹/₈ in. (48.5 cm.), W. 23³/₈ in. (59.4 cm.)
Published: Bibl. 11, pl. 120; Bibl. 15, pl. 43;
Bibl. 18, pl. 242
Tokyo National Museum
Important Cultural Property

42 Aoki Mokubei New Verdure Wet with
   Rain, 1826
Hanging scroll, ink and light colors on
   paper
H. 52¹/₂ in. (133.4 cm.), W. 11 in. (28 cm.)
Published: Bibl. 11, pl. 114; Bibl. 14, pl. 59
   (detail); Bibl. 18, pl. 254
Idemitsu Art Museum, Tokyo

43 Aoki Mokubei Heaven Protects the
   Nine Similitudes *(Tempō Kyūjo),* 1830
Hanging scroll, ink and light colors on
   paper
H. 41³/₈ in. (105 cm.), W. 20¹/₂ in. (52 cm.)
Published: Bibl. 8, pl. 9; Bibl. 18, pl. 258
Mrs. Fumiko Yoshikawa, Tokyo

44 Aoki Mokubei Clouds around the Base
   of a Mountain *(Unshutsu Sanyō)*
Hanging scroll, ink and light colors on
   paper
H. 12-1/16 in. (30.6 cm.), W. 14³/₄ in.
   (37.2 cm.)
Published: Bibl. 14, pl. 56; Bibl. 15, pl. 27;
   Bibl. 16, pl. 55; Bibl. 18, pl. 268
Mr. Genichi Tōyama, Tokyo

45 Tanomura Chikuden (1777-1835)
   Autumn Landscape, 1827
Hanging scroll, ink and light colors on
   paper
H. 20⁷/₈ in. (53 cm.), W. 39³/₈ in. (100 cm.)
Published: Bibl. 18, pl. 291
Mr. Yoshirō Hasegawa, Yamagata-ken

46 Tanomura Chikuden A Boat Trip on the
   Inagawa, 1829
Hanging scroll, ink and light colors on
   paper
H. 52³/₈ in. (133 cm.), W. 18-5/16 in.
   (46.5 cm.)
Published: Bibl. 11, pls. 149, 150; Bibl. 14,
   pl. 73 (detail); Bibl. 17, pl. 51 left; Bibl.
   18, pl. 301
Mr. Tatsuichi Kataoka, Yamaguchi
Important Cultural Property

47 Tanomura Chikuden Returning by Boat
   on a Cold River
Hanging scroll, ink on silk
H. 48-9/16 in. (123.4 cm.), W. 19-3/16 in.
   (48.7 cm.)
Published: Bibl. 18, pl. 348
Mr. Hikoshirō Nishitani, Chiba

48 Tanomura Chikuden Feeding Cranes
   Beneath Pine Trees, 1830
Hanging scroll, ink and light colors on
   paper
H. 49¹/₂ in. (125.8 cm.), W. 14-15/16 in.
   (37.9 cm.)
Published: Bibl. 18, pl. 307
Mr. Gihei Hamaguchi, Chiba

49 Tanomura Chikuden Living in
   Seclusion *(Kōban-zu),* 1832
Hanging scroll, ink and light colors on

paper; forms a pair with a hanging scroll
   of calligraphy
H. 69³/₈ in. (176.1 cm.), W. 18-9/16 in.
   (47.2 cm.)
Published: Bibl. 11, pl. 139; Bibl. 18, pl. 363
Idemitsu Art Museum, Tokyo

50 Tanomura Chikuden Yet Again One
   More Pleasure *(Mata-mata Ichiraku-jō),*
   1831-1832
Albums of thirteen paintings, ink and light
   colors on paper, and seven leaves of
   calligraphy
Each leaf, H. 8¹/₈ in. (20.6 cm.), W. 9-3/16
   in. (23.4 cm.)
Published: Bibl. 11, pl. 169; Bibl. 14, pls.
   70, 98 and figs. 53, 54; Bibl. 15, pl. 32;
   Bibl. 17, pls. 48, 49; Bibl. 18, pl. 370
Neiraku Art Museum, Nara
Important Cultural Property

51a, b Takahashi Sōhei (1802-1833)
   a. Peonies and Hydrangeas; b. Birds in a
   Flowering Tree, 1832
Pair of hanging scrolls, colors on silk
Each, H. 48¹/₈ in. (122.1 cm.), W. 14-9/16
   in. (37 cm.)
Published: Bibl. 16, pl. 83; Bibl. 17, pl. 57
   right
Mr. Hikoshirō Nishitani, Chiba

52 Okada Beisanjin (1744-1820) Landscape
   with Pine Groves, 1807
Hanging scroll, ink and light colors on silk
H. 51-7/16 in. (130.6 cm.), W. 19-15/16 in.
   (50.6 cm.)
Published: Bibl. 8, pl. 17 (detail); Bibl. 16,
   pl. 76; Bibl. 17, pl. 35 left
Mr. Ichiyō Matsushita, Hyōgo
Important Art Object

53 Okada Hankō (1782-1846) Crows
   Taking Flight through Spring Haze
   (Shunai Kia), 1841
Hanging scroll, ink and colors on silk
H. 51-11/16 in. (131.4 cm.), W. 14-5/16 in.
   (36.4 cm.)
Published: Bibl. 8, pl. 8 (detail); Bibl. 14,
   pls. 77, 78; Bibl. 15, pl. 34 (detail), fig. 9;
   Bibl. 16, pl. 77; Bibl. 17, pl. 59 right
Mr. Genichi Tōyama, Tokyo
Important Art Object

54 Tani Bunchō (1763-1840) Landscape
   with Figures, 1793
Hanging scroll, ink and colors on silk
H. 27 in. (66.5 cm.), W. 11 in. (28 cm.)
Published: Bibl. 14, pl. 79; Bibl. 16, pl. 69
Tokyo National Museum

55 Tani Bunchō Travel Sketches of
   Kōnodai
Handscroll, ink and light colors on paper
H. 6-7/16 in. (16.3 cm.), L. 128¹/₄ in.
   (326.3 cm.)
Published: Bibl. 14, pls. 102, 103
Miss Yoshiko Hosoya, Yamagata

56 Watanabe Kazan (1793-1841) Playing
  Fish, dated 1834 but probably painted
  in 1840
Hanging scroll, ink and colors on silk
H. 44³/₈ in. (112.7 cm.), W. 21-9/16 in.
  (54.8 cm.)
Published: Bibl. 5, pl. 7; Bibl. 17, pl. 71 right
Seikadō, Tokyo
Important Art Object

57 Watanabe Kazan Weaving by
  Moonlight, dated 1829 but probably
  painted *ca.* 1840
Hanging scroll, ink and colors on silk
II. 49-15/16 in. (126.9 cm.), W. 22-1/16 in. (56 cm.)
Published: Bibl. 5, pls. 4, 58, 59; Bibl. 17,
  pl. 65 left
Seikadō, Tokyo
Important Art Object

58 Sakurama Seigai (1786-1851) Landscape
Hanging scroll, ink and light colors on
  paper
H. 51-3/16 in. (130 cm.), W. 19³/₈ in. (49.1 cm.)
Published: Bibl. 16, pl. 93; Bibl. 17, pl. 78
  left
Tokyo National Museum

59 Nakabayashi Chikutō (1776-1853)
  Summer Mountains Washed by Rain
Hanging scroll, ink on silk
H. 48-15/16 in. (124.3 cm.), W. 16-15/16 in. (43 cm.)
Published: Bibl. 16, pl. 85
Zakke-in, Kyoto

60 Yamamoto Baiitsu (1783-1856)
  Bamboo Groves and Waterfalls
Hanging scroll, ink on silk
H. 51³/₈ in. (130.5 cm.), W. 20-3/16 in.
  (51.3 cm.)
Published: Bibl. 8, pl. 21; Bibl. 16, pl. 86
Umezawa Memorial Hall, Tokyo
Important Art Object

61 Yamamoto Baiitsu Birds and Flowers,
  1837
Hanging scroll, ink and colors on silk
H. 64³/₈ in. (163.5 cm.), W. 28¹/₈ in.
  (71.4 cm.)
Mr. Sōshirō Yabumoto, Tokyo

62 Tomioka Tessai (1837-1924) Fishermen
  on the Great River, 1916
Hanging scroll, ink and colors on paper
H. 58⁷/₈ in. (149.5 cm.), W. 31⁷/₈ in. (81 cm.)
Published: Bibl. 16, pl. 102; Bibl. 17, pl.
  102 right
Tokyo National Museum

63 Tomioka Tessai Hakuin Visiting the
  Hermit Hakuyūshi, 1920
Hanging scroll, ink and light colors on
  paper
H. 52¹/₄ in. (132.6 cm.), W. 20³/₈ in.
  (51.8 cm.)
Published: Bibl. 16, pl. 103; Bibl. 17, pl.
  103 right
Eisei Bunko, Tokyo

Bibliography

General

1. Akiyama, Terukazu. *Japanese Painting.* Geneva, 1961.

2. Covell, Jon Carter. *Japanese Landscape Painting.* New York, 1962.

3. Ijima, Isamu. *Bunjinga* [Literati Painting]. (*Nihon no Bijutsu,* [Arts of Japan], No. 4.) Tokyo: Shibundō, 1966.

4. Matsushita, Hidemaro. *Ikeno Taiga.* Tokyo, 1967.

5. Suganuma, Teizō. *Kazan.* Tokyo, 1962.

6. Suzuki, Susumu. *Buson.* Tokyo, 1958.

7. ________. *Chikuden. (Nihon Keizai Shimbun.)* Tokyo, 1963.

8. ________. "*Nanga (Bunjinga),*" in *Nihon: Edo II* [Japan, Edo Period II], ed. Susumu Suzuki. (*Sekai Bijutsu Zenshū* [Arts of the World], Vol. 10.) Tokyo, 1963. Pp. 148-159.

9. ________. *Uragami Gyokudō Gashū* [Collection of Paintings by Uragami Gyokudō]. Tokyo, 1956. With English summary.

10. Suzuki, Susumu *et al. Ikeno Taiga Sakuhin-shū* [Collection of Works by Ikeno Taiga]. Tokyo, 1960.*

11. Tokyo National Museum. *Nihon no Bunjinga* [Japanese Literati Painting]. Tokyo, 1966.

12. Watson, William. *Yosa no Buson.* London, 1960.

13. Yashiro, Yukio, ed. *Art Treasures of Japan.* 2 vols. Tokyo, 1960.

14. Yoshizawa, Chū and Yamakawa, Takeshi. *Nanga to Shasei-ga* [Nanga and Realistic Painting]. (*Genshoku Nihon no Bijutsu* [Japanese Art in Original Color], Vol. 18.) Tokyo, 1969.

15. Yoshizawa, Chū and Yonezawa, Yoshiho. *Bunjinga* [Literati Painting]. (*Nihon no Bijutsu* [Arts of Japan], Vol. 23.) Tokyo: Heibonsha, 1966.

Catalogues

16. *150 ans de peinture au Japon: de Gyokudo à Tessai.* Catalogue of an exhibition in the Petit Palais, Paris, 1962.

17. Tokyo National Museum. *Nihon Nanga-shū* [Collection of Japanese Nanga]. Tokyo, 1951.

18. Tokyo National Museum. *Nihon no Bunjinga-ten Mokuroku* [Catalogue of Exhibition of Japanese Literati Painting]. Tokyo, 1965.

*The same material published earlier in larger plates, as: Tanaka, Isshō *et al. Ikeno Taiga Gafu.* Tokyo, 1957-1959.

Credits

Catalogue designed by Joseph del Gaudio
Production supervised by Françoise J. Boas
Photographs courtesy of the Agency for Cultural Affairs (Bunka-cho), Tokyo
except for No. 10, by Otto E. Nelson, New York
Composition by York Typesetting Co. Inc., New York, N.Y.
Printed by Eastern Press, Inc., New Haven, Conn.
Bound by Publishers Bookbindery, Inc., New York, N.Y.